WARRIOR,
WIMP,
OR
WINNER

WHAT ROLE DO YOU PLAY IN THE BATTLE OF THE SEXES?

E. EDWARD REITMAN PH.D.

Library of Congress Control Number: 2013907132
CreateSpace Independent Publishing Platform
North Charleston, South Carolina

DEDICATION

I dedicate this book to my grandchildren, Melissa, Jessica, Lauren, Reese, and Miles. It is my hope that it will not only give them something to remember me by, but that it will also provide them with one thought they may choose to use in the process of sculpting their own destinies:

Be yourselves! Don't hide, apologize for, or exaggerate yourselves, because who you truly are, what you think and feel, the talents you have, along with any shortcomings and scars you may possess, all contribute to you being far more worthwhile persons than any false images you could create.

In short, you needn't be warriors or wimps; you only need to value yourselves as much as I value each of you. That will make you winners.

Papa

If you live life as a warrior, you are prone to fight and manipulate. If you live life as a wimp, you will rationalize and capitulate. But if you choose to be a winner, you will live life according to what your heart and brain dictate.

—E. Edward Reitman

TABLE OF CONTENTS

ACKNOWLEDGMENTS   ix

PREFACE   xi

INTRODUCTION   xv

Section 1   How Did It All Come About?   1

Chapter 1   Men As We Knew Them   3

Chapter 2   It's Difficult To Be A Man   9

Chapter 3   Women Emerging   17

Chapter 4   Where Do Women Stand?   27

Chapter 5   The Warrior   35

Chapter 6   Dealing With A Warrior   41

Chapter 7   The Wimp   53

Chapter 8   Dealing With A Wimp   61

Chapter 9   Warriors And Wimps Are The Same   71

Chapter 10   The Winner   85

Chapter 11   Marriage Can't Survive Warriors
                 And Wimps   93

Section 2   Marriage Is A People Problem   105

Chapter 12   What Do You Want To Be?   107

Chapter 13   People Of Chaos   115

Chapter 14   You're Not Trapped   125

Chapter 15   Yesterday's Cures And Tomorrow's
                 Problems   133

Chapter 16   The Ordeal Of Change   139

Section 3	What You Need To Do	149
Chapter 17	Behave Abnormally	151
Chapter 18	Run Toward Your Fears	159
Chapter 19	Don't Be A Victim	169
Chapter 20	Little Things Mean A Lot	179
Chapter 21	Dare To Be Selfish	191
Chapter 22	Set Limits	201
Chapter 23	Choose Liberation Over Rebellion	209
Chapter 24	Tell Them Who You Are	215
Chapter 25	Have The Courage To Face Your Own Truths	225
Chapter 26	Tell The World That You Matter	231
Chapter 27	Accept The Unacceptable	237
Chapter 28	Learn To Float	243
Section 4	Everything In A Nutshell	249
Chapter 29	Why Relationships Don't Work	251
Chapter 30	Easy Solutions Are Attainable	259
Chapter 31	Your Losses Can Be Your Gains	265
Chapter 32	Grow Up Before You Grow Old	273
Chapter 33	Three Major Gifts	283
Chapter 34	Trust Yourself	297
Chapter 35	Twenty-Four-Cow Partner	307
Chapter 36	Thoughts On Becoming A Winner	317
Chapter 37	So, Who Are You?	323
INDEX		329

ACKNOWLEDGMENTS

Although *Warriors, Wimps and Winners* was only written over the last eight months, it was a long time in the making. Most of the credit for this book needs to be given to the numerous patients I have seen in therapy over the past 45+ years. It is their story. It depicts their successes and their failures, both of which ultimately contributed to their growth, of either a positive or negative nature.

Along the way, I shared their anxieties, panic attacks, addictions and a myriad of neurotic behavioral patterns. But, in almost every instance, our interactions consisted of a relationship between two human beings who trusted each other sufficiently to be open and vulnerable. Never mind that one was called a therapist and the other a patient. Never did I in any way feel or look upon them as any different from myself, and probably any of you. We were, similar to everyone else in the world, individuals who were wounded in our pasts, because no one escapes childhood without some difficulties, problems or baggage that they carry with them the rest of their life.

Our purpose together wasn't to change the past but, instead, to recognize and accept that baggage and to deal with life in spite of it, and in spite of the fears and threats it contributed to.

In every case, their courage to face themselves, to risk change and to make themselves vulnerable in the therapeutic relationship and in a world that wasn't always friendly or supportive has always awed me and even contributed to helping me to grow, as well.

There are also a number of special individuals - friends and family who have always been there for me to lean on, to reassure me, and to encourage me, even when they weren't aware of the extent to which their presence, support and love were both needed and appreciated. Additionally, I need to single out Amber Lane, my office manager and secretary, who fought, criticized and provoked my thoughts throughout the entire creative process. By the time the book was complete, she was as sick of the manuscript as I. Nevertheless, her efforts strongly contributed to the final results. I also appreciate the editorial suggestions and positive reinforcement I received from Jana Whitby, who, after the book was written, looked at it with fresh eyes and provided considerable help in rearranging and organizing the chapters.

However, most of all, there is one person who is always there, who has been there for me for almost 52 years. She willingly gave up countless evenings and Saturday and Sunday mornings so that I could devote the time to writing. She did so without creating guilt, or expecting special favors. She is my rock, my no-nonsense source of common sense, my travel buddy and my love. She understands me, knows my weaknesses and, most importantly, accepts me in spite of them.

To her, and all the rest of you, let me unequivocally say,
Thank You.

PREFACE

believe that everyone walks down the aisle with the partner they love, want to share their lives with, raise a family together and live with until death they do part. The question is, is that possible or even probable today? I think it can be. That's why I wrote *Warrior, Wimp, or Winner?*

Fifty years ago, when I initially opened my office, you could have shot off a cannon in the waiting room and never killed a man, because men didn't come to therapy. But their unhappy, discontent and depressed wives did.

Today, that isn't the case. There are as many, if not more, unhappy men in my waiting room, as there are women. Why? Mostly because times have changed. Today, there are many men walking in what were originally women's moccasins, who are not finding them at all comfortable. Even more, where once divorce was considered a sin, it is now common for almost 50 percent of the population. The result is that most people are no longer trapped in what they believe is an unhappy marriage, they are instead victims of divorces which I feel they too readily jumped into.

Figuratively speaking, I am saying that, frequently, those individuals who stay in a leaky ship and repair it, become the survivors, as opposed to those who abandoned the ship.

Let me quote a great number of my patients who said:

"I wish I'd known then what I know today. If I had, I would probably never have divorced the first time."

Those are words I've heard on countless occasions, from individuals whose second or third marriages were finally on the right track. It wasn't that they were dissatisfied with their present partners. Instead, they regretted the ordeal they experienced to get where they were. In most instances, they came to see that:

1. The problem wasn't their first spouse's alone.
2. They recognized the part they played and the extent to which their behavior contributed to both their initial choice of a spouse and to their spouse's reactions.
3. Most of all, they regretted the hurt they caused all of those individuals affected by their divorce, i.e, their spouse, their children, their parents, in-laws, friends, and most of all, themselves.

This isn't to say that every divorce can or should be avoided, but it does say that, if you come to recognize the source of your own behaviors, beliefs and feelings, the likelihood of your relationship ending in divorce will be greatly diminished.

It doesn't matter if you're single and looking forward to marriage, married and displeased, want to improve your relationship with your present spouse, or even involved with someone outside your marriage; before you take the next step, please read *Warrior, Wimp or Winner?*. It will make that step a far more positive one. My suggestion, with regard to the best way you can absorb and apply the content presented within this book is to read the whole book once, then go back to more carefully examine the particular areas that are of interest or concern, that apply to you. The benefit will be that you become a winner in your first, present, or next and, hopefully, last relationship.

INTRODUCTION

Pick up any newspaper, and the front page will be filled with articles about war, global warming, drugs, increasing crime rates, and the terrible state of the economy. But there is another epidemic that is threatening our world, one that is spreading at an alarming rate. Instead of responding to it, people take it in stride. They accept the notion that nothing can be done about it. As a result, nothing is.

That epidemic is *divorce.* Today, one out of every two marriages ends in divorce. In fact, recent speculations suggest that the rate of divorce is now up to 54 to 56 percent. It's alarming, but few people even take notice anymore. If the headlines in our newspapers read that 54 to 56 percent of the oak trees in the country were dying because of a particular form of blight, every tree hugger, myself included, would be up in arms, shouting, "Do something about it!" Yet, professionals and laymen alike watch the institution of marriage deteriorate at the same rate and ignore it. All the while, the consequences of this disease continue to affect our whole society. It impacts the growing fear of commitment demonstrated by single people, the destructive way in which men and women interact in relationships, and the way our children are hurt by broken homes. To say the least, something drastic needs to be done. It's time to wake up to the crisis marriage is facing.

The first step in this direction is to search out the major factors contributing to this epidemic, foremost among them a significant change in the age-old battle between the sexes. *Warrior, Wimp, or Winner* will expose men for who they really are: frauds who are strong on form but weak in substance. It will further suggest that close to but just beneath the surface of their masculine image lies a strong sense of false pride, excessive vanity, and a desperate need for nurturing, all of which have for years been obscured by an air of pompous superiority, accompanied by the erroneous but widely accepted notion that women are basically weak and dependent on men to protect them.

The problem with this point of view is simple: men haven't been able to live up to the picture they painted. During the last fifty years, women have experienced greater opportunities to grow. Instead of secretaries and heads of classrooms, they are now secretaries of state and heads of multinational corporations. They are now better represented in many professions, such as medicine, law, and business. With that have come higher-paid positions in the work world and an increased sense of self-confidence. Given these advances, together with the introduction of effective methods of birth control, women found themselves liberated and independent. Men have felt threatened by this development. Without stereotypes about power to hide behind, man's true identity has emerged.

Take, for instance, Jennifer Homans's article in the *New York Times Book Review on September 3, 2012,* about *The End of Men and the Rise of Women*[1], by Hannah Rosin:

> According to Rosin, the revolution feminists have been waiting for…is happening now, before our very eyes. Men are losing their grip, patriarchy is crumbling and we are reaching "the end of 200,000 years of human history and the beginning of a new era" in which women—and womanly skills and traits—are on the rise. Women around the world, she reports, are increasingly dominant in work, education, households; even in love and marriage.

Rosin isn't alone in seeing this trend. David Brooks, in "Men Are Falling Behind, as Women Learn to Adapt," states that:

> Women are thriving in the new economic quarter, by being flexible, while men attempt to cling to outdated ideologies. In elementary and high schools, male academic performance is lacking. Boys earn three quarters of the D's and F's. By college, men are clearly behind. Only 40% of bachelor's degrees go to men, along with 40% of master's degrees. Thanks to their lower skills, men are dropping out of the labor force. In 1954, 96% of American men between the ages of 25 and 54 worked. Today, the number is down to 80%. In a recent job report, male labor force participation reached an all-time low. Millions of men are collecting disability. Even many of those who do have jobs are doing poorly, according to Michael Greenstone, of The Hamilton Project. Annual earnings for median prime-age males has dropped by 28%

over the past 40 years. Nevertheless, men still dominate the tip-top of the corporate ladder, because many women take off time to raise children. But women lead, or are gaining, everywhere else. Women in their 20's out earn men in their 20's. Twelve of the fifteen fastest growing professions are dominated by women.

These changes didn't happen overnight. Nor did any one factor alone contribute to the end of the illusions of male supremacy and female frailty. But over the past thirty to forty years, the consequences of the gender shift have proven far greater than might have been initially predicted, particularly with regard to the impact it had on the institution of marriage. The turmoil, anxiety, and depression brought about by these changes have had unintended repercussions across every facet of society.

But, if the old adage that "when a door closes, a window opens" holds any truth, it's also true that the demise of the notion of male superiority isn't all bad for men. It is forcing men and women to deal with one another in an altogether different fashion. Men and women no longer have to live up to archaic roles that obscure who they are and what they feel. As a result, members of neither sex have to choose between being a warrior or a wimp. Instead, they can both be winners because they can finally view and deal with each other as emotional equals.

"That's the evolution," the novelist Karl Taro Greenfeld said recently in the *New York Times* of the gender shift. "Whoever has more time can take on more of the domestic role. There isn't any shame, or even any social awkwardness. It's not even observed as being anything distinctive or worthy of comment." It's an admirable goal that Greenfeld outlines—to make changing gender norms unworthy of comment—but not everyone is onboard yet. And because, as the same article states, "federal statistics show that men lost two and a half times as many jobs as women did in the recession," there may be a great deal more conflict before we reach a solution.

The primary goals of *Warrior, Wimp, or Winner* are, first, to help eliminate the need for men and women to live up to false gender norms by helping them recognize, accept, and value who they really are, and, second, to help men and women to see and appreciate the sensitive and loving person inside of their partners. Every man and every woman has to recognize that somewhere inside every warrior is a wimp who doth protest too much. Conversely, inside every wimp is an angry, resentful warrior, whose resentments and frustrations have smoldered for years. Neither coping mechanism is right or wrong; they're just behaviors learned early in life. In fact, there isn't even a difference between the two. When you look inside and examine each of their emotional dynamics, they're the same. They are emotionally insecure, needy individuals who desperately require and want recognition, sympathy, and love. This book's goal is not to exacerbate this gender war or to claim a victor but to show just how similar men and women are, the ultimate goal being to stem the tide of divorce by helping partners recognize that they're on the same team and they can *win* only by working *together*.

This book isn't a panacea for all the difficulties people encounter in their relationships, but it can provide you with a very specific set of guidelines to help you see and accept yourself for who you truly are. The goal is to help you begin to work on those things that you alone determine need changing in you. In turn, your growth can serve to enhance your relationships with others. If you're a wimp, you will begin to stand up. If you're a warrior, you will learn to stand back. As a result, you and your spouse will be loving partners who find it easier to compromise with and understand one another, while standing together.

HOW DID IT ALL COME ABOUT?

Fifty years ago, you could have entered my waiting room any day of the week and never seen a man. They didn't come to therapy back then, because you either had to be certifiably crazy, or weak and desperately in need of help to do so. That's not the case today. Oftentimes, I'll have a day when my schedule primarily includes men.

How did it come about? Women slowed flexed their muscles. They no longer need physically strong men to fight off tigers, hunt their dinner, or protect them from the world. They became educated, practiced birth control, and learned to say "NO!" All the while, men held onto the past, hid behind their physical prowess, and resisted change.

This section of *Warrior, Wimp, or Winner?* will detail how those stereotypical roles came to be, and how they contributed to the erosion of the old institute of marriage.

CHAPTER ONE

MEN AS WE KNEW THEM

What happened to men as we once knew them? Where are they hiding? Have they disappeared altogether? Were they a mirage that you could only clearly see from a distance, who when viewed up close, revealed themselves as an illusion?

Throughout the centuries, we've paid homage to the brave, fearless individuals that men portrayed themselves to be. Our hearts beat faster as we envision the thundering hordes of Genghis Khan's warriors crossing parts of Asia and Europe, conquering, pillaging, and mastering all that they encountered. We glamorize the Samurai warriors, the French Foreign Legion, the Musketeers, the Roman gladiators, the Knights of the Round Table, even the cavemen, whom we depicted as strong and rugged. Every picture showed him carrying a club over his shoulder and dragging a woman by the hair behind him.

The flip side, of course, is that women have always been portrayed as weak and subservient. *Soft, delicate, gentle, docile, submissive*—these have all been used as synonyms for "feminine." Paradoxically, women have also been perceived as beguiling, seductive individuals of whom one should be wary. Remember that even the mighty Samson could be seduced by Delilah, just as Napoleon Bonaparte was by Josephine or President Clinton was by Monica.

It's no wonder then that throughout the ages, man, because of his acute but often covert awareness of his vulnerability to women, has subjugated, dehumanized, objectified, and tried to physically control them. People need to control whatever they fear or whoever makes them feel vulnerable. Recent years have, however, brought about a radical change in man's reign over woman, a change that has slowly eroded his self-image and the status he has claimed for himself. It started subtly in the media. The list is long, and the themes are repetitive, but to name just a few: Ricky and Lucy, Fred and Ethel, Archie Bunker and Edith, and Ralph Cramden and Alice, not to mention Fred Flintstone and Barney Rubble, whose wives, Wilma and Betty, were the strength behind their blundering behavior. More recently, television has perpetuated the pattern, with programs, such as *Everybody Loves Raymond, Frasier,* and *The Kings of Queens.* All have examples of men who take the limelight, are loud, seemingly authoritative, often rude, and always insensitive and weak in their dealings with women.

When they do achieve success, it's because of the old adage, "Behind every good man is a better woman." Or is it that she's a controlling, manipulative, surreptitious, designing, bright, cunning, sensitive, aware femme fatale who knows how to handle her man? History is replete with examples of these relationships— Marc Anthony, who lost his empire because of Cleopatra; John the Baptist, who lost his head because of Salome; Sir Lancelot, who wasn't quite as virtuous because of Guinevere; the Duke of Windsor, who gave up the crown for Wallis Simpson; Juan Peron, who gifted his power to Evita; and countless other men in every walk of life, who have defamed their reputations, lost their families, embarrassed their children, and jeopardized their careers for the so-called love of a woman.

So where are the real men, the ones who have true inner strength, who are noble, virtuous, strong in character, dependable, rational, and able to live up to the image of masculinity that men have proclaimed from time immemorial? Is it possible that they were only an illusion to begin with? Is it that men are really just peacocks, who strut, fan their tail feathers, and proclaim their beauty in a fruitless search for acknowledgment and attention, while, in reality, they are shams, bumpkins, buffoons, and weak, indecisive individuals whose strength is derived by virtue of the image they created, the physical strength they possessed, and the illusion they projected? Perhaps their real strength came from the women who supported them, followed them, were there to bear their children, raise their families, and provide sound counsel when they lost their confidence, broke their stride, or wavered in the quests they followed.

No matter the reality, it's apparent that the tide has changed significantly. On the political front, women are increasingly playing pivotal roles. Golda Meir, Margaret Thatcher, Madeleine Albright, and Condoleezza Rice are all examples of women who have risen to heights never before seen. The concept that a woman who is subject to menstrual periods once a month could never be a ruler of a country is now an all but archaic notion to be laughed at. It holds no credence.

In the entertainment industry, Oprah has taken the place of Phil Donahue. In the business world, the name Martha Stewart has become as commonplace as Donald Trump. In politics, Hillary Clinton came very close to winning the race for president of the United States. And who would ever have believed that in February 2007, Harvard University would name historian Drew Gilpin Faust as their first female president?

"I hope my appointment can be one symbol of an opportunity that would have been inconceivable even a generation ago," Faust said at the time. "I'm not the woman president of Harvard; I'm the president of Harvard." Half of the eight Ivy League schools now have a female president. It's evident women are making marks for themselves in medicine, dentistry, law, education, law enforcement, and even as religious leaders. The world is theirs for the taking, and the direction they're taking is upward and onward.

This is not to say, however, that these changes have come without a price. Many of today's women are as confused regarding what role they need to play to be an adequate woman as men are concerned about what constitutes a positive masculine image.

On the surface, men's reaction to this change appears to be positive. Men voice encouragement for women to get an education and get involved. But, behind locked doors, in male-dominated boardrooms, and, most important, in their hearts, men are threatened. They're like the stereotypical movie cowboy who kissed his horse instead of his girl. In his own way, he was saying to the world, "I will not be controlled, dominated, or seduced by a woman. I won't let my guard down or my emotions out." It's no different from the forceful physical and emotional stance that some men take with women in order to perpetuate an illusion of strength.

It's no surprise then that the mixture of men and marriage adds up to problems and conflicts, which frequently result in divorce. Nor is it difficult to understand why fear of commitment increasingly makes itself evident in intimate relations. To make matters worse, the more the illusion crumbles, the more we see a greater number of men waiting longer and longer to marry, fearful to enter into meaningful relationships and unwilling to give up their freedom to become a paycheck or to lose their independence.

The consequence is that a majority of the men who do choose marriage unconsciously enter into a power struggle with wives whom they perceive as trying to control them. It's not an altogether crazy notion, because the first woman they met, their mother, established that precedent much earlier in their lives. It's no wonder that, in retaliation, they typically exert their prowess by controlling family finances; assuming rigid, overbearing positions; or exhibiting passive-aggressive behavior. In both cases, they still wind up feeling trapped in relationships from which they can't extract themselves.

Men aren't in this alone, though. Women tell men they want sensitive, feeling, caring partners who show their emotions. But when men are fearful, indecisive, unable to take charge, make less money than they do, or are inept in dealing with others, they see them as weak, incapable of protecting and standing up for their families or spouses, and lacking insight and sensitivity. The end result is that males have become confused individuals who have lost their age-old image of what it takes to be a man. Even more, they have no idea what it takes to be a truly loving spouse or partner. They don't know how they should act or what they need to do to be seen as adequate. They mistakenly view the amount they earn, the position they achieve, the physical strength they possess, the volume of their voices, the degree to which they can intimidate, and the number of gifts or pieces of jewelry they bestow on others as indices of their worth. When that doesn't suffice, they frequently search for sexual challenges outside their marriages to prove they're adequate.

Ironically, most men are unaware of these factors. Instead, they tend to blame women for the difficulties they experience in their everyday lives and interpersonal relationships. Needless to say, that hasn't solved the problem. What both men and women have to do is gain greater insight into their own behavior. Men need to better understand the increasing amount of confusion they feel regarding their roles as males, the despondency they experience in their interpersonal relationships, and the sense of helplessness these issues create intra-personally that undermine their everyday happiness and their intimate relationships. At the same time, women need to recognize the emotional confusion that their partners experience. It will help them to comprehend why men need to compensate through sports, outside activities, and controlling or addictive behaviors.

This mutual understanding might provide a common ground from which men and women can take the steps together to finally become what they should have been from the very beginning of time—human beings first and males or females afterward.

CHAPTER TWO

IT'S DIFFICULT TO BE A MAN

A patient recently came to me after staying up all night, saying to himself, "I should have said *this*. I could have said *that*. It would have been better if I had told my boss…"

This went on for hours. "I could've, I should've, I would've, but…" As he lay there, unable to go to sleep, mumbling these same words over and over again, he inadvertently woke his wife, who turned to him and said angrily, "Why don't you just drop it? You've spent the whole night talking about what you could've, should've, might have done, would've done, but didn't do. I'm tired, and you keep waking me up. Stop it, and go to sleep." With that, her head hit the pillow, and she was in slumberland. The man spent the rest of the night tossing and turning in the bed, saying, "I should've told her *this*. I could've told her *that*."

I listened to the story and, sadly, could relate. It brought back memories of an incident that occurred over twenty years ago, one I hadn't thought of in years. I was standing in line with my wife outside a movie theater. The line was long, and we had been waiting for a considerable amount of time when a man pushed his way into the line three or four places ahead of us. My wife nudged me and said, "Did you see that? Look at what he did." I looked at this individual, who was large but has, over the years, grown in my mind to the point that I now think of him as six-eight and well over three hundred pounds. I also recall at that time thinking he could well be a lineman for the Dallas Cowboys. I remember thinking, *I wish I were Rambo. I wish I could go up to him, all five-eight of me, and tell him what I think, how rude his behavior was, and how inappropriate it was for him not to go to the end of the line.* But I rationalized the whole thing away. After all, he was a foot taller. This was Texas; he could easily have had a gun, and, well, it wasn't worth having an altercation that might result in physical harm. Still, it bothered me emotionally that I wasn't a hero, someone who could have taken him by the arm and forcibly steered him out of line. The fact was, I couldn't stand up and be as lionhearted as King Richard or as fearless as Superman. That night, I lay in bed, saying, "I should have said...I could have said, but I didn't."

It can be difficult to be a man, to feel the constant burden of having to live up to the stereotypical demands the image imparts and to fulfill its obligations. Most men think they need to be macho, strong, fearless, wise, successful, powerful, and gallant. They must be able to protect their families and provide for their emotional and financial needs. At the same time, they're expected to possess sufficient ability to play the role of an objective judge, a stern but compassionate disciplinarian, and a coach who is physically fit and has an innate wealth of knowledge regarding all sports. Fat, scrawny, or nerdy men don't fulfill these criteria. A man is required to be an all-around handyman with the ability to deal with all problems involving carpentry, plumbing, electrical wiring, and gardening. Sons will invariably say to their friends, "My daddy can beat up your daddy," and daughters will expect their fathers to be the best dancer at their father-daughter dances. Last, but certainly not least, a man is supposed to be a "stud," who is sufficiently virile to provide his wife with the ultimate sexually satisfying experience.

There may be more, but you can readily see why a large number of men feel inadequate and use critical or controlling behavior to bolster their sense of masculinity or choose to capitulate to appease the opposite sex. When that doesn't work, they hide at work until late at night, travel for their jobs, surround themselves with an endless list of projects, become promiscuous, drink, gamble, fish, or golf to excess, or they sit in their offices, staring out the window, dreaming of running off to some exotic, faraway place where they can live out their lives without responsibilities while drinking tropical beverages served up by scantily clad native women. Years ago, that may have been a fantasy of mine, but today, I know that it isn't a solution. The real problem is that men have bought into the very image they created. They believe their own PR. Men play the masculine role to the hilt until, as in the Wizard of Oz, the curtain is raised and they can no longer hide behind the all-powerful image they create. This isn't surprising. If you tell yourself a lie a sufficient number of times, it winds up being your truth.

Men are now angry. They resent the burden they placed on their own shoulders. Their anger erupts when the bills come in at the end of the month and they can't meet them; when the credit cards are charged to their limits; when they feel overwhelmed and defeated and see no end in sight; when their wives and children want a new house, clothes, or jewelry. If they can't meet their family's emotional or financial needs, make their wives happy, and compete with other males, they're failures. They're fakes. Similarly, when their wives earn more than they do, down-deep inside, they resent it.

In his book, *Us Guys: The True and Twisted Mind of the American Man*, Charlie Le Duff, the Pulitzer prize–winning reporter for the *New York Times,* says, "I don't like the place [men are] headed. You know? Fat, stupid, scared, and masturbating to porn." Taken as a whole, it's not hard to feel that American men have lost their central place in the culture and, as a consequence, have drastically demeaned themselves.

At another point in his book, Le Duff joins a circus to be trained as clown but comments, "I am already a clown, a stupid man who hides behind his outrageousness. A scared, stupid little man who would rather people laugh at what he does than at who he is." It's apparent that, although Le Duff uses the first-person pronoun "I," he is really speaking for most men of the present generation.

As a clown, LeDuff could draw attention to himself, act the fool, be the butt of his own jokes, and endear himself to others without exposing his true self. I know several individuals I am very fond of who fit that description, and I'm positive you do as well. And this is only one of the roles open to men who are reluctant to expose their vulnerability. There are countless others, such as the overachiever, who constantly works to prove his adequacy; the underachiever who fails at everything he tries or never tries at all and proclaims his disdain for the demands society places on him; the bully, who demeans others physically or intellectually in an attempt to prove his own adequacy; the vain individual who takes far longer to prepare to go out than his female companion; the controller; the pleaser; the hostile; the fearful; the compulsive; the chaotic; and countless others.

They all share two things in common: first, they hide behind excessive behavioral patterns, either too little or too much, in order to create an image of adequacy they really don't own; second, the facade they present is far less palatable to others than the person inside, whom they are trying to obscure.

Their behavioral patterns are difficult to discard because they stem from deep-rooted feelings of insufficiency that are hardwired into them. It is the psychological equivalent of the religious notion of original sin, for which you must repent for the remainder of your life. These men feel destined to live, hide, run from, and/or compensate for any evidence of behavior, thoughts, or feelings that imply weakness, insufficiency, or inadequacy. To that end, men are willing to risk destroying reputations they have spent a lifetime building, to behave inconsistently with their own values, to set aside their own good common sense, and to live on the edge, even to the point of risking physical harm or death, to establish an image that attests to their strength, bravery, and courage. It's understandable why men behave the way they do, but it's a terrible price they pay to prove their adequacy. There needs to be another alternative, something far less self-destructive.

The solution consists of the demise of the *warrior* or *wimp* and the emergence of the *winner*: a person who sees, accepts, and respects who and what they are in spite of and because of his fears, warts, scars, and shortcomings. Winners don't need to prove who they are. They already know who they are and accept themselves.

If this proves to be the case, the demise of the male image needn't be viewed as all bad. Instead, it might more accurately be seen as fortuitous, as a catalyst forcing men and women who truly desire a positive relationship to alter their archaic perceptions, expectations, and communications with one another. Hopefully, these changes will enable them to establish healthier interactions in the future.

Whether you are a man or a woman, *Warrior, Wimp, or Winner* can help you avoid becoming a victim of these changes by giving you a better understanding of why they are now taking place and the role you play in this process. The key is that you take control of yourself, not your partner, see each other as equals despite your differences, and, most important, learn to respect those differences so they can be utilized in a more positive fashion. As a result, rather than engage in emotional power struggles, you will be able to interact with your partner in a healthier way. Men can learn to accept that they needn't hide behind a curtain and build their worth on a powerful voice, the illusion of infinite knowledge, or the bestowing of gifts. They will realize their true worth stems from being real instead of right and believe that they can be loved for who they are, instead of who they pretend to be.

Finally, you will see that the evolution of winners need not represent the decline of the masculine male. Instead, it may more accurately be viewed as a major step in the development of the male image from a counterfeit hero to a genuine human being: a person whose intimate relationships can be healthier and more positive than ever before.

CHAPTER THREE

WOMEN EMERGING

Picture a field shrouded in the early morning fog. At the far side, you see figures bent over, working, with large baskets strapped over their shoulders. Depending on your geographic location and what time period in history you imagine, they could be gathering firewood, harvesting crops, or picking cotton.

One figure emerges from the fog: a woman, with a sling across her chest, which gently moves, as though some living creature inside is slowly awakening. No men are in sight. They're off hunting. If the child in the sling is female, she may still be sacrificed or left to die. If she survives childhood, years later, if she cannot produce children or is unable to bear male offspring, she will be discarded and replaced by someone who can. Throughout the ages, her own female children and grandchildren will be bought with a dowry, sold for men's pleasure, raped, beaten, burned, or beheaded. Life isn't going to be easy for her and those yet to come. Considerable time will pass before she will have the right to own property or, for that matter, before she isn't considered property herself.

Generations later, her descendants will still feel discontent and disillusioned, despite the fact history will have brought about many changes. They'll be entitled to vote and to get an education, even at once exclusively male universities. They may even find employment that equals some of their male counterparts', but something will be lacking. Marching for equal rights, smoking cigarillos, wearing pants, going out unaccompanied, cursing, adopting the same sexual attitudes as men, and ridding themselves of husbands they view as weak—none of this will solve their discontent. In addition to the benefits, the changes also brought a markedly greater number of divorces, more single-parent homes, and a greater susceptibility to stress-related illnesses previously considered to be the exclusive province of men.

Many will resent having to clean or cook and will view the ideal home as one without a kitchen. Their preference for dinner will be reservations, takeout, fast food, or something that can be defrosted in a microwave. Where once they cowered, they can now be heard telling their husbands, "I want you to come home at night and help with the children. I expect you to give them baths when they're young, help them with their studies, attend their games, and participate in their religious training. At the same time, I need you to be understanding, sensitive, supportive, nurturing, ambitious, financially successful, physically strong, protective, and manly."

I'm exaggerating to make a point, but I've heard these words in therapy on all too many occasions. They were uttered by women who still feel the pain of watching their mothers' servitude to their fathers, and they compensate by criticizing their spouses to ensure that they do not find themselves in the same situation. They are also spoken by women who have, themselves, been severely hurt, emotionally or physically, in a previous relationship. And for every woman who had the courage to speak out, I've seen dozens of others who share those feelings privately in therapy sessions but are too frightened to verbalize them. You can accurately say that life still isn't easy for women.

The men on the receiving end will view these things as demands, as opposed to desires. If they acquiesce, they usually do so with strong feelings of resentment toward their partners. If they object, they are invariably accused of being argumentative, chauvinistic, and unloving. In the end, they wind up either hating themselves for being weak or feeling rejected by their wives. As a result, they often feel it's a hopeless struggle. Life isn't easy for them, either.

Obviously, neither side really wins. Instead, they engage in a long series of battles where one gender "rules the roost," whatever that means, for an extended period of time, and then the tide turns and the roles are reversed. The battles are fruitless and futile, and they exacerbate the trend Rabbi Shmuley Boteach speaks about:

> Women are abandoning men in droves and learning to find happiness completely on their own. Two astonishing studies show just how alarming the trend has become. First, there was the study, from the National Marriage Project at Rutgers University and others, that two-thirds of all divorces today are initiated by women.

Research shows that when a man leaves his marriage he is usually leaving for another woman. Often he trades in the mother of his children for someone who is younger and more submissive, who will eventually prove to be emotionally similar to the wife he left. But that's the subject of another book.

For wives, the very opposite is true.

Ninety percent of all women who leave their husbands go out into the wild blue yonder. They are leaving their husbands and accepting what is often life-long single status. They would rather be alone than stay with a man who does not appreciate them. They would rather live by themselves than with a husband who doesn't speak to them, who won't share of his inner self, and who chooses the company of the TV over theirs.

The single woman may live in loneliness. But she lives with the hope that one day she will find a soulmate who cherishes her. But what does the married woman who lives with a man who has abandoned her have to look forward to? In my 20 years of counseling, I have discovered that the loneliest women of all are married!

An even more shocking statistic was recently released by the *New York Times*. For the first time in American history a majority of women are living without a husband. The *Times* reported that 51% of all women are living without a spouse, up from 35 percent in 1950 and 49 percent in 2000.

How could this possibly be?

Simply stated, women are giving up on men. Whereas they once harbored hope that men could satisfy their needs and make them feel appreciated, today they are finding far greater satisfaction in career over companionship and from female friends over husbands.

These are the consequences for a culture that has mercilessly exploited women as a man's plaything. The net result is that the average man has no idea of how to please a woman. He doesn't even know how to talk to her. On a date he uses compliments not to make her light up, but to make her lie down. After marriage his purpose is not to attend to her emotional needs but to get her to attend to his domestic wants, as she slowly becomes his maid.

If Rabbi Boteach seems to be overstating the situation, consider *this: Somewhere in the midst of papers I've collected over the years, I came across a pamphlet, quoting a high school book on home economics from the 1950's. I'm sorry to say I have no idea of its original source, but I think it's important for you to read.*

THE GOOD HOUSEWIFE
HOW TO BE A GOOD WIFE

HAVE DINNER READY: Plan ahead, even the night before, to have a delicious meal—on time. This is a way to let him know that you have been thinking about him and are concerned with his needs. Most men are hungry when they come home, and having a good meal ready is part of a "warm welcome" that is needed.

PREPARE YOURSELF: Take fifteen minutes to rest so that you will be refreshed when he arrives. He has just been with a lot of work-weary people. Be a little gay and a little more interesting. His boring day may need a lift. Greet him with a smile.

CLEAR AWAY THE CLUTTER: Make one last trip though the main part of the house just before your husband arrives, gathering up children's books and toys, papers, etc. Then run a dust cloth over the tables. Your husband will feel he has reached a haven of rest and order, and it will give you lift too.

PREPARE THE CHILDREN: If they are small, wash their hands and faces and comb their hair. They are his little treasures and he would like to see them playing the part.

MINIMIZE ALL NOISE: At the time of his arrival, eliminate all noise from the washer, dryer, or vacuum. Encourage the children to be quiet.

SOME "DO NOT'S": Don't greet him with problems and complaints. Don't complain if he is late for dinner. Count this as a minor problem compared to what he might have gone through that day.

MAKE HIM COMFORTABLE: Have a cool or warm drink ready for him. Have him lean back in a comfortable chair or suggest that he lie down in the bedroom. Arrange his pillow and offer to take off his shoes. Speak in a low, soothing voice. Allow him to relax and unwind.

LISTEN TO HIM: You may have a dozen things to tell him, but the moment of his arrival is not the time. Let him talk first.

MAKE THE EVENING HIS: Never complain if he doesn't take you to dinner or to other entertainment. Instead, try to understand his world of strain and pressure and his need to unwind and relax.

THE GOAL: TO MAKE YOUR HOME A PLACE OF PEACE AND ORDER WHERE YOUR HUSBAND CAN RELAX IN BODY AND SPIRIT.

It may seem we've come a long way from these mid-century mores but, as Boteach goes on to say, "men have to be honest":

> We are part of a new generation of males who have silent contempt for women. At college we use them for sex. At work we reduce them to body parts. In marriage, we push them into domestic servitude. Is it any wonder they're telling us to drop dead?
>
> And it's not the women who suffer most. It's the men.

Is the solution, as Boteach goes on to say, "having a noble knight whisk [women] off their feet to a state of everlasting bliss"? I certainly hope not! After all, isn't that what brought us to where we are today? Elevating men to their former status as warriors and returning women to hero-worshiping wimps won't solve a thing. It will only perpetuate the problem the institution of marriage faces today. It is my hope that before marriage as we know it takes its last breath and is identified with a headstone saying *"the way men and women used to live,"* we can construct a new model of marriage that is less demanding of men, more palatable to women, longer lasting, emotionally constructive, and more enjoyable.

To that end, I believe that *Warrior, Wimp, or Winner* will provide you with a new, viable paradigm for creating a successful, healthy marriage. The basic factor contributing to the demise of the institution of marriage is the war between warriors and wimps, and warriors and wimps come from both genders. As such, the major factor undermining meaningful relations between loving individuals is a battle of the sexes.

Neither warriors nor wimps, whether men or women, will ever effectively love others_unless they are capable of loving themselves. That means that they must recognize and own their shortcomings, fears, and feelings of insufficiency. They may not be able to change or fix them, but they can learn to alter how they react to them. They need to accept and forgive (if necessary) who they perceive themselves to be in order to be able to laugh at themselves and then fully share themselves with others. Until the day when they are all able to recognize that who and what they are is basically worthwhile and deserving of their own love, they will never be able to trust or accept the love someone else offers them.

Unfortunately, for most of us, that day is a long way off, but if you worry or know you're one of those people, you can work to shorten that period of time. The initial steps in that direction involve you putting yourself and your partner on the same page at the same time. It can only be achieved by ending, forever, the historical competition between men and women. This requires that both of you face the way you feel toward the opposite sex, the role you play with regard to the age-old battle between the sexes, and the inner conflict between your emotionally motivated feelings and your intellectually driven thinking. The goal is an acceptance of self, whether you are male or female, tall or short, fat or thin; the mitigation of your need to defend yourself by assuming the role of either a warrior or a wimp; and the elimination of fear and dependency as two of the primary motivating factors governing your interactions and relationships.

As you can probably see, this process involves major adjustments in your emotional orientation and behavioral lifestyle.

You might view it as getting a PhD in yourself. It will require intense introspection, commitment, and follow-through. But it's worth it. The self-satisfaction you derive from each step along the way will be emotionally exhilarating. The end result is almost impossible to put into words. You will have overcome your major obstacle in life: *yourself.*

You will discover a deep, satisfying sense of peace in your world because you no longer need to compete or do battle with your partner—all because you became strong enough to become vulnerable with him or her. That means each of you will be able to bare yourself emotionally to those you love—not as an act of submission, but as one of trust. This act signifies:

> "I am a worthwhile, loving partner who means you no harm and whom you need not fear. Therefore, we need not battle or compete to see who will be the warrior or the wimp. Instead, we can interact as equals who have our own faults as well as our unique talents that can be of benefit to each other."

What I am saying is that there is a solution to your marital problems. But, to avail yourself of it, you need to recognize that the institution of marriage, as it now stands, has all but failed. Think about it once again. Over 50 percent of all marriages end in divorce. How many of the remaining marriages are unhappy or consist of men and women who only *live together alone?* Perhaps a better question would be: "How many happy marriages do you really know of?" or "How many marriages would you use as a model for the marriage you'd like?"

I suspect your response would be very few. That being the case, it would seem you have only three alternatives to choose from: never get married; accept marriage as imperfect and tolerate its imperfection in order to perpetuate the institution and the species; or—the only truly viable solution—work to resolve the age-old power struggle between men and women.

How would you do this? By recognizing that this power struggle is the core reason for the endless conflict between men and women. It ran rampant throughout Greek mythology. It made its presence known in the Judeo-Christian world from the time Eve enticed Adam to take a bite of the apple, and it has reared its head in almost every marital conflict since then. The solution isn't easy. Committed partners can only successfully coexist when each is a separate entity, independent and able to survive on his or her own but also able to benefit from the relationship with the other. They cannot be victims of one another. (At this very moment, I can hear Adam saying, "If it hadn't been for you, we'd still be living comfortably in that wonderful garden.") Even more, they must take individual responsibility for their own actions (i.e., Eve may well have enticed Adam, but Adam ate that apple of his own accord).

After fifty-seven years of marriage to the same person and fifty years as a practicing clinical psychologist, it is apparent to me that the vast majority of the arguments, conflicts, and problems I've seen, both professionally and personally, could have been resolved if people directed their energy and efforts toward the real problems, instead of attempting to place the blame on their partner.

In the age-old tug-of-war, both men and women want to win. They both can, but only if they find a way to stop pulling against each other and learn to pull together. That means they both have to learn to be *winners*.

CHAPTER FOUR

WHERE DO WOMEN STAND?

Ask any woman, and, if she's truly honest, she'll tell you that most men are wimps. Science backs her up: every study of survival rates of infants demonstrates a very large advantage for females over males. And when it comes to multitasking all of the responsibilities involved in running a household and holding down a job, there is no contest. Women come out ahead, hands down. In the words of Margaret Thatcher, "If you want something said, ask a man. If you want something done, ask a woman."

There is no doubt that women are becoming more independent. They're able to get an education and compete with men in the workplace. So where's the bad news? Well, women are able to get an education and compete with men in the workplace. You see, the times have changed, but most men haven't. Some are able to support the change intellectually and verbally, but most can't accept it emotionally. Others are confused. They didn't know how to be a man before, and now they're befuddled about what it takes to be an adequate husband or father. As a result, they can be described as confused human beings who have difficulty communicating about anything other than their jobs, politics, money, taxes, automobiles, or sex. In marriage, they think they communicate, but they don't. A large number of them articulately mouth words but can't express feelings. They justify not saying anything because they don't want to get a divorce, hurt their wife, or upset their children, parents, or friends. But, in truth, they're afraid of what people will think if they speak up and say what they honestly feel. Those remaining behave in a controlling or hard-nosed manner. Underneath the surface, they're weak and frightened. That's why most men rarely exercise honest give-and-take communication with a woman. They know that women who are controlled or intimidated won't speak up.

Today, those threats aren't nearly as effective. Why? For several reasons.

First is the advent of birth control. Once it became readily available, women didn't have to stay home, or have half a dozen babies. Today, increasing numbers of women leave home, get an education, and earn as much as or more than their spouses. The number of women who are economically dependent on men in this country is rapidly diminishing.

Second, *the financial gap between the genders is closing.* Women in 2005 earned 81 cents for every dollar men made. That was up from 76.1 cents in 2001 and 66.6 cents in 1983. The Bureau of Labor Statistics also reported that these changes are most beneficial for workers aged twenty-five to thirty-four. They earned 89 cents for every dollar earned by men, as opposed to women aged thirty-five to forty-four, who earned only 75 cents per dollar. Moreover, shifts in educational and job market patterns are fueling a growing change in the number of marriages where women are sole or primary breadwinners.

In 1987, only 17.8 percent of working women out-earned their partners. In 2005, the number rose to 25.3 percent. In a study by the Pew Research Center, reviewed by the Associated Press on May 29, 2013, it was reported that women are more likely to hold bachelor's degrees than men, and these women make up almost half – 47 percent of the American workforce. They stated further that in more than one in five married households with children, wives out-earn their husbands. It's good for women and, hopefully, will eventually prove good for men. In the meantime, husbands who earn less than their wives are often the butt of ego-deflating jokes.

There are still some women depending entirely on men, but there is little doubt that as time moves on, even they will liberate themselves. Men will have to recognize and adjust to that. What does that mean? First, men need to learn to deal with women as equals, not a population they can subjugate or control. This is a totally new orientation, one that requires interpersonal skills that very few men possess, because they never learned them. Their role models only provided them with two images: a milquetoast, passive father, or a dominating, controlling one. The sensitive, emotionally demonstrative, flexible but strong father figure capable of interacting meaningfully with a woman as a partner in marriage and parenting of children was, and is, a rarity.

Third, *men are still primarily raised by women.* As a result, though they may not admit it, they are accustomed to trying to please them in order to get the approval and love they desperately need. Despite the fact that they experience a stage commonly referred to as "teenage rebellion," their attempt at independence is, for the most part, only evident on the surface. Underneath, they go through their lives still wanting and needing a woman to look up to them, to love them, to attend to them, to be enamored of them, and to acknowledge their adequacy. Thus, throughout their lives, they essentially do what they learned at home as children: "Be good, be nice, be kind, be sweet," or rebel, be cantankerous, be argumentative, be dominating and controlling, whichever behavior best elicited their mother's attention.

An accommodating, compliant, jellyfish husband is a grown man still behaving the way he did as a child. He's filled with inner resentment and anger that he often doesn't quite understand. For a moment, think about the conflict he experiences. If he gets too angry, too vocal, or too critical, he'll lose the love that he desperately needs. So, what choice does he have? He either becomes an obedient, compliant, capitulating person, who then sees himself as a weak man, which contributes to self-loathing, or he gets angry at his wife because he perceives her as manipulating and controlling him. In truth, he's really angry at himself because of his lack of backbone, his depreciated sense of self-adequacy, and his loss of self-worth. If he's a difficult, critical individual, he's certain to perceive his wife as someone who resents him, who isn't loving, attentive, involved emotionally, or sexually responsive, all of which he'll wind up resenting her for. More often than not, he demonstrates so little insight into the part he plays in the equation that he believes he's the victim.

In either case, he winds up angry, unhappy with himself, and resentful toward his spouse. So, what does he do? Too often, he divorces, goes out, finds another woman, and feels loved and manly. Eventually, however, he reproduces the very same relationship that he left. But before that occurs, he usually gives the other woman things he never gave his first wife. He buys her gifts, takes her on expensive vacations, and tries to purchase her favor. As time progresses, he increasingly succumbs to all of her wishes, which he later perceives as demands, and the cycle begins again. In most cases, she is initially appreciative, attentive, and sometimes even subservient, but there is eventually a second divorce, only this time, the marriage is shorter because it's easier to leave the second time around. No wonder the divorce rate for second marriages is even higher than it is for first ones.

Physical or emotional abuse, infidelity, or addiction to alcohol or drugs top the list of reasons for divorce, but other so-called "soft reasons"—such as lack of communication, insensitivity, and loneliness—are also frequently given as grounds for ending long-term relationships.

A 2004 study by the AARP found that, in recent years, an increasing number of men were listing these same soft reasons for getting a divorce. In other words, both sexes contribute equally to the problems in a marital relationship. Often, their words and their actions don't coincide. I cannot begin to count how many times I have heard a woman say, "What I'm looking for isn't a wonderful body, a 'jock,' or a financially independent individual. What I desperately want is a feeling, sensitive, caring man who will love me, cater to me, care for me, become a partner in making a home and a marriage, and who will share responsibilities insofar as rearing children. I want someone who smiles and laughs, who can cry at a 'chick flick' and isn't necessarily consumed by action flicks, sports, or sex. Someone who would prefer me to the Super Bowl."

The words sound so genuine and sincere, but their behavior belies their credibility. On far too many occasions, I have seen women in therapy who have joined dating websites with a written a description of the partner they were looking for. It sounded quite similar to the one I just mentioned. But when they received replies to their inquiries, they turned the man down.

"He seemed too nerdy, too weak, too compliant, too agreeable, too nice."

"He wasn't manly, successful enough, or assertive and aggressive. He's just not my type."

Interestingly, some of these patients divorced because their previous spouse was always at the gym or the golf course, hunting or fishing a workaholic, or too aggressive. There is a sane explanation for these occurrences. Pay attention. *Human beings marry individuals who are exactly like themselves.* That won't be the last time you hear me say that in this book.

Many of you may immediately object. "I'm not at all like my spouse! I want a social life. I want to go out. I want to dance. I want activity. My spouse wants to stay home, be a couch potato, take care of the kids, sit by a fireplace. I want to go to a concert, get involved with others, go skiing. My spouse is the exact opposite of me."

That may, in fact, be true superficially. But *the very same gift can be presented in two different packages.* On the surface, you and your partner may appear radically different, but underneath, the emotions, motivations, and dynamics that contribute to your behaviors are the same. We marry people with similar backgrounds, goals, expectations, and desires—at least emotionally. But on the surface, we behave differently.

You always marry someone who is exactly like you, and then you spend the rest of your days punishing him or her for what you perceive in him or her that you can't stand in yourself. This is a statement worth giving thought to. On the one hand, throughout time immemorial, men have tried to present themselves as strong, masculine, fearless individuals. They've hidden the sensitive person inside because it didn't fit the image they thought society demanded of them. Even more, men have often criticized and belittled their wives for their perceived weakness and frailty.

It's no different from what you see in the animal kingdom. The strongest stallion, bull elephant, or lion leads the pack and has breeding rights with all the females. Weakness isn't valued in the wild, and, sad to say, despite the maturity and greater level of development we human beings would like to think we have, it isn't fully acceptable in our society either.

Perhaps, over the years, when men played the dominant role, women complemented it by appearing weak, subservient, and obedient—in fact, a vow of obedience was even a part of the marriage ceremony. But most women resented the role they played and the lies they lived. Although many women today may utter words that suggest that intellect, sensitivity, good humor, and compassion are valuable attributes in a spouse, they still look down on those characteristics and see them as signs of weakness. They are the same feelings they felt throughout the ages. They didn't like them in themselves in the days when they felt trapped and obliged to comply with the demeaning role society and men designed for them, and they don't like them now. Being unable to accept them in themselves, it's understandable why they cannot accept or appreciate these characteristics in the males they date or marry. As a result, just like men, women are either unaware or unsure as to how they should act and what they should feel.

In order to change this situation, women have to learn to appreciate and accept their emotions and feelings, whether they're deemed desirable or not. They need to learn that they can be soft, feminine, sensual, loving, compassionate, and caring without giving up their independence or feeling trapped and controlled in a male-dominated society. After all, if warrior behavior didn't work for men, it's not going to work for women either.

Basically, warriors and wimps are of the same ilk. Their behaviors differ, but their motivations are the same. Heretofore, warriors were usually males. Women were the wimps. Today, warriors and wimps can't be classified by gender. It's their coping techniques and behaviors that give them away.

If that sounds confusing and complicated to you, you're not alone. What I'm suggesting in *Warrior, Wimp, or Winner* is that everyone else is confused, too. That's the problem. Most people don't know who they are or what they should be, so they go through life playing roles, acting parts, and feeling disappointed, cheated, and misled. The rules and roles they were given to follow were lies.

CHAPTER FIVE

THE WARRIOR

Beware of warriors! They're dangerous, hurtful, controlling, and angry. To say the least, they're difficult to live with, particularly when they're wounded, which is most often the case. As a general rule, warriors exhibit few signs of self-awareness or sensitivity, but they are acutely aware of the actions and words of others. Their behavior is typically highly egocentric and defensive in nature. Moreover, they tend to view a potential threat in almost every interpersonal relationship. As a result, loving relationships are difficult for them.

Because the notion of vulnerability is a totally foreign concept to them, warriors thrive on conflict. They almost *enjoy* a battle, are quick to enter one, and are reluctant to lose it, even if it means they will lose the war. Because they are unable to trust, their relationships are fraught with feelings of rejection, anger, and tremendous pain. Because they perceive love as a form of control, it's only when they are able to control the people they love that they feel safe and at ease. However, when they can control the people they love, they doubt the love they receive. For them, it's a logical conclusion. *After all, these people have no choice but to love me. They need me. They're fearful of me. Thus, their display of love is suspect.*

When they can't control someone, they go on guard, thinking, *This person can hurt me.* Therefore, they push the other person away, criticize, belittle, or intimidate him or her. As a consequence, warriors rarely afford themselves the possibility of getting love from someone they can't control. It's sad, because that love might, in fact, be more sincere.

Emotionally, warriors are very fragile individuals. Their outward behavior totally belies the feeling person inside. In actuality, they are far more sensitive than most individuals realize, and they are often extremely generous, even though they conceal it well. However, if you know where to look, you will find that they wear their feelings on their sleeve. Their egos are broken, and their sense of lovability suffers from pain experienced early in childhood. The rule of thumb is that the degree of insufficiency the warrior feels is equal to the thickness of the outward shell he or she displays. In truth, warriors are emotionally wounded individuals who feel unworthy and undeserving of the love they desperately need and desire. Rather than admit to this, they deny their need and present themselves as self-sufficient, strong, independent, and able to make it entirely on their own. Although these declarations are false, people tend to accept them as truths, which only serve to further estrange and distance warriors from those around them.

To make matters worse, warriors more often than not believe their own facades. They put out little or no effort to lean on anyone. Their usual approach is to wait for others to initiate relationships. Think of the warrior as an armadillo with a very soft underbelly covered by a hard shell and sharp claws.

Warriors are basically depressed people. Little, if anything, ever fully appeases their emotional neediness or their desperate desire for love and affection. Despite that, most warriors go through life playing the role of benign dictators, who, in their own minds, do everything for others, hold things together, and work harder and achieve more than anyone else but get no real thanks or appreciation for what they've done. The sad fact is, even when it's there, they can't believe the appreciation they get. The only role they know is to do for others; they need to be the benefactor, never the beholden. That stems from their need to prove to themselves and the rest of the world that they're self-sufficient and adequate. But it paints them into a corner. If no one is allowed to do for them, they can never feel fully appreciated, genuinely loved, or recognized for their efforts. To compensate, they need and expect others to feel indebted to them and make their own lives a continuous stream of projects designed to reinforce their facades of strength and success. It also keeps them involved to the point they are so preoccupied with their activities that they have neither the time nor the opportunity to get close to their inner feelings of despair and loneliness.

Truly, warriors are sad individuals. On one hand, all they desire and desperately need is love and affection, emotions that, more often than not, they are truly worthy of. On the other hand, they are blind to the fact that the love they want and need would be there if it weren't for their controlling behavior and their inability to ask for what they need. In the end, those who love warriors often avoid or tiptoe around them because of their false sense of pride and their critical, demanding, and oftentimes hostile behavior.

Warriors' underlying goodness doesn't excuse their outward behavior or the damage that they perpetrate on others, but it does explain the reasons for it. It also provides a better understanding of their motivations and feelings. Sadly, there is little hope for warriors unless they can permit themselves to look inside and get in touch with the emotions and feelings that they themselves can't accept and learn that they can't change or outrun what's imprinted on their emotional hard drive.

What warriors can do is learn to accept the hurting child inside, divest themselves of their armor, and allow others to see them for who they are. To be sure, it's difficult and frightening for anyone to do, but it is almost impossible for the warrior. There is, however, a saving grace: after warriors try, they can discard those who reject them and cling to those who genuinely accept them.

The words sound easy, but the fear of exposing oneself to others is so great that most warriors never take their armor off. They live emotionally sad, lonely lives, constantly putting out effort to prove their worth and feeling dissatisfied after every success they achieve. Life for warriors is a series of mountain climbs. When they reach the top of one, they celebrate for a brief time before an almost gut-wrenching feeling of despair takes over. "What's it all for?" they ask. "Is that all there is?" Then, for a period of time, they submerge themselves in a world of martyrdom and anger toward the very people whose affection and nurturing they desire. Emotionally, warriors are bottomless pits. There is never going to be enough success, money, sex, food, alcohol, houses, attention, or love to satisfy the emptiness inside them or to hide their inner fears of being seen as weak, emotionally needy, and out of control. It is no wonder that they compensate by needing to control others and the world.

If this description depicts your partner, even in part, you are faced with a mighty challenge. Either you have the courage to leave him or her, or you use that same courage in a more positive manner; despite your fears, you choose to stand up to him or her. Give your partner the gift of his or her own reality; tell him or her you're not fearful of his or her anger or rejection and, although you know you can make it on your own, you don't want to. Further, tell your partner you are not going to leave him or her, because you love him or her, despite the hurtful behavior. Let your partner know you see him or her for the person inside that he or she can't accept, but you also clearly see and value the person he or she is. If, on the other hand, this description fits *you*, open your heart to the hurt inside you. Drop your guard, and share that hurting child inside you with those you love. You may be pleasantly surprised by how forgiving and receptive they'll be.

CHAPTER SIX

DEALING WITH A WARRIOR

How do you deal with warriors? My first thought is that you never take them on head-to-head, because you'll be competing on their terms, and you're bound to lose. Remember, warriors are experts at confrontation, intimidation, and control. Therefore, you have to mentally and emotionally prepare yourself when you finally decide to honestly confront a warrior.

The first step is for you to repeat after me, "What is obvious isn't always accurate." Helen, for example, described her husband this way:

"Joseph is a bear. He's irritable, critical, and quick to explode. Whenever I even slightly question his behavior, he becomes defensive and refuses to answer. He either draws up inside or estranges himself. He doesn't interact with anybody, because he doesn't care. No one matters to him."

It's true that Joseph appears to be a wolf. After all, he snarls and growls, bares his teeth, and, in some instances, even bites.

But inside every warrior is a wimp. If there wasn't, they wouldn't have to put up such a tough exterior.

So while everything Helen said regarding Joseph's behavior was accurate, her interpretation was way off base. Whenever you want to communicate with people who are upset, argumentative, or difficult to deal with—and warriors definitely fall into this category—the rule of thumb is you must look beneath the surface to understand who they are and how best to approach them. For example, Joseph's behavior had little to do with his complaints. When I spoke with him, he said, "I feel as though I don't matter. I'm just a paycheck, a meal ticket for the whole family." But what was scaring him to death was that his job was about to end, and at fifty-five, he had strong doubts about his ability to find another position at the same level with an equivalent salary. Without a job, without a position, he feared he would no longer even be a meal ticket or a paycheck. The thought was devastating. He wondered, *If I can't be that, would she want me at all?* But he was incapable of sharing his fears with her.

Another patient's behavior was very similar in nature. However, Roger's actions more closely resembled those of a fighting dog. He was quick to attack and vicious to the point of frightening his wife and children, as well as anyone else with whom he came in close contact. Nothing pleased him. He found fault with everything and everyone. He hadn't always been that way. His extremely hostile behavior started about six months earlier and seemed to get worse with every passing day. His wife said, "I don't know if I can live with him anymore. He's unbearable. I don't deserve this kind of treatment from anyone, let alone this ungrateful SOB."

Similar to Helen, her interpretation was inaccurate. After several sessions, Roger confided in me that, following his annual physical six months earlier, his doctor referred him to an oncologist because he believed Roger had prostate cancer. Roger never went back to the doctor or to the specialist, nor did he inform his wife or family. Instead, he tried to deny it, even to himself. But it was apparent his denial wasn't working. His fears were manifested by his hostility. What he needed was someone to support him, but he drove everyone away. Ironically, the person he most wanted support from but feared to be honest with was his wife, who was now threatening to leave him. He, too, found it almost impossible to communicate his feelings.

Then there was Arnie, whose daughter was getting married but whose tuxedo no longer fit. He hated buying clothes, and he was particularly embarrassed about the weight he had gained. As a result, he put it off. One week before the wedding, his wife insisted they go shopping. His response was, "Okay, *Mother*, but I'm going alone." He stomped out of the house, and the next thing she heard was the screeching of tires as he pulled out of the driveway. Two hours passed before the phone rang. Arnie's voice was somewhat contrite but at the same time, cool and impersonal. "I'm not going to buy a tux. I'll just wear my old one. It's only one night, and it really doesn't matter."

He had pressed the right button, and, in short order, he got the response he wanted: an angry reproach for acting like a child, running out of the house, and not buying a tux.

After eliciting her anger, he asked, "Why don't you stop screaming and have dinner with me?"

Her response was, "I don't want to be with you when you're rude and arrogant. You think you're better than anyone else, you're always perfect, always right, and everyone else is always wrong." Then she hung up the phone.

Once again, the interpretation was inaccurate. Her description only reflected his external behavior. Inside, emotionally, he was an insecure individual who functioned successfully at work but not at home. In intimate relationships with people he loved, he was fearful of not being sufficient and desperate to appear strong and in control. As a result, he acted in an arrogant manner and projected a false air of confidence. It was far from the truth, but it was his cover story and he was sticking to it, even if it pushed his loved ones away.

Melanie never complained, but her work at school began to deteriorate. She was less and less the energetic, happy-go-lucky kid she had been. She kept to herself, verbalized less, and seemed to have more problems in her relationships with her siblings. Her mother suggested that the problem was hormonal in nature, that it was the typical behavior you might expect from a young lady who was just about to start her period. "She is undoubtedly reacting to problems associated with puberty," she told me.

Wrong. Her explanation was too easy. Had her mother tried to read between the lines, she might have learned that Melanie's lifetime playmate had moved to another city and that, where once there were four girls who were close to one another, there were now only three. Melanie's best friend was gone. Her other two friends preferred each another, and she felt left out and pushed away. In her mind, it was because something was lacking in her. She perceived herself as the odd man out and proceeded to act that way. Her behavior wasn't acceptable, but once again, the real problem was not the obvious one. Melanie couldn't bear to reveal how inadequate she felt and how badly she wanted to be included, but the manner she went about trying to be noticed was noxious to others and self-destructive.

There are dozens of other examples I could cite, but you've probably got the idea. *What is obvious isn't always accurate.* When it comes to interacting with warriors in particular, you need to step back, take a deep breath, and ask yourself, "Where are they coming from?"

Too many people, particularly warriors, are severely lacking the wherewithal to recognize their own inner feelings, let alone share them with someone else. Nor are they able to read between the lines and discover the hidden agenda underlying their behavior. They are more prone to respond only to what immediately comes to their mind, is right before their eyes, or is dictated by old—often non-constructive—coping techniques. Consequently, their reactions are frequently distorted, biased, misdirected, and justified by faulty reasoning. The problem is that they can't emotionally afford to see themselves, so they believe their own rationalizations, which aid them in avoiding coming in contact with what is really of concern to them. I cannot stress that fact enough. If there is one cardinal rule to follow when responding to warriors, it would be that, before you react to the obvious, stop, particularly if their behavior is excessively hurtful, unwarranted, or inappropriate, and try to determine where they are coming from. At the same time, you need to take care because, in too many instances, your own emotional orientation can determine not only what you hear, but, more important, how you interpret and later react to their behavior. You need to stand strong because, in some instances, their intelligence and forceful personality may cause you to accept their rationale as truth, which will prevent you from helping them.

The truth is when you are in a good place, you hear more accurately. You don't personalize things, and you don't take criticism quite so harshly. As a result, you needn't defend yourself. Instead, you are able to be more objective, read between the lines, and determine what is really being said and, on many occasions, why it's being said. Again, that doesn't excuse or justify unacceptable behavior, but it does explain it.

When the person you're attempting to resolve a conflict with is a warrior, he or she is by definition a difficult person. Fortunately, there are some specific guidelines you can follow that will enhance, but not guarantee, your chances of reaching an equitable solution. These guidelines apply no matter what gender your partner is or how intelligent or successful he or she may be.

1. Avoid discussing issues, facts, or who is right or wrong. That will only heighten the conflict and magnify the problem. Even more important, in most instances, the issues and facts aren't pertinent to the conflict itself. They are only smoke screens around which an argument can take place and behind which the warrior can hide his or her fears and feelings of insecurity.

2. When you speak with difficult people, completely eliminate the word *you* from your vocabulary. It will only serve to provoke the other person, cause him or her to be anxious or feel accused, and, as a result, raise his or her guard.

3. Do not take any damaging statements personally. First, that's exactly what your opponent wants. He or she needs you to lose your cool, which will result in placing you onto the battlefield—where warriors feel most comfortable. War is their game, and, in most instances, they're better at it than you. Remember, they've had far more experience. Second, you need to recognize that their statements are either meant to anger you or are more a reflection of where they are coming from than they are about you. It isn't a personal attack. It only demonstrates how hurt and threatened they feel and the low level to which they will stoop to defend their weak ego. Defending your position, trying to set things right, or responding to personal remarks will only give credence to, not invalidate, their statements.

4. Keep in mind that the conflict is not based on intellectual factors. It is almost always purely emotional in nature. Therefore, realize that trying to talk rationally with an out-of-control emotional person will get you nowhere. Consequently, you must communicate emotionally. But when you do, unlike the warrior, you must be in control of yourself. Your goal shouldn't be to change the other person or his or her position. Let me assure you that no matter what you do, you won't be able to control a warrior. Your job is to speak on an emotional level about your feelings, perceptions, cares, and concerns. You see, there is no way to argue about him or her. There is no right or wrong. Your concerns are solely yours. The same can be said about your perceptions and your feelings. They may be inaccurate or distortions of reality,

but they're yours and you can't be blamed, punished, or devalued because of them.

5. Never create a win-lose situation, because the end result is always that both parties lose. You may win short-term and feel good, but the loser feels badly and winds up resenting you and negating any possible long-term resolutions. When you lose, the result is essentially the same, but the shoe is on the other foot. The only desirable solution to any conflict is one where both individuals win. Win-win situations can only occur when issues and facts are minimized and emotions are maximized and shared.

How can you create a win-win situation? Wayne Dyer said it best. Let me try to paraphrase him: Listen intently to the other person. When you disagree, take a deep breath. After he or she has finished speaking, whether you agree or not, your first response needs to be, "You may be right." Notice, that's not an apology, a statement of agreement or disagreement, or a personal attack. It merely says, "You may be right, but more importantly, I heard you." It can be followed up with, "Now I'd very much appreciate it if you would hear how I feel. It's difficult for me to tell you honestly all the emotions inside me, but I'd like to try. And I'm asking that you listen, not interrupt, in fact, not say anything till I'm done. Then I promise you, I will listen to anything you have to say." I should add that you can even make notes prior to your encounter and tell the other person ahead of time, "I'm so nervous in this situation that I made several notes to help me recall the things

I want to talk about. So forgive me if I refer to this paper in order to help me remember my thoughts."

6. Speak from your heart. Doing so requires that you be able to access your own feelings. That means that you must have the wherewithal to recognize where you're really coming from inside, what emotions are driving you, and what you want to accomplish during your discussion. But before you verbalize your feelings, take the time to ensure that you truly see yourself for who you are, that you're aware of your own hidden agendas, and that you're willing to expose them openly. It's easier to do when you can forgive and accept yourself despite your shortcomings, acknowledge your attributes, and, most of all, value your feelings—the good ones, bad ones, strong ones, and weak ones. Notice, you can be frightened, wrong, or out of step with popular thought or moral dictates, but you can't live ashamed of who you are and what you feel. Nor can you share who you are if you haven't looked directly at yourself in the mirror and decided, "I'm okay in spite of and because of who I am."

7. After accepting and coming to peace with yourself, you will be ready to speak from your heart. You will no longer have to hide or defend yourself or your feelings, nor will you have to push others away for fear they'll see the real you. Quite the contrary. You'll be able to open up, be vulnerable, and expose the emotions inside you without embarrassment or apology. As a result, you will be able to say something like the following:

I know there have been problems between us. It concerns me, and I'd very much appreciate your listening to what I have to say. I promise that, when I'm done, I will then listen to anything you want to communicate to me. You can call me weak, neurotic, emotionally needy, whatever, because, in part, they all apply to me. It's who I am. It's the way I feel, and it causes me to think and behave in the manner I do. I know that I haven't always had the strength to stand up for myself, or to tell you or others what truly matters to me, who I am or what I think and feel, let alone what I want. As a result, I suspect you've had to deal with me based on assumptions about all those things. If I've appeared distant, estranged, silent, or rejecting, it wasn't a true reflection of where I'm coming from. It was my way of hiding my fear of being hurt and rejected and of losing a relationship with you. As a result, I feel that I've lost the relationship by default. I promise you, despite my inside inclination to run and hide, in the future, I am going to try to behave in a more constructive manner. I don't know that you'll always agree with me, but that isn't necessary. I don't know that you'll always like what I say. But I do know that in the future, you'll know where I'm coming from. More than anything, I want an honest, meaningful relationship with you. I want to feel comfortable with you and accepted by you. I never have. I'm sure a good deal of my doubt has come about because of my own fears. But I'm going to change. I'm more than willing to do my part to reach out, to try to be a better partner, and to let you know how much you mean to me, how much I need you, and how much I care. At the same time, I hope that you can hear what I'm saying and that you will choose to do your part because you want the same things I do. I think the reason I can say it now is because, for the first time in my life, I know that I can make it without your love and acceptance. I'm now willing to take the risk of losing you. But that's not what I want. It's just that knowing I can make it on my own gives me the strength to tell you I'd like to make it together.

Obviously, these are all my words, appropriate to a hypothetical conversation. You have to fill in the spaces with what's inside you. You have to be honest, even if it hurts. And you have to take the chance of being rejected. I can't guarantee what reaction you'll receive. I can, however, assure you that you will feel much better. Although you may not get the results you want, it won't devastate you to the point of life or death. Why? Because having the courage to be yourself and taking the risk of being totally rejected has its own reward. It will result in you being proud of yourself.

While not always successful insofar as the other person is concerned, this approach will definitely contribute to your sense of self-worth. At the same time, it may enhance any chance you do have of truly resolving the conflict you're experiencing. It is, by far, the best and most effective way to reach someone, but it doesn't always work.

Warriors can be so fearful of your honesty that they retreat behind a wall of anger or silence or push you away emotionally. Despite that risk, it is still the best path to follow; honest communication from another human being is always more palatable than coping mechanisms, such as playing a warrior or a wimp.

The moral is: to communicate effectively, you need to see yourself, accept yourself, forgive yourself, and share yourself, which is easier said than done.

CHAPTER SEVEN

THE WIMP

You know them. They're the ones who always defer to their partners, voice few opinions, laugh halfheartedly, agree consistently, and deny feelings of anger or resentment over being controlled by a husband or wife who runs the show, calls the shots, sets the pace, and often seems totally insensitive to their feelings. They are the compliant male, the spineless female—*the wimp.*

These individuals capitulate, compromise, and rarely voice their real thoughts or feelings. They rationalize their behavior with statements like, "It isn't worth the effort," "These are little things that truly don't matter," "I do it for the sake of peace," or, "It's not worth starting World War III over inconsequential matters."

They justify their position with, "I really don't care. It doesn't matter to me. I've got bigger issues to deal with." However, one rarely hears what these issues are. Despite their outward appearance of intelligence, their level of education, their good nature, or how they contribute to the relationship, they assume a secondary position, content, at least on the surface, to be the dutiful, compliant, passive spouse who is looked upon as "a gem."

"She takes an awful lot," their friends say, "but she does it well," or, "You can't help but like him and admire him for his tolerance."

Most of the time, however, the tolerance is a facade. Underneath, there is passive resentment. On occasion, it may escalate into an angry tirade or an outburst of frustration and hostility, which is short-lived on the surface but omnipresent in their underlying feelings and emotions.

In many ways, the picture isn't radically different from the position women assumed only a couple of decades ago. I cannot begin to count the number of wives I've known professionally and personally who felt insignificant, inadequate, and dependent on men who ran the show. They gave up any sense of personal rights. They felt they contributed little because they earned little. They saw themselves as dependent on their husbands, without whom they couldn't survive or raise their children. They were the quintessential "Stepford Wives."

In today's world, the positions previously held by men and women are often reversed, but the emotional dynamics are the same. Today, more men are willing than at any time before to openly verbalize their need for care, nurturing, and acceptance. Sadly, their attitudes haven't kept pace with their behavior. As a result, at some level of awareness, these individuals see themselves as subservient and emotionally dependent. They feel threatened by the potential loss of their spouse's approval or acceptance and try harder because they perceive themselves to be in second place. All the while, underlying resentment makes itself apparent in passive-aggressive behaviors, withholding of affection or sex, and occasional vitriolic outbursts. The result is marital relationships that suffer enormously.

In past years, it was wives who redirected their attention to their children in lieu of their spouses. Their husbands may have felt jealous but were reluctant to express it. After all, how does one say, "You're too good to your children. I resent it"? It wasn't politically correct then, and it isn't today. But now, on an increasing basis, I see women complaining about men who aren't interested sexually, are more emotionally expressive toward their children than they are to their wives, and display little real affection or caring for their spouses. Ironically, these attitudes aren't always apparent by the outward behavior of such couples. They still give presents for Christmas, anniversaries, and birthdays. They take vacations together. Friends, children, and social acquaintances often view them as "golden couples." But in the bedroom, behind closed doors, the story is different. Honest conversation is rare. Intimacy is absent, and emotional interactions, aside from occasional angry outbursts, are not to be heard. Their time and attention are primarily directed toward maintaining the outward facade of the relationship without any effort being directed toward emotional growth, acquiring greater sensitivity to one another, or changing behaviors.

Sadly, a majority of married partners aren't aware of how their spouses feel. Instead, they're fully engaged in emotionally protecting themselves. But that's not something new. Today's marital problems are no different from the ones I saw in therapy ten or twenty years ago, except the shoe is sometimes on the other foot. Now, it's as likely to be wives instead of husbands who come in stating, "I can't understand it. I had no idea how angry or upset he felt. Then, out of the blue, without telling me, he filed for divorce."

My response is typically, "No wonder he filed. You were so unaware of his feelings that you never saw how discontent, hurt, and angry he was."

"But if he was so unhappy, why didn't he tell me?"

The answer these people usually elicit from their spouse is the same that I heard decades ago. "I did, time and time again. But you never listened." For the most part, both statements are true. Both partners fill up a one-hundred-pound sack with pain and irritations that they never openly, honestly, or clearly discuss. Then, when they have 120 pounds crammed into that sack, the seams split.

In the end, wimps wind up being depressed, passive-aggressive "good guys and gals" who never win. Why? Because they generally tend to deny their emotions to themselves as well as to others. They keep their own counsel and, as a result, rarely share their true feelings with anyone. Although they often boil inside, they don't allow their emotions to govern their behavior. Except for infrequent angry outbursts, they don't see their lives or behavior as necessarily bad. Then again, they rarely perceive them as joyous. For them, life is mainly tolerated, rather than desired. They learned this coping pattern early in life, and it often follows them to their graves. To alter this condition, they must learn to open themselves up emotionally, share whatever they discover inside them, and be willing to be flexible, all of which are possible if they are committed to solving their problem.

The first step in this process involves being able to recognize the problem. That's not necessarily easy to do. Most individuals automatically focus outward, on the people around them, the place they reside in, and the situations they feel are contributing to their stress or conflict. That's the wrong direction. To find the way out of their problem, they first need to look inside.

Let me provide a couple of examples to help you to see this more clearly.

Beverly described Phillip as having always been a wonderful husband. Maybe he worked too hard, but he was a good provider and a generous man, who never objected to what she purchased for herself, the kids, or their home. The children adored him, and her friends had commented more than once that they wished their husbands were as kind and considerate. From her viewpoint, they had an ideal marriage. In their friends' eyes, they were the "golden couple" with a perfect family. No wonder she found herself in a state of shock when he came home late from work one evening, after he had obviously been drinking, and announced that he wanted a divorce.

When she came to her senses sufficiently, she questioned his reasons. All she could get him to say was that he was unhappy and there was nobody else involved. He added that, even though he needed his freedom, he would always take care of her and the kids. Her family and closest friends questioned if he was being honest about there not being another woman. All agreed that he was going through a midlife crisis.

She stated her reason for seeing a therapist was that she wanted to know what she could do to bring him back to his senses. After further questioning, she indicated that she had no idea what might be upsetting him, except that a good friend, two years his junior, had recently died of a heart attack. She also stated that Phillip agreed to see me after her first appointment but only to discuss how to make their divorce easier on the children.

Interestingly enough, Phillip had little more insight regarding his own behavior than his wife. He knew he felt trapped, wanted his freedom, and had felt that way for at least five or six years. He reiterated that he had no other romantic interest and he loved his wife, but he wasn't "in love" with her. As the picture unraveled, it became apparent that he was the "good kid" in the "emotional family portrait." He was the baby in the family, and according to his siblings, he was Mother's favorite.

Beverly wholeheartedly agreed and stated that during several arguments, she had even asked him who he was really married to, her or his mother. In my opinion, it really didn't matter. He felt as controlled by his wife as he had by his mother. In either case, his emotional conditioning was complete by the age of six. Whenever he felt love for or from a woman, he was filled with an overwhelming feeling of guilt if he did not please them, as well as a strong need to capitulate, along with an inability to hurt or disappoint them. The overt expression of anger was foreign to him, and his own desires were always secondary to the wishes of those he loved. In the eyes of others, however, he was perceived as boyish, a bit of a nerd, but a good guy.

It was apparent that the death of his friend introduced a harsh note of reality into Phillip's life. He knew he was unhappy, but he was unable to emotionally accept the reasons underlying his feelings of depression. To do so would necessitate recognizing his own weakness, expressing his unconscious feelings of anger and resentment, and changing his mode of behavior. Divorce was his way out. It was a form of coping that enabled him to escape the situation and the truth of his own being. There were, of course, other avenues he could have chosen. He might have behaved promiscuously, adopted a passive-aggressive lifestyle, or compensated by interacting in an authoritarian, hostile manner. After considerable therapy, Phillip and Beverly developed a new means of relating. She learned the problems in their marriage were not solely the fault of her husband. She also recognized that his superficial "agreeability" was a perfect match for her need to control and to feel self-righteously burdened with still another child to raise. Conversely, he discovered his wife wasn't his mother, he did not need to live the rest of his life as a passive-aggressive teenager, and love is available only when you're able to freely express honest feelings.

This phenomenon is not strictly limited to one gender or even to married couples. Liz was as much a martyr as Phillip. Every one of her relationships was fraught with conflict. Illustrative of the fact was the recent problem she had experienced with a friend who invited her to spend a weekend with her at her family's ranch. Liz immediately agreed, but as the day approached, she found herself inundated with work and deadlines. The thought of leaving for the weekend increased her normal amount of stress tenfold. She needed that time to catch up. The anxiety she experienced because of her conflict over whether or not to cancel pulled her in opposite directions and further increased her stress. True to form, she found it impossible to change her mind or go back on her word. She simply couldn't do what was best for her.

As a result, Liz reluctantly spent an alcohol-filled weekend with a very depressed friend who needed a sounding board for her lamentations about her single life, her divorce, and the way she was treated by men. As the weekend progressed, Liz became increasingly anxious. She wanted to leave. She knew that staying was doing her no good, but she was afraid to lose her friend's "love." Consistent with a long-established pattern of behavior, she did what she didn't want to do, and thus, she became angry at herself, her friend, and even God, for not giving her a strong enough backbone to stand up in the world.

What she needed to learn in therapy was that she already had a backbone. She was just too frightened to use it. Consequently, she lived a lie, hated herself, and eventually resented everyone she cared for. The solution was simple. Doing it was difficult. Liz had to learn to live according to what she knew and let her good common sense govern her emotions and behavior.

The lessons Phillip, Beverly, and Liz eventually learned from therapy are important to every one of us but particularly to wimps. They teach us that when you can't say "no" to the people you love, you can't say "yes" to genuine joy and love. Instead, you will constantly question whether your every "yes" is a "no" in disguise. As a result, your heart will be filled with self-resentment for being a wimp and, illogical as it may seem, anger toward your partner because you are unable to deal with him or her.

Sadly, when you are incapable of standing up to someone for yourself, that person will interpret your inability to stand up as a sign that you are also too weak to support him or her. If you're a wimp who truly wants to experience a meaningful, interactive relationship with a partner, take heart. You must behave according to the following axiom: "If a relationship is worth having, it is worth fighting for."

CHAPTER EIGHT

DEALING WITH A WIMP

I t seemed like Chuck's world was falling apart—not in slow motion, but almost all at once. Every support system, everything that helped hold him together all these years, was crumbling at the same time. It was difficult for him to determine what initiated the slide. The more he spoke about it, the more he decided it was like the chicken and the egg—he didn't know which came first, the hurt he felt as a child or the loss of a man he called father but had been physically estranged from for years. His biological parents divorced when he was only three, and all that remained of their relationship were bitter feelings his mother still expressed years later. His father moved away, remarried, started another family, and only after experiencing considerable success in the oil industry, decided to revisit his past. At that point, he attempted to get involved with his then fourteen-year-old son. He started to provide child support and requested visitation rights, but by that time, the emotional damage to his son was complete. Although there were occasional Thanksgivings or Christmases together, Chuck felt only a semi-closeness with the man he called "Father." It provided him with some degree of emotional support but never fully repaired the damage caused by his father's leaving in the first place.

In contrast, his mother was always there, at least physically. In some ways, Chuck often saw her as being there too much of the time. She overprotected him, made excuses for his misbehavior, and failed to provide real boundaries or limits for him. All of this stemmed from her love for him and her attempt to make up for the guilt she felt over choosing to divorce and cheating Chuck of his father. Years later, his mother's role was still the same. She continuously built him up and praised him for his achievements, often to excess. In fact, he even questioned the sincerity and credence of her words. As a result, it was difficult for him to derive any real sense of confidence or benefit from them. He wanted to believe her, but too often, her gushing was so outlandish that he couldn't help but see her and her words as strong on form but lacking in substance. In many ways, that was also the way he saw himself. He perceived his life as a sham, a facade giving the impression of diligence, commitment, and a strong desire to achieve. All the while, inside, he felt himself a failure.

The unexpected death of his father left Chuck feeling a loss that didn't make sense to him. It wasn't as though they were really close, yet something was missing. He finally concluded it was the end of an era. With Dad gone, Chuck would never be able to show this man he was worthy of his love and to verbalize through actions, rather than words, "You shouldn't have left. I was worth staying for."

At the same time, his career seemed to be plummeting. His company had merged, and his position was being taken over by the controlling entity. As a result, not only was he in the dark regarding what position he might fill in the future, he was unsure as to whether he still had a job.

To make matters worse, his wife had been experiencing medical problems that were not covered by his insurance. Last, his son was graduating from high school and wanted to go to college out of state, which would cost considerably more than Chuck could afford. Everything seemed to be coming to a head. And, as usual, there was Mom hovering in the background, wanting to come to his aid, to provide financial support, and, with it, at least in his mind's eye, assume total control of his life, increase his feelings of responsibility to her, and reinforce his feelings of insufficiency.

From Chuck's viewpoint, his life wasn't worth living. He had lost a parent he never had, had a parent he sometimes didn't want, and anticipated financial obligations he felt inadequate to meet. To make matters worse, he was becoming increasingly argumentative and dissatisfied with his home, life, and marriage. He felt alone, with no one to lean on, and he was angry about it. Thus, there were times he would explode for no reason at all—at least that was his conclusion several days after each blowup. But at the time he erupted, he felt entirely justified. After all, he was married to a woman he perceived as dependent, needy of his attention, and unable to support herself emotionally. It was no wonder she was willing to take anything he dished out. Nor was it surprising that he didn't feel he could lean on her. The curious paradox was he had unconsciously chosen her for those very reasons. Yet, there were times he wished she were stronger, someone who could support him. But even if she were, his childhood experiences with his mother would have made it difficult for him to lean on her. That, however, was something he didn't have to concern himself with because his wife lacked the backbone to stand up to him. Therefore, he questioned whether she could stand up for him. As a result, he felt there was no way for him to win. There was no one he could lean on, and even if there were, leaning only exaggerated his feelings of weakness and insufficiency and perpetuated his fear that he couldn't make it on his own. Nothing helped. The arguments with his wife increased by geometric proportions, and his feelings of depression and helplessness overwhelmed him. In his own words, "There is absolutely no light at the end of the tunnel."

His plight is not as atypical as it may appear. All too many men (and many women, as well) find themselves in the same position. They see themselves as trapped in situations that they fail to realize are of their own making. They feel unable to leave but are unhappy about staying. On the one hand, they look for support that isn't forthcoming from a spouse they belittle, criticize, and find fault with. It doesn't matter they do so in order to cripple their partner emotionally to ensure they'll stay with them. No matter what the motivation is, that type of behavior doesn't elicit a positive response. On the other hand, they find fault with their spouse for being weak and unsupportive. But once again, it's of no matter, because for most individuals of this type, no amount of reassurance is ever given credence or accepted as truth.

In Chuck's case, you need to bear in mind that all his life his mother built him up and then found fault and pointed out his shortcomings. All of which was carried out, at least in his mother's mind, in order to "motivate him to achieve." It only stands to reason that later in life, when his wife tells him how much she cares, he doesn't believe her. Somewhere deep inside, at some level of awareness, he feels he hasn't made it; he's a failure who never fully lived up to his mother's expectations or achieved sufficient success to compete with his father. After all, if he had achieved, his mother wouldn't have had to build him up with false or faint praise. The obvious conclusion was she felt he needed it, not because he deserved it. As strange as it may seem, Chuck may appear to be a warrior, but, as you can see, he's really a wimp.

How many men find themselves in this situation? More than you realize. But, if you found it difficult to relate to his situation, you may be able to see yourself in Judy's marriage:

"Doctor Ed, I don't know what to do. I've been married to Jack for 20 years and I doubt he'll ever change. He doesn't talk. He keeps everything inside. It isn't like it's only me. He does the same thing with our children. They don't know him. He's like a mechanical man. He doesn't have any friends to speak of, just a few people at work. I've only seen him cry once, when his mother died. And that was only for a short time. I'm a feeling person. I need people and conversation, but when I'm with him, I feel lonely. I really don't know how I wound up in a relationship like this. I know I'm not alone. A lot of my friends say the same thing. I think most men must be like Jack. They don't have any feelings. It wasn't so terrible when the kids were young. My life was full. I was busy with them. Now they're married, they have their own lives and I'm left with this silent body. At my age, I certainly don't want a divorce. But I do want someone to talk to. I'm not the kind of person that would go out and have an affair. That's not me, but......."

I've heard statements similar to Judy's dozens of times. All of them included the notion that men are devoid of feelings. At the same time, the women stress they have an over-abundance of emotions. The curious paradox is why so many feeling, caring, emotionally expressive women wound up marrying these "unfeeling" men. Oddly enough, the notion that men are lacking in feelings is a prevalent one. It's not only generally accepted, but often used as a criticism by female wimps. It may well be a sham perpetrated by women who portray themselves as victims, perhaps even martyrs, who have to suffer throughout life, due to the lack of involvement and/or sensitivity of the men they married. It provides them with a right to complain, to estrange themselves and even punish their spouses because they're emotionally lacking. But, it's in sharp contrast to a concept we've already discussed: *human beings marry individuals who are exactly like themselves.* The "wimps" feelings are "If he weren't so closed up, uncommunicative, uninvolved, or difficult, I'd be open loving and kind." My thought is, it sounds right, but it doesn't fly.

Individuals marry someone who is exactly the same emotionally, on the inside, but someone who manifests those dynamics outwardly in a precisely opposite manner. Generally speaking, it might be said women show their feelings on the surface and are better able to share and discuss what's going on inside them than men. In part, society gives women permission to do so, and condones their behavior. At the same time, it considers them less stable because of it. In the end, it often uses their emotionality as justification for discrimination. In contrast, men who talk about feelings are criticized. Is it possible that women demean and chastise wimps for the weakness they see in them that they can't abide in themselves? Thus, they expect men to follow Teddy Roosevelt's example, "Speak softly and carry a big stick." In the movies, women are always drawn to "the strong, silent type." It's no wonder men emulate the role model society sets up for them. Being a wimp isn't rewarded, it's punished.

Imagine for a moment a city whose inhabitants build a 15' seawall around its perimeter. Essentially, this wall is designed to protect it from flooding. The next town over builds only a 5' retaining wall around its perimeter. Which one perceives itself to be in more danger? The answer is obvious. The higher you see fit to elevate your home, the stronger and taller you build your perimeter defense, the greater the perceived threat and the more you feel the need to protect what's inside the walls. Is it possible that men who build high walls, who hold their feelings inside and are reluctant to share them, are persons who have just as much inside to protect as those who express feelings freely? Could it be that men who learned from society that expressing inner thoughts and feelings isn't manly, may build their defenses because of the flood of potential criticism they might experience if they didn't? They have just as much to protect behind their walls, but the danger they perceive is greater. In some ways, the wimp may be more courageous than the warrior.

If that's true, then I would suggest, whether you are male or female, if you're married to someone who is emotionally locked up inside themselves — if they're a wimp — the way to reach them isn't to criticize, find fault, put them down or leave them to their own devices and create your own life. All of those behaviors will only serve to further reinforce their notion that when you open up to someone, they'll hurt or reject you. A far better approach might be to reassure them of your involvement, your concern for them and mostly your belief that they are far more of an emotional human being than they demonstrate. You also need to assure them that by expressing their feelings, they won't be providing you with ammunition to find fault or to put them down. The best way to their heart is through caring, reaching out, them know they matter and that their feelings are valuable and desirable. That doesn't mean that they'll immediately respond. Quite the contrary. They're more likely to question your truthfulness by testing you or pushing you away. But, with persistence and gentle persuasion, I promise they will eventually respond.

You can see in both Chuck's and Judy's cases, the solution isn't easy. It's apparent that excessive praise doesn't work. Put-downs, as you know, are even less effective. So, what can you do if you're married to someone like that? Be real, be honest, be strong for both of you. That means speak honestly, criticize things if it's needed, praise when it's deserved, but always do it with love. Then, after you've shown you see for what he or she is, and you recognize how he or she feels, you can add, "You've acted like a horse's butt, and I'm strong enough to leave you. I don't need you. I can make it on my own. But I want you, because I love you in spite of and because of your shortcomings." It's only then that your partner might believe you. You see, the solution for both of you is to be real, not right. So tell him or her how it is forthrightly and honestly but with compassion, desire, and love. It works with either gender. The problem, however, is you must gain the courage to be honest without expressing anger or resentment. Too often, we speak the truth only in a rage, in a fit of anger, under the influence of alcohol, or when we want to hurt our partner and not when we want to help. You need to recognize that when anger is substituted for courage and mixed with honesty, the result is a toxic combination. However, when genuine courage, which always includes vulnerability on the part of the giver, is combined with honesty, you can frequently harvest love.

There is, however, one gigantic problem that has to be overcome. Before you can harvest a truly meaningful relationship with anyone, but particularly with a wimp, there is a great deal of work that must be done. You have to clear your own emotional land and remove old roots in order to prepare the soil for planting. You have to ask yourself, "Am I capable of that? Am I willing to explore my own feelings, to plow inside myself and bring to the surface things that I've kept hidden from others, and even from myself?" You have to know where you're coming from, what your inhibitions are, and why you chose and stayed with a partner whose feelings and behaviors you have difficulty accepting. All of which you do to stop explaining yourself or blaming your situation on your partner. Recall, you made your bed, but you *needn't* lie in it. You aren't a victim; you're a volunteer.

Conversely, your partner, the wimp, essentially has to look inside him- or herself. The initial step in this process involves him or her recognizing and accepting who he or she truly is—a feeling, hurting, needy, sensitive human being. Your partner, particularly if he is male, must realize that he or she is an individual who has rarely been given the opportunity or had the courage to expose him- or herself honestly, with all his or her shortcomings, insufficiencies, and failings without the risk of being perceived as weak, wimpy, nerdy, panty-waisted, or power-less. All these characteristics are foreign to society's traditional concepts of independence and strength and, unfortunately, are generally viewed by the public as noxious and unbecoming.

CHAPTER NINE

WARRIORS AND WIMPS ARE THE SAME

B y now, you've broken the code. Not all warriors are men, and not all wimps are women. To distinguish between warriors and wimps, you have to observe their behavior, not whether they're wearing trousers or a skirt. You see, behavior knows no gender. You have probably also come to realize that you rarely come across a 100 percent warrior or wimp. In the course of a lifetime, most individuals vacillate between the two extremes. They become blends. Their roles alter, depending on whom they interact with and the situation they are in. Therefore, if you want to describe yourself accurately, the question you need to ask is: "What percentage warrior or wimp am I?" Eventually, you'll learn that it doesn't matter. The terms are only definitions, which reveal how you hide, cope, or defend yourself. They say little about who you really are. You can only discover that after you determine why you needed to become a warrior or wimp in the first place.

When you give it additional thought, it also becomes evident that the underlying emotional dynamics of warriors and wimps are really very similar. However, the manner in which they deal with their fears and insecurities are 180 degrees opposite. Warriors compensate by developing a mixture of combative, unemotional, critical, authoritarian, and controlling behaviors, which they use as a form of self-defense. Thus, they are often rigid, unbending, and seemingly insensitive. Wimps are generally acquiescent, compliant, agreeable "good guys or gals." They do what's right, say what's right, and even punish themselves for not totally believing or adhering to what they think is right. They allow themselves little room to deviate from the beaten path. Yet, wimps and warriors are both basically martyrs. Warriors perceive themselves as having exerted tremendous energy to care for, support, direct, and help all those around them. Wimps believe that they have acquiesced, capitulated, given in, and allowed others to control them in order not to rock the boat or cause people pain or difficulty.

As a result, both warriors and wimps harbor great resentment and anger toward people they believe have used them and never reciprocated or appreciated them. In reality, they are both wounded individuals who react out of their hurt, albeit in opposite directions. In either case, they fail to see the impact they have on the people they live with and the people they claim to love.

Oddly enough, warriors and wimps can equally be described as selfish, egocentric people who either do whatever they want to do, with little regard for others, or who live in their own world, locking other people out and never getting involved. In either case, they are viewed as uncaring and unfeeling.

The truth is quite different. Speak to any warrior or wimp for a prolonged period, and, at one point in the conversation, he or she will say, "It's time for me to start living for myself." There's some truth to that statement. Despite outward appearances to the contrary, warriors and wimps are both outside-in people—individuals who behave and act in accordance with what's going on outside of them, such as how they assume others will react to them, rather than on the basis of what they're feeling, what they desire or want. In that respect, they live for others, even though they don't openly show it. You mustn't be fooled by the fact that one is often overtly angry, hostile, and controlling, while the other is passive-aggressive, resentful, and withdrawn. Inside, they're both filled with hurtful emotions, so much so that they can ill afford to face themselves honestly. Nor can they own up to the fears causing them to hide their true feelings from themselves and others.

Their only salvation, as noted in a previous chapter, is to recognize themselves, take off their armor, come out of their caves, and share who they are and what they have discovered about themselves with the people to whom they want to relate. However, there are several problems. For one, sharing is such a fearful behavior that most human beings rarely attempt it, which undoubtedly accounts for the fact that there are so many divorces and so few happy marriages. You see, sharing of self is the key to closeness and intimacy in every relationship for every human being, not just for warriors and wimps. However, few people have the necessary courage to look at themselves. Of those who do, even fewer have the additional courage required to share what they discover with the individuals they want to get close to. The second problem is that much of what goes on inside them never comes to the surface. Consequently, they aren't in touch with the unconscious thoughts, feelings, and hidden agendas influencing or even controlling their interactions with others.

Two of the best examples I can give you are short vignettes of situations that occurred between several couples I've seen in therapy. They're good people who are working at establishing relationships with their partners that are healthy, open, and long-lasting. But, too frequently, their conscious desires conflict with their unconscious needs to protect themselves. The first is a late marriage, involving a man who is somewhat older than his wife. He has two children from a previous marriage. As a result, much of their finances involve private property owned by the husband and his two daughters. One of these assets is a country house that they rarely visit as a family. He built it, and she decorated it, but they never use it. It sat idle for months at a time. All the while, property values increased to a point where the house and land became a valuable asset. Thus, he put it up for sale. He briefly mentioned to his wife that the asking price of adjoining properties had almost doubled and there was a sizeable profit to be made, but he never actually told her he was considering selling it.

Several weeks later, he contacted a real estate broker and listed it. When she heard about it, she said. "You put the house up for sale?"

His answer was, "Yes. When I bought it for my daughters and me, I thought it would be something we could all use. But no one seemed interested in it, so I thought this is the time to take advantage of the market." That was the conversation. There was another message that both conveyed, however: "You put it up for sale?" really meant "I can't believe you did that without telling me or discussing it, in terms of 'This is my plan.' I understand that it's not my property. I understand that it belongs to you and the kids. But you know something? It hurts me that you find it necessary to continuously refer to it as belonging to the three of you. It leaves a bad taste in my mouth. It hurts. I feel left out. Maybe that's the reason I never really wanted to go, never used it, and never expressed an interest in it."

His statement, "I bought it for the three of us, and since no one used it, I thought, *Let's take advantage of the increased property values going on there*," meant "You know, it hurt me. I built that place; I put my heart in it, and I thought you'd think it was wonderful, that you'd want to be with me and want to enjoy it with me. But you never did. It didn't matter to you. You didn't care. That's why I never told you that I'd put it up for sale. I was hurt and angry at the attitude you expressed toward the place and me." Those were their feelings on the inside, but that wasn't what either of them verbalized.

Let me tell you about a second example of the same type of behavior. A husband and wife who were experiencing serious problems came to see me. Initially, their issues worsened. There were numerous emotional swings and frequent conflicts. Then, on a holiday weekend, Leslie went to visit her folks because her father had taken ill and she was concerned about his health. Her husband stayed home. During the time she stayed with her father, she removed her wedding ring and left it in the bedroom she was using. After she returned home, she called about her ring. Her mother, who had been so distraught about her husband, had never checked on it, and it turned up missing. Whether one of the medical care people or one of the workmen who had been around the house took it or whether it was just misplaced was never determined. When she told her husband, "I lost my ring. I left it at my folks' house, and now it can't be found," he said, "Easy come, easy go." She took it as a sarcastic remark, one she assumed implied, "You just think money grows on trees and that whatever you want, I'll give you. As a result, it's no big deal if you lose something like that." But what he really meant was, "The whole thing angers me. It pisses me off that you took it off in the first place, didn't even think to search for the ring before you left, and then took three days to even call about it. It makes me feel that you don't care about me, the marriage, or everything else the ring symbolizes." When I suggested that alternative meaning to her, she was shocked.

Her eyes opened wide, and she said, "I never considered anything like that. He's not that caring and emotional."

In the end, it doesn't matter whether you're talking about country houses or wedding bands. It's all the same. People don't share themselves or their inside feelings because they're frightened of being exposed, of being vulnerable, and of being hurt.

When I look at my own life, I recognize how arduous a task revealing oneself can be. My wife and I are now celebrating fifty-seven years of marriage. I sometimes joke, even though it's not too far from the truth, that it took that long for me to show all of myself to her. Even then, I only did it little by little, checking, each step of the way, to make sure that she could accept who I am on the inside, what I really feel, fear, and need. As I wrote this, I began to feel uncomfortable. It is probably more accurate for me to say "almost all of myself."

Nevertheless, one example stands out above the others; it is an incident that will seem so trivial and inconsequential that many of you will initially ask why it was so difficult to communicate in the first place. But you will discover that there's a vast difference between saying words and sharing feelings. To make a long story short, I had written the book *Games Lovers Play*, published by William Morrow, which was sold in bookstores around the country. A local department store wanted to promote the book and asked me to give a luncheon speech in their store auditorium and then sell autographed copies of my book. I agreed, and it went so well that they requested I repeat the program in Austin and San Antonio. The day before I was to leave, I got out of the shower early in the morning and said to my wife, the primary caretaker for our two children, two dogs, and the house, as well as a full-time special education teacher in public school that I was out of shampoo. It was an off-handed comment, merely a statement of need, not in any way a request that she get it. The next morning, very early, I showered, dressed, and packed for the two-day trip to Austin and San Antonio. There on my counter was a new bottle of shampoo. I know that doesn't seem like very much, but I knew my wife had not only worked the previous day but had also picked up our children from school, taken them to the doctor, and prepared dinner. Therefore, she had to have exerted conscious, deliberate thought and effort to make time to go to the store to buy shampoo.

I must admit, at that time, I was on an emotional high, having just published my first book, but the thought that went through my mind was, *I have to thank her for getting the shampoo*. Now, that isn't so very difficult. It would have been easy to say to her, "Hey, thanks for getting the shampoo; I really appreciate it." But that wasn't what I wanted to say. In fact, I could hear the words inside me. I wanted to say, "Harriet, I know how much you had to do and I can't begin to tell you how much you getting that shampoo means to me. It really says you care, what I said was important to you. It tells me that you heard me and took the time and effort to act on it. It touches my heart. It makes me feel loved and appreciated, and I want you to know that."

I have, on many occasions, gone out and brought something home that I knew my wife might want or would like. But if you know me, you're aware that I brought it home and presented it as though there were a full orchestra playing a marching tune while I stated, "Look what I've done! Here's the thing that you wanted! See how great a person I am!" But that isn't the way my wife did it. She just left it on my counter— no fanfare, no orchestra, no speech. That touches me. Believe it or not, it's easier to write about this incident in this book than it was to communicate those feelings to her. Since it was 4:00 a.m. when I left and she could sleep a few hours longer, I promised myself I'd tell her that evening. So, I drove to Austin in time for a radio show in the morning, followed by a TV program before my speech and a book signing. On the way, I told myself, "I have to tell her tonight when I call her after dinner." That night, I called to tell her all about the day's activities—the TV and radio shows, the book sale, and the speech.

The next morning, I thought, *Oh, my God, I forgot to tell her about the shampoo!* But I was already on the way to San Antonio. This was in the days before anyone had a cell phone. Later that day, I thought, *I'll tell her when I call to let her know what time I'll be home.* Would you believe I forgot again? I'm not saying this with pride. I'm saying it to show you how difficult it is to share your soul. It's somewhere between heart and brain surgery. You open yourself up, but what if she says, "No big deal. I just happened to be at the store to get something for dinner and I picked it up"? That wasn't what I wanted to hear. What if she didn't hear my real message at all or thought that I was being too melodramatic or weak? I do know that sometime during the following week, I said something about the shampoo. It wasn't as eloquent as I would have liked it to have been. It wasn't as emotionally revealing as I wanted it to be, because I was back in the real world and back to protecting myself.

I've thought about that incident many times since and wondered how I would change myself if I ever had to live my life over again. Or, God forbid, if my wife leaves this world before I do. I know that I'd want somebody else to share my life with, but the next time around, I'd have to do things a lot faster, because I wouldn't have another fifty-seven years to do it a little bit at a time. I'd have to follow the rule I set out in one of the chapters in *Hungry for Love,* in which I talked about honesty in labeling. Essentially, I said that when you go to buy a plant, there's always a tag that says, "Hi, I'm an Ivy. I need my soil damp, but I don't fare well when my roots are wet. I grow best in the shade, and I'll thrive if you water me every two weeks and don't let direct sunlight burn my leaves." Then I suggested that people need tags. For instance, my tag might say, "Hi, I'm Ed Reitman. I'm a desperately needy, emotionally dependent, loving, sensitive-to-a-fault guy whose bark is far worse than his bite. I'll give an awful lot of love back if you'll just pat me on the head, hug and kiss me, nurture me, tell me I'm all right when I am, and let me know when I've goofed up, which I will." Then, if she doesn't want someone like me, she can just leave and I could choose a partner from the people who are willing to accept me that way. I'd want her to know that I'm not the most refined person in the world and that I'm still suffering from childhood pain, which will never be fully resolved but which I try not to behave in accordance with—at least not all the time. All that information could be delivered up front, directly, so I wouldn't have to put my best foot forward and drag the lame one in long after she thought she knew me.

That's what I mean when I say that warriors and wimps have to drop their cover and show who they are. It's a matter of taking the risk of exposing yourself to a world filled with people, not all of whom will love or want you, but one of whom might. That's the one you need to cling to.

This brings to mind a question Wallace, a newly divorced, fifty-year-old patient asked me. He said, "I really am concerned. You know my wife complained, throughout the marriage, that I was emotionally detached. Now, I've just briefly dated a woman who is complaining about the same thing. And I'm wondering, is there some imperfection in me that I can't and will never be able to change, or are they both wrong? Are they both looking for and expecting more than they have a right to?"

My answer was, "No, they're both right. You are emotionally detached, invulnerable, and imperfect, but a very nice human being. The fact that they're both right doesn't necessarily mean that you shouldn't have left your wife or that you have to marry the woman you're dating. Truth be known, their observations are accurate. But note that both of them chose you the way you are, for the person you show yourself to be. One stayed almost thirty years and would never have left had you not finally asked for a divorce. The other only recently met you and decided that she'd like a long-term relationship with you. More important than looking at them is to look at yourself. You are the quintessential people-pleaser. You go through the world attempting to be socially and politically correct. Your decisions, your behavior, your verbalizations, everything that you do has to fit in those categories. That being the case, you're always on stage, playing a role, albeit that of a nice, good guy. But *good guys, bad marriages.* Why? Because good guys aren't real. As a result, people don't know them for who they are. They hide themselves. How can they be vulnerable when all of their activities are directed toward hiding who and what they really are or feel?"

Like most people, Wallace couldn't appreciate his own worth because of his imperfections. What he didn't realize is that we are all imperfect. We are human beings, not gods. We have shortcomings and inadequacies. We are, without a doubt, less than perfect, because we are human. And, as such, we have a right to our imperfections and an obligation to own them, to wear them well, and to share them openly. In the course of living our lives, there will be times when we look back and regret our actions, speech, and thoughts. We can change them if we have the desire to. But more important than any step you will ever take toward improving yourself is recognizing, accepting and owning the you that's there inside. If I've said this once, I've said it a million times over the years I've been in practice: "The acceptance by you of the imperfections (i.e., the humanness) in you is the only real actualization of you."

So, it would seem that you need to start today to actualize *you,* to allow people to know who you truly are, what you feel, and what you desire. You don't have to be perfect or totally politically correct, or what society deems self-sufficient, or a real man—the stereotypical warrior. Instead, you can say, as I've heard it said to me in therapy, "I want somebody who knows me for who I am, someone who will kiss my forehead, hug my shoulders, touch my hand, and tell me that I'm worth loving; who will praise me for the good things I do because I sometimes do good things; and who will help me see my own reality when I mess up and when I make mistakes but will do it with kindness instead of criticism, put-downs, or aggressive behavior. I need someone whose shoulder I can lean on when I'm tired or scared, whose lap I can rest my head in when I'm sad, and who will enjoy laughing and exploring whatever life has left to offer us. As imperfect as it may be, it's me. If it doesn't suit you, if I'm too weak, don't date me, don't hang around, and please, don't try to change me. If there are things that I deem unacceptable, I'll try to change myself. If I can't, I'll even enlist your aid. But there are other things so basic to me that they can't be altered. If you cannot accept them, you would do well by each of us to find someone else to share your life with." That's the step that starts you on the road to being who you are—to being a *winner*—and allows others to love you for who you are.

You might ask, "How do you go about doing that? Where do you get the courage?" Well, you go about it slowly, three steps forward and two steps back. You don't live in yesterday and lament the past. Nor do you punish yourself for what you didn't do. You don't live in the future and keep planning what you're going to do but never get around to. You live in the present. Along the way, there are certain things you can do to learn to be someone you can accept and love. I'll talk more about those steps in later chapters. When you get to that point, you no longer have to worry about being a wimp or a warrior, because you're no longer compensating for what you can't accept inside of yourself. You no longer have to because you recognize that, despite the imperfect you inside, you're still worthy of being loved. Even more, you'll discover that, on many occasions, you feel differently than you think. For example, you may know that you're capable and smart, but you feel frightened, insecure, and dumb. In spite of your feelings, you choose to run through your fears—not be embarrassed by them—share them, and give someone a chance to love you for who you are. That makes you a winner, a person who has won the battle between your feelings and your emotions and is in control of yourself instead of being controlled by your emotions.

CHAPTER TEN

THE WINNER

Winners, whether they're male or female, are unique individuals. They're radically different from warriors and wimps, in that they don't have the need to defend or justify their feelings or actions. The reason being that they their orientation and focus is primarily directed toward themselves; the goals they want to achieve and the ways in which they can best reach them. They aren't concerned with competing, hurting, depreciating, or finding fault with others because, for the most part, they have come to peace with themselves. They're individuals who direct their energy toward coping with whatever the world throws at them without complaining, because they know that it does no good. As a result, they don't concentrate on "woe is me" behavior, or present themselves as victims. Instead, they see their shortcomings, recognize their insecurities and fears, and accept them. When it's possible, they alter non-constructive or destructive behavior. Most of all, winners realize that they are human, and that humans have faults, make mistakes and, on occasion, fall short of their own expectations. But they don't blame or punish themselves, as wimps often do, or take it out on others, the way some warriors behave. Instead, they look inside self and ask, "How can I do this differently? What can I do in the future to improve my behavior, alter my reactions, and make my life more constructive and positive?"

Similarly, they are aware that others are also human; that they'll make mistakes, speak out of turn, accuse, find fault, or behave in critical, hostile manners when they're threatened or insecure. As a result of this awareness, winners are more forgiving and understanding of the shortcomings of others, because they're understanding and forgiving of themselves.

To become a winner, you can't just flick a switch. You can only reach the status of winner through personal growth, trial and error behavior, and the realization that life is a series of three steps forward and two steps back. The wondrous part of this orientation is that winners don't focus on the two steps back, they're appreciative, pleased, and proud of the step forward they achieve.

If you want to become a member of this unique group, Warrior, Wimp, or Winner can definitely show you the way. It includes numerous examples of problems experienced by many of my present and former patients in their interpersonal and marital relationships. I feel certain you will be able to relate to many of them and gain understanding from all of them. Your job is to learn from them and to see that there is no shame in having made previous mistakes. Shame only comes from not learning or benefitting from them.

How do you deal with a winner? Easily. What you see is what you get. They don't play games, hide their feelings, or pretend to be what they aren't. They're strong in form, but also in substance.

Therefore, they're easy to trust. Be aware, however, that they aren't perfect and won't act like winners 100 percent of the time. Nevertheless, that should be encouraging to you. It says you don't have to be perfect, either. It gives you breathing room to fall short, to fail, and to be human while still being a winner yourself.

Let me add that, in almost every instance, winners marry winners. As a result, their relationship, the way they interact, and the children they rear are also winners. The reason for this is that winners have learned a secret that I'd like to share with each of you, regarding how to deal with a partner during troubled times. When things go well, human beings tend to experience fewer difficulties in their interactions and have more satisfaction with their relationship. But, when things go askew, people, particularly warriors and wimps, deal with each other in non-constructive, sometimes even destructive, manners that serve to destroy or cripple the relationship they desire.

> The secret that winners inherently know is that <u>you do not do battle or resolve problems with a partner by standing up to, competing with, or depreciating them. Instead, resolution comes about from being able to communicate effectively by standing up for yourself.</u> I'd have you note the difference between the two. When you attempt to stand up <u>to</u> someone else, you are almost implying that the interaction you're creating involves conflict. When you stand up <u>for</u> yourself, you do not engage in, or find fault with another individual. You explain to them what you think, where you're coming from, what you feel and, if you have sufficient insight to your own being, why you feel and act the way you do.

Words alone don't fully convey this notion. Therefore, I'd like to share with you a letter written by an individual who had been in therapy for a considerable length of time . By virtue of that therapy, he had learned to recognize and forgive his own shortcomings and failings, but who, in spite of his self-acknowledged shortcomings, had learned that he still had worth and deserved to be loved by another individual. He also realized that he had to take full responsibility for his own behavior, not respond out of his fears, and direct his energies toward achieving the goals he had for himself, as opposed to those his partner had for him.

You see, in healthy relationships, you don't have 51/49 partnerships. Nor do you have 50/50 relationships. Neither works because, at one time or another, the partners are bound to interact in combative ways in an attempt to prove that they're right and that what they feel is also right for their partner. As a result, their interactions are often fraught with competition, intimidation, subordination and/or manipulation. In healthy relationships, each individual is 100% responsible for his or her own behavior. They have no need to convince their partner that their thoughts or actions are right or wrong. Their primary responsibility is to ensure that they do an adequate job in conveying their thoughts, feelings and emotions. If you're one of those healthy individuals, please try to remember that your partner doesn't have to comply, agree, or see merit in your words, because you aren't saying them to change their position. You are expressing your views, to openly communicate where you're coming from.

Sometimes an example is worth a thousand words, so let me share my patients' letter to his spouse:

My dear _____,

> *I would like to share my thoughts and feelings regarding our discussion last night.*
>
> *Before I start, I want you to know that I love you and want to be with you for the rest of my life. I want you to know that I'm aware that you're scared of being made a fool of again, after what happened in our relationship in the past. I also know that you do not feel worthy of being loved, because of your painful childhood.*
>
> *It also shows me that you have a great deal of resentment toward me. Not only for my leaving you years ago, but for all the things that you felt you did for me before I left. Now, I believe you want me to do similar things for you, but that's not healthy. You originally gave to me in order to justify your demand that I behave the way you wanted me to. Then, you resented me when I didn't. Now, if I were to do the things for you in order to get you to love me, I know I would wind up resenting you. I now know that it isn't healthy for me to feel resentment, or to accept resentment from you, or anyone else.*
>
> *I cannot change the past, mine or yours, but I have been able to change the way I see myself. Please know, I don't mean this in a threatening way, but I have learned that I am a good man, even a good catch, and I don't deserve that resentment any more. It has to go away. Because the more you resent me and treat me badly, the more I resent myself for taking it and staying with you.*
>
> *Now I want you to know what I discovered about myself. I learned to feel badly about me from a very early age, possibly 3 years old. I was beaten, I was yelled at, I was criticized. I felt I was hated. All I knew to do was try to be "perfect", to be the good little boy; because I must have been a bad boy to get all the criticism*

thrown at me. But it didn't work. All I got were restrictions and control. I was told, "don't look at women the wrong way; don't be too warm around girls, it always leads to something; don't be the center of attention; don't be........" Every day, I was, and believe it or not still am, nervous and scared. Despite all the success I have experienced, I recognize that I loathed myself for everything that I believed I was inside. Even now, I try to be perfect enough to deserve to be loved, and I don't want to do that anymore, because I'm imperfect, and I've discovered that my imperfection is okay.

I also learned that I recreated the abusive environment with my mother and stepfather with you. You may not know this, but I feel physically threatened by you. When you assume that angry posture, or have that negative expression on your face, it scares me as much as when my stepfather stood over me with a belt in his hand, and my mother did nothing to stop it. I don't know if you realize it, but you yell at me and I feel like I'm the scum of the earth. You are critical of me and my actions and almost everything I do, and every move that I make. It's constant. You make my mistakes bigger than life, and I wind up feeling that you hate me. For years, I accepted this, loathed myself, and acted out. But now, I realize I never deserved it, from them, or from you. I didn't deserve it when I was 3 years old and I don't deserve it now.

If I want to look at a good looking woman, I'm going to. I'm going to enjoy her beauty in its full glory. It's really okay. If a woman's breasts are on display, I'm going to look. I like breasts. God made them for man to like, and I'm a man and I like them. If I want to share my warm, caring personality with others around me, I'm going to, because, believe it or not, it still surprises me that people love me. They're drawn to me. And I've learned that it's a wonderful gift that I want to take advantage of. Your fear of me leaving you will no longer make me hide me. If I can make people smile through the day, I'm going to. I'm not going to worry about what you think is appropriate, or what you are fearful of. I'm going to be me.

But, at the same time, at the end of every day, I want and intend to come home to you, because I care for and love you. This is what I wish. This is what I want for me and this is what I wish you would want for yourself. I expect us to learn to encourage each other to be who we really are. The us that we are, despite how scared we are, and how reluctant we can be to show the real us to the outside world. I want us to rally to each other's aid, and to share ourselves, because you know something? We're good people.

I will not accept a relationship with a person who is trying to hide me, and is so scared that she doesn't want me to "talk to girls." We (you) have to leave the past in the past. If there are issues in our relationship, they need to be addressed on an even playing field. They do not need to be avoided by you beating me up over what I did to you years ago. Those mistakes don't define me to me. They do not define me to anyone who knows and cares about me today. But, sadly, if they define me to you, we are wasting our time. You (and I) have to own our successes and our failures. We have to be able to say we're sorry and I would hope you would own up to the fact that a lot of the pain and suffering that you play such a victim to, has a lot more to do with the baggage you brought with you than the baggage I've created. Your shortcomings and missteps, your terrible way of treating me, and your bad decisions are yours to own. I can't take credit for them. Even more, my mistakes DO NOT make your mistakes okay. I'd hope you learn to say, "Yup, I don't want to behave the way I am, or treat people I care about like I treat you. I love you, and

I'm sorry." That's what I need to hear. If you don't, or can't trust me, please go get someone you can trust. Someone you are secure enough to encourage them to be themself. Someone you would love to see in the spotlight. Even though you may be in the shadow, you can feel really, really happy for them. If you can't, please go get someone who doesn't scare you so badly, so that you can minimize your fears and don't have to be angry at them.

I want to sum up by saying, unequivocally, I love you. I want to spend the rest of my life with you. There is no question about that. The real question is, do, or can you love you, and then me?

For me, this letter is as honest, open, loving, respectful and committed as a person (a winner) can be. It is also an example of someone who has come to peace with who he is; who recognizes that he has worth, despite his feelings from the past. Perhaps it takes knowing that you are okay before you can genuinely make a commitment to someone else.

Having said all this, I encourage you to closely examine the content of the rest of the book, to benefit from those examples which you can relate to, and to understand that there will be situations and interactions that have little to do with you. That isn't the fault of the book or you, it's just testimony to the fact that each of us is a unique individual. A person who can't be described by one generalization, but who shares with every other human being, common feelings and emotions that need to be openly shared in order for you to live together with your partner or lover in a harmonious fashion.

CHAPTER ELEVEN

MARRIAGE CAN'T SURVIVE WARRIORS AND WIMPS

Warriors and wimps don't relate well with others. They either subjugate, control, and demean or manipulate and resent. Warriors can be argumentative, competitive, and vicious. Wimps are passive-aggressive, devious, and pitiful. They rarely see themselves for the victimizers or victims they are, because they lack introspection and honesty and are highly egocentric in nature. None of these behavioral characteristics are conducive to establishing healthy relationships or rewarding marriages. Despite that fact, warriors and wimps continue to marry each other and reinforce the belief that the majority of marriages are doomed to fail. Janice and Robert's marriage is an excellent example of this behavior. I'd like to share their story with you.

Robert was the quintessential example of a male warrior whose armor obscured the emotional wimp inside. In therapy, he stated that his dissatisfaction with his marriage started over ten years earlier. He indicated that he had left his wife, Janice, on three different occasions but returned each time because of his children. Unfortunately, it was to the same wife, the same problems, and the same solutions, all of which he said stemmed from his wife's lack of support, lack of emotion, and lack of understanding. As a result, he had little or no feelings for her, no interest in her sexually, and only a modicum of appreciation for her role as a mother and parent. Janice said that when she approached him physically, his body would tense, his arms would remain at his side, and his face displayed no expression. If she attempted to hug him, he would move away. She stated further that each night when he entered the home, he greeted his three children with effusive emotional affection and physical closeness but totally ignored her.

For the better part of ten years, Janice accepted this behavior, hiding her pain, refusing to let him know how rejected she felt or the anger that rejection provoked. Then again, rejection was a behavior with which she was very familiar. As a child, she had experienced a mother who was as cold and distant as her husband and a father who was consistently busy and uninvolved. Her only solace was the attention she received from an older sister. It met a basic need but never filled the hole left by the absence of nurturing parents. No matter how hard Janice tried, no matter that she excelled academically and never caused a problem, there was no acknowledgment of her accomplishments or her behavior from either of her parents. Thus, her marriage was only a continuation of the same pattern of behavior she had learned to live with throughout childhood. For the most part, Janice survived by hiding her true feelings behind a veil of complacency, cool disdain, and emotional distance. On our first meeting, she appeared shy and totally ineffectual—so much so that you would initially wonder why her bright, Harvard MBA husband with his dynamic personality, his ability to articulate, and his apparent insight would have chosen her for a partner. Over time, however, you would discover that beneath her bland exterior was a warm, extremely bright, and very competent human being with a dry sense of humor. In contrast, over time, her model husband would prove to be the quintessential example of the old adage, "You can't judge a book by its cover." Despite his keen understanding of others, he was blind to his own emotions. In reality, he lacked self-confidence and doubted his ability to really succeed. He was strong on form but weak in substance.

Janice was Robert's scapegoat. He blamed all of his shortcomings on her, at least until they entered marital group therapy. There, she learned to recognize, possibly for the first time, that his rejection and denigration of her was, in fact, emotionally abusive behavior. Sometime later, she entered law school, graduated near the top of her class, and was hired by a prestigious firm. Within a short period of time, she was not only making more money than her husband but was on the fast track to becoming an equity partner.

With each success she experienced, Robert's criticism, put-downs, and rejection magnified until she finally confronted him with her decision to leave the marriage. What she said was, "I see no other alternative than to leave. I can't stay the way things are. If they can't change, I'll have to get a divorce."

His response was, "Since you've made that decision, you'd best get on with it."

He later expressed considerable anger toward her, stating that she was the one ending their marriage and that her decision was another blatant example of her lack of support for him. She said, "That isn't the case. If you'll work on the marriage, I'll be here. I gave you every chance. Divorce isn't what I wanted; it isn't what I was looking for. I was hoping that it would shock you into caring. I can't live with someone who rejects me on a continuing basis. I deserve more. At work, I'm appreciated. I'm told how adequate I am, what a good job I'm doing, and the reinforcement causes me to work even harder. At home, I'm treated as though I'm invisible. I feel guilty about wanting to leave, and I'm worried about the effect it will have on our children, but I see no other alternative."

Their divorce was finalized a year ago. Robert immediately went out and found another woman. After all, on the surface, women saw a good-looking, articulate, Harvard-educated man who appeared to be their dream come true. He was actually a mirage; when seen from a distance, he instilled hope and promise, but when viewed up close, he proved to be a poisoned well.

Janice is on her way to becoming a partner at the law firm. Last year's bonus was more than 40 percent of her annual salary. But more important, the new relationships she has begun to form with coworkers and friends provide an opportunity for her to show herself for the woman she is inside. On the positive side, the intimidated, inadequate-feeling little girl she was for so many years is gone. The sadness is that still another divorce has taken place, because her spouse could ill afford to build her sense of adequacy and encourage her to grow. Unconsciously, he feared that once she realized how adequate she was, she wouldn't want him. Her threat to leave actualized his fear to the point that it was impossible for him to ask her to stay, even after she gave him the opportunity. In the end, his false pride was his undoing. It caused him to cling to an image that was only an illusion, a cover-up for the insecure guy on the inside.

Many more men than you might suspect share Robert's problem. They appear to be an oasis—strong, nurturing, loving, and wise—but when you reach for them, all that's there is emptiness and sand. There are no palm or date trees, no springs or water, only an illusion. How many times do you reach out to a mirage? How often do you race toward it before you lose heart and interest? How long before you're angry at the mirage, because it isn't what it promised to be? How much disappointment will you tolerate? And, if men are a mirage and appear to be warriors but wind up being wimps, think of the emotional distrust and hurt it breeds and the resentment it elicits.

In many ways, it's similar to the resentment that many people now have, particularly toward male physicians. Recall the time when a "doctor" was a man who could be trusted and depended upon? He never made a mistake, and you never questioned his advice. He was seen as wise beyond medicine. It was almost as though he had a direct connection with God. Because of that, you would willingly place your life in his hands. Doctors perpetuated that image. They would write their prescriptions in Latin so the patient couldn't read or understand what they were getting. They took your blood pressure and temperature but didn't tell you what it was because it was a secret. Those were the old days, but those days are gone.

Why? Because popular periodicals like *Reader's Digest* published articles about medical treatment, and the average citizen learned that certain medicines didn't work, that doctors were human and subject to error, and that it was okay to seek a second opinion. These realizations were accompanied by an underlying attitude of resentment toward doctors, who heretofore had been portraying themselves as the ultimate father figures, making you believe they would protect you, save your life, and never make a mistake. When the public realized their fallibility, they became angry and litigious. It was the beginning of a new orientation between doctors and patients.

It's the same for men and women. Today, just like Janice, more and more women are entering the world of business, industry, and politics. They're learning that men aren't all-powerful, fearless warriors. They're cognizant of the mistakes men make, and they no longer believe or are willing to support the myth that "Father knows best." They know how women suffered in the past. They recognize the pain their mothers experienced, and they worry about the world their daughters are going to inherit. It's no wonder women are resentful toward men, who, they now believe, have deceived them and let them down.

There are other reasons for what's happening between the sexes. Recent technology has shown that men and women are definitely different—not just emotionally and behaviorally but neurologically. These differences are reflected by specific patterns of development in the connecting tissue of the brain, as well as in brain activity. Studies of the brain are now unearthing evidence that supports previous clinical observations that physicians, psychologists, and teachers have made for years regarding differences between boys and girls with regard to learning ability, physical growth, and emotional maturity. These studies have also unveiled surprising revelations in opposition to the stereotypical picture we hold of men and women. All of this strongly suggests that the way we deal with men and women early in life, in infancy, and in childhood has to be revamped.

Of particular relevance to our topic are studies which have shown that early experiences of either a highly stressful or catastrophic nature affect the way various parts of the brain develop. The results demonstrate unique growth patterns in certain areas of the brain, due both to the gender of the subjects and the nature of the stress that was experienced. For example, little girls who have been sexually abused show a very specific but atypical pattern of growth in the connective tissue in the brain between the frontal lobe and the amygdala. Interesting, however, is the fact that young males who have been sexually abused do not demonstrate that atypical growth pattern, with one exception—when the sexual abuse is associated with hostile or physically abusive behavior.

Of even greater importance is the fact that little boys who have been emotionally rejected in their youth, who have experienced neglect, emotional deprivation, or lack of involvement or nurturing demonstrate the same atypical pattern of growth as do little girls who have been sexually abused. The initial conclusion is that, while sexual abuse has an acutely negative and stressful impact on little girls, emotional rejection and neglect has the same effect on boys. Researchers have also determined that male infants are far more emotionally vulnerable than baby girls. On a personal level, I cannot begin to count the number of patients I have seen with marital difficulties stemming from the acute sensitivity of men who perceive themselves as rejected, unappreciated, and not listened to. *It isn't that women don't need attention, involvement, and gratification, too. It's just that they cope better than men do when they don't get it.*

These observations are consistent with numerous clinical surveys indicating that later in life, men don't fare well when they live alone. The life span of married men and the level of health they experience is greater than that of single or divorced men living on their own. Women fare much better on their own than do men. They network better; they socialize more and become involved with other activities. They seem to cope more effectively and to live just as long whether they're single or married. All of which is in sharp contrast with the way the socialization of boys and girls is carried out. Boys, who would seem to be more emotionally needy, are instructed to mitigate their emotions and to deny their vulnerability. We teach them to refrain from expressing feelings, with the exception of anger—one of the six fundamental characteristics associated with masculinity. The remaining five—power over women, violence, dominance, emotional control, and a disdain for homosexuality—are, interestingly, generally viewed by society as negative behaviors.

If you give serious thought to these studies, you begin to see that child-rearing practices and the socialization process, as applied to young men, do them a tremendous injustice. Despite the fact that clinical observations and neurological studies show that little boys are more emotionally vulnerable than little girls, they're trained to deny their feelings, not to cry, to hold their emotions inside and "keep a stiff upper lip." Later in life, they're expected to act tough and "be a man," an attitude that often contributes to a general disdain for anyone appearing less than masculine. It also explains why many men fear or resent women who demonstrate they can compete with and even surpass them in the workforce, economically or professionally. At the same time, young men who are viewed as intelligent, obedient, passive, or sensitive are looked down upon. Instead of being called "daddy's big boy" or "a chip off the old block," they're described as "a goody two-shoes," "a weakling," or "effeminate." Thus, we have a curious paradox. The would-be, masculine-oriented male has to constantly prove his masculinity—by prowess over women, dominance over his peers, denial of emotions, and acting tough, while the sensitive, outwardly emotional, less physical male is forced to perceive himself as weak, inadequate, and even possibly gay. As a result, many of these men tend to have unconscious but excessive self-doubt, feelings of insufficiency, and disdain for themselves. All of this is frequently reinforced by women who are predisposed to accept sensitive men as friends but to discard them as lovers. In order to compensate for these feelings, some men push the limits on masculine behavior in order to prove they're acceptable. They're the ones who are prone to be vitriolically anti-gay, tend to bully their peers, and have to control women. Because of their self-doubts, many of them find it necessary to control and subjugate women in an attempt to punish the weakness they perceive in them that they can't accept in themselves. The majority of the remaining men are often passive-aggressive individuals who live out their lives filled with unconscious resentment toward women, which they have difficulty expressing openly. The end result is that a majority of men, without realizing it, walk a narrow line in their attempt to portray what society deems a healthy, desirable "male" image (i.e., the warrior).

Lest you see me as partial to women, let me tell you about the other side of Janice. It won't alter anything you've heard about Robert. He still needs to look at himself. But Janice picked Robert, stayed with him, complained about him, and openly stated, "If he'd get help," she would stay. So, in her mind, who had the problem? That was obvious to her, but not to me and, I hope, not to you. You have to give it to her. She's smart, personable, socially adept, and able to succeed in a professional environment. But can she perform in a similar fashion in a meaningful relationship? Will her fear surface again and cause her to look for shortcomings in her next choice of a spouse? Can she risk being vulnerable, being open emotionally, or being sexually vulnerable? That remains to be seen. In my opinion, it's almost certain she won't, unless she looks at, recognizes, and accepts the part she played in the downfall of her marriage to Robert.

While the trend of emotionally liberated women continues to grow, it has a profound effect on more than just the divorce rate. The number of attacks on students at school may also be a result of these same feelings of inadequacy. A review of some of the major incidents of on-campus violence reveals that most of the attacks were made by males primarily targeting females. In a Montreal massacre, a young man in engineering school separated young men and women and killed fourteen women before killing himself. In 1998, in Arkansas, two male shooters, ages eleven and thirteen, also targeted women. Four middle school girls and their female teacher died in that attack. Nine of the eleven wounded were also female. Girls were the only targets in the shooting at an Amish school in Pennsylvania in 2006.

It is evident that the problem between the sexes is far more complex than any one book can discuss. It involves many contributing factors of a sociological, psychological, and even neurological nature. The solution, I should add, is equally complex and very difficult to achieve. It will only come about when men and women commit themselves to understanding instead of competing, recognize that on the inside, warriors and wimps are the same, and each strives to become a winner.

For marriages to ultimately survive, men and women have to first learn what a winner is, and then use what they've learned as a role model for the persons they want to be. Essentially, they need to learn how to be honest with themselves and to be real with each other. They must see themselves as adequate human beings, despite their perceived shortcomings, failings, and fears. Women and men need to view each other as people who love and care for them, someone who isn't always right but has good intentions. As partners, they need to openly convey the message, "Even though I may have different attitudes or opinions regarding the world, politics, and finances, I can still love you and be here for you. I know I make mistakes. That's because I'm human. I also hurt and feel unloved and rejected just like you, but I demonstrate it in different ways. Despite my failings, there is one thing I want to reassure you of: you're important to me. Your love is important to me, and I will do a great deal to deserve that love and to give you love in return." Messages of that type mitigate attitudes of superiority, which only create competitive interactions, emotional disappointment, resentment, and hurt. Sharing these messages can openly serve as a testimony to the humanness shared by the sexes. It establishes a common ground on which men and women can build new, healthier relationships. Without it, the power struggle between the genders will only continue to grow for years to come. It will create an environment in which warriors and wimps can thrive, but where marriages can't survive. There is no other alternative but for males and females to learn new coping skills, which will enable them to function in a world of winners, who can be transparent and vulnerable because they have nothing to hide and nothing to prove. Then know and accept themselves for who they are; winners in the fullest sense of the word.

MARRIAGE IS A PEOPLE PROBLEM

B y now, you can probably see that healthy relationships can't survive in a world of warriors and wimps. But that doesn't mean marriage is doomed. If you truly desire a long-term, meaningful relationship, it's there for the taking, and not because a prince or princess suddenly appeared on the horizon. Even they aren't perfect. The ability to establish a long-term, positive relationship is dependent upon how well you are able to deal with the imperfect person you choose to have as your partner. That, in turn, will be determined by your willingness to look inward at who you really are—a warrior, a wimp, or a winner. It is also dependent on the degree to which you are aware of the pitfalls and obstacles that interfere with creating a healthy relationship and how committed you are to making that relationship work in spite of those hazards.

It doesn't matter how many times you have tried and failed in the past. In fact, each of the disappointments you've endured can be looked upon as experiences from which lessons can be learned. What matters instead is whether or not you're ready now to face the ordeal of change.

The following chapters provide you with numerous examples of individuals who have probably experienced many of the same problems you have lived or are living through and have dealt with them in a similar manner. I hope you will be able to relate and to see that there are lessons you can learn from their experiences that can not only help you in your quest to become a winner but ensure that the relationship you have right now or that you hope to establish in the future can be a healthy and loving one guaranteed to last.

CHAPTER TWELVE

WHAT DO YOU WANT TO BE?

I recently came across an anonymous slice of wisdom that started the wheels in my head spinning. It said, *"Going to church or synagogue doesn't make you a Christian or Jew, any more than standing in a garage makes you a car."* It seemed applicable to so many facets of peoples' lives. Too often, they only go through the motions of living, rather than the emotions. They go to weddings, christenings, celebrations, testimonials, and funerals only to be seen and counted, not necessarily to be involved, contribute to, or to learn from the occasion. It's as though they dress up in costumes and go about acting a role. In a house of worship, they're religious. At work, they're a doctor, teacher, or clerk. At home, they're a wife or a husband, and emotionally, they're either a warrior or a wimp, or a little of both. But they never sit down and consciously ask themselves, "What kind of person do I want to be?" and then go about becoming that person.

Marie was one of my patients who never acted on becoming the person she wanted to be. She absolutely knew what was right for her, but time after time, she disappointed herself as well as those she loved. Despite her resolve to be punctual, something always occurred that prevented it. Then, when she was really late, she often blew the meeting off entirely because of her remorse and embarrassment. She initiated and almost brought to fruition countless creative projects that would have—if she had completed them—brought her financial success and a great deal of self-fulfillment, goals she claimed to desire. Although her promises were genuine, her follow-through was terrible. Her performance was similar to a quarter horse entered in mile-long races. She ran spectacularly for the first quarter mile, but she always arrived late at the finish line. In Marie's particular case, fear of failure, feelings of insufficiency, and a desperate need for approval paralyzed her somewhere between the starting gate and the finish line. The anguish she later felt was emotionally devastating, but her fears continued to control her behavior.

There may be a little bit of Marie in all of us. Just think about the multitude of New Year's resolutions you have made but never stuck to. Consider how many times you've said, "I'm going to start next week," "We must get together sometime," "Do drop in when you're in the neighborhood," "I'll call you back tomorrow," or "I'm sorry about your loss, and I'll be there to support you." They are all well-meant, socially acceptable statements, which, more often than not, you fail to actualize. How often have you made sick calls and bought flowers when a person was in the hospital but failed to visit when he or she was recuperating and even more in need of your visit? In the same vein, you quickly gather together to support someone who has lost a loved one but forget that mourning doesn't end with interment or burial and that your care and presence is needed over a much longer period of time. It isn't that your intentions are lacking, but that, in so many instances, you act for the moment, extend yourself only after a catastrophic event, or respond best to a crisis. Maybe you are a "life sprinter," a person who looks for immediate rewards, sets short-term goals, and rapidly runs out of steam. Too few people have the mentality of the long-distance runner who knows that if he wants to finish the race, he has to commit to long-term goals, overcome numerous obstacles, and experience failure before he attains the reward he desires. Saying the words, or just being there, isn't enough. It's the follow-through that makes someone a winner.

Think about it. Most anyone can make a child, but only a few very special people are willing to exert the energy and devotion necessary to rearing one properly. For every one hundred couples who run off to the altar and vow to live their lives together in sickness and health, in good times and bad, fifty wind up getting divorced. The rest lament, tolerate, and torture each other because they are too fearful or lack the knowledge and commitment to work on the relationship that they originally claimed to want. Consequently, their marital vows become empty words, no different than the promises made by politicians during an election year. No wonder human beings find it difficult to trust one another, to commit to a relationship, or to depend on others' promises, let alone to expect them to act on them. How many times has a repairman promised to return to your home at a specific time but failed to do so or failed to even inform you he would be late?

You must do more than stand in your garage hoping to grow wheels. You have to follow through on your commitments despite your fears, the inconvenience, or the obstacles. You have to do what you know will make you the person you want to be, rather than live under an illusion.

You must be thinking, *How do I go about doing that?* I've already noted that most other people let you down and that you can't trust your resolutions. The outlook seems pretty dismal as a result, but you are capable of taking that second step—the one that comes after asking yourself what kind of person you want to be.

Picture this scenario: Carl came home to a state of total pandemonium. There was his wife, holding their eight-month-old in one arm, frantically trying to shove the dog out the back door before he made another mistake on the carpet, while on the stove, a large pot of water was boiling over. Meanwhile, their three-and-a-half-year-old twins were running through the kitchen. There seemed to be a commotion in every corner of the house. The thought going through Carl's mind was, *I can tell what kind of an evening I'm in for,* and he was probably right. Carl's expectation was typical of an individual who feels victim to the world around him. In reality, Carl just reacted to the situation he found himself in and allowed it to govern his thinking and predict his future.

Now consider that Carl comes home to the same situation, but this time, he says, "My God, things are a mess! Here, let me take the baby, and let the dog out. You tend to the pot on the stove, and I'll grab the other kids and take them into the bedroom with me while I change clothes. Then I'll come out, and we'll make dinner together."

In the initial situation, Carl reacted. As a result, he was of no help to either Janet, their children, or himself, because reactors rarely feel good about themselves. They always blame their actions, thoughts, and feelings on someone else and, eventually, try to get even, either passively or aggressively. One way or another, they make others pay for their ineffectuality. Moreover, they generally complain and criticize others for the problems in their lives but rarely see themselves as responsible. In the second illustration, Carl took charge of the situation. He obviously knew what kind of person he wanted to be, and he acted accordingly.

You can do the same. It all starts with making the decision to be the person you want to be. The best illustration I can give comes from an email I received from my daughter. It is a story about carrots, eggs, and a cup of coffee. Once you read it, you will never look at a cup of coffee in the same way again. It may also cause you to consider your own behavior and the manner in which you cope with your world. At least, it did for me.

The Carrot, The Egg And The Coffee Bean

A young woman went to her mother and told her about the marital problems she was experiencing. She felt totally defeated and wanted a divorce. She said she was tired of fighting and struggling. It seemed as soon as one problem was resolved, a new one arose.

Her mother took her to the kitchen, filled three pots with water, and placed each on high heat. When the pots came to a boil, she placed carrots in one, eggs in another, and coffee grounds in the last. She let them sit and boil without saying a word.

After about fifteen minutes, she turned off the burners. She fished the carrots out and placed them in a bowl. She pulled the eggs out and placed them in a bowl. She ladled the coffee out and placed it in a bowl. Turning to her daughter, she asked, "Tell me what you see."

"Carrots, eggs, and coffee," the daughter replied.

Her mother brought her closer and asked her to feel the carrots. She did and noted that they were soft. Her mother then asked her to take an egg and break it. After removing the shell, she observed a hard-boiled egg. Finally, her mother asked her to sip the coffee. The daughter smiled as she smelled its rich aroma.

The daughter then asked, "What does it all mean?"

The mother explained that each of these objects had faced the same adversity, boiling water, and each reacted differently. The carrots went in rigid. After being subjected to the boiling water, they softened and became weak and limp. (The wimp?) The egg was fragile; it's thin outer shell was all that protected it's liquid interior. After sitting in the boiling water, its inside hardened. (The warrior?) The ground coffee beans were different. After fifteen minutes, they changed the water around them. (The winner!)

"Which are you?" she asked her daughter. "When adversity knocks on your door, how do you respond? Are you a carrot, an egg, or a coffee bean?"

Ask yourself, what you want to be: the wimpy carrot that seems strong but when faced with pain and adversity, wilts, becomes soft, and loses its strength? The warrior egg that starts out with a malleable center but quickly hardens? Or do you want to be a winner like the coffee? Do you want to be someone who changes the environment when adversity strikes? When things get hot, do you release a positive fragrance and flavor? When things are at their worst, do you get better and alter the situation you find yourself in? I've had a lot of patients who have, and you can, as well. All you have to do is ask yourself: "When the hour is darkest and my trials are their greatest, do I elevate myself to another level?"

CHAPTER THIRTEEN

PEOPLE OF CHAOS

L ife is not easy for any of us. We not only have to carry the baggage we've been burdened with from childhood, but we have to face a constant battle against the forces of nature, the whims of others, our DNA, and circumstances that often come about without our having had anything to do with them. That should be enough of weight for any one person, but there are many people who make every day a catastrophe of one type or another. They view their world as being in a constant state of flux and turmoil. Their emotions are stormy, mercurial, frantic, agitated, and conflicted. Their home, car, and financial records are totally disorganized and in disarray. They view life anxiously, are prone to making molehills into mountains, and overreact to any inconveniences or disruptions in their plans. Being depressed and feeling in a state of constant upheaval is normal for them. Their life is filled with unrest and bedlam, all of which contribute to a constant state of stress. Yet, it does not happen by accident, because people of chaos, be they warriors or wimps, need the "noise" to avoid being in touch with themselves or their true emotions. No matter the nature of their noise—be it depression, worry, drugs, drinking, financial problems, anger, marital discord, or sexual entanglements—it helps to drown out their inner feelings of fear, inadequacy, isolation, or unlovability. Sad to say, there is a little bit of this chaotic person in all of us.

When I suggested this to Michael, he refused to accept the fact that he contributed to the emotional turmoil in his life. That isn't unusual. When you are in a forest of this type, it is difficult to see the trees of your own creation objectively. It is far easier to see yourself as a victim and to feel controlled and trapped by every situation in which you find yourself. At the same time, Michael had no other explanation for his periodic bouts of depression, his inability to structure his life, and his more than occasional emotional outbursts. It is worth noting that, prior to his explosions, he always experienced a financial crisis, an argument with his wife, or an overwhelming feeling of despair, loneliness, and emotional estrangement from his parents, who, even in his childhood, were unable to satisfy his emotional needs. Oddly enough, his financial problems never seemed to right themselves. Every ten to twelve months, Michael would become so overwhelmed by them that he felt forced to disclose all the details to his wife and beg her to come to his rescue. Eventually, she would but not before their relationship spiraled down to a new emotional low. Arguments seemed to permeate their every interaction, and their children suffered terribly from their exposure to these explosive conflicts. In the end, Michael and his wife always laid out a workable plan for avoiding future financial problems. He never fully followed the plan, and the result was that, before long, he found himself needing to be rescued from the same financial difficulties. Once again, his wife would reluctantly offer up the money she had squirreled away, and the scenario would repeat itself.

Although there were occasions when Michael's world appeared peaceful and free of stress, they were short-lived. Before he could fully reap the benefits of these times, he would sabotage himself. He would go on another spending spree or contact his parents for help. It was his way of trying to establish the loving relationship he always longed for. It was, of course, to no avail. They once again proved they were the same individuals who had failed to meet his needs years ago and were still incapable of doing so. Even worse, despite the fact that his attempts to contact them left him feeling weak and guilty about asking for help, he still felt angry over being rejected and unworthy of being loved because, in his own words, "If your parents don't love you, something must be wrong with you." If he had not contacted them in the first place, he might have avoided the pain he experienced. It was obvious that the pain was something he needed. Although he maintained that his emotional strife was his own fault, his repeated financial difficulties and his frequent attempts to search for emotional support from his parents reinforced his wimp status and the notion that his chaotic world was of his own making.

Amanda was in the same boat. In fact, Michael's life pales when compared to hers. Chaos reigned supreme in her life. She was desperately hungry for love, but when she received it, she was unable to recognize it or was so fearful of losing it that she ran from it. Her behavior screamed, "You can't reject me because I don't care!" Then, when she found herself alone and distant from those whose love she desired, she lamented the estrangement she felt and expressed anger toward them for not contacting her and reassuring her. Whenever Amanda was invited to a luncheon or meeting, she was overwhelmed by what to wear, whether or not she'd be accepted, even whether or not she'd be able to find the restaurant. She invariably arrived later than might be considered fashionable or polite, the reason always being that she lost her way or some emergency had occurred. In effect, her desperate need for involvement and acceptance caused her to become so anxious over establishing relationships that she sabotaged them before they could start. Her life was rarely stable or peaceful. It was, instead, forever disappointing and always anxiety-producing. In her own words, "I feel like something is getting ready to explode inside." She saw herself as a victim in every relationship she entered and clung to pain from her past stemming from the rejection she experienced as a child. She may have been a victim of her past, but she was also a volunteer in the present.

Joe was no different. Although he was a respected physician, he had difficulty sticking to a goal. Consequently, he changed his area of specialization more times than he could count. He switched his place of employment on more occasions than that. In every instance, he started out enthusiastic, motivated, goal-oriented, and successful. Two to three years later, he was disenchanted, disappointed, and searching for a new horizon. This behavior pattern wasn't limited to his work alone. The last time I saw him, he was convinced that he needed to divorce another wife. All the while, he constantly sought answers from therapy, religion, and philosophy. However, no matter where he went or what he did, confusion followed him.

Alex was the same. For years, he hid behind his work and his affairs with other women. His actions and his words never coincided. "I definitely want my kids and my family," he would say, but he was rarely home. He worked all the time. He vowed his love for his wife, but he did little to hide his extramarital involvements, even flaunting them in front of her until she felt forced to file for divorce. Then, fearful of losing her, he promised he would immediately end the relationship with his lover. All the while, he reassured his lover that he still cared for her and would end his marriage in the near future. Neither was a promise he intended to keep. They were only statements designed to diminish the emotional pressure he felt. In the long run, his words and promises only served to create and perpetuate his chaotic existence. Both women eventually became angry while he perceived himself as being pushed and pulled by two controlling, hostile females he saw as very similar in nature. Of course they were; he picked them both. In his eyes, he was the victim. It was better than taking responsibility for the part he played in creating the turmoil. In that respect, Michael, Amanda, Joe, and Alex were similar.

Although the source of their pain—problems with spouses, children, parents, friends, or jobs—may vary, people who thrive on chaos tend to share five characteristics in common:

1. *They are all "horrible-izers" and worriers.* They are unable to see goodness in the world, instead seeking out the negative in even the best of situations. They find things to be concerned about, even though they may be positive in nature. They are the type of people who win the lottery and then complain about the taxes they will have to pay on the winnings.

2. *They overreact.* Their problems are, for the most part, genuine but would appear like mere stumbling blocks to others. They envision the slightest cough or pain as pneumonia or cancer. They view mild criticism as permanent rejection. They interpret a simple difference of opinion as anger and hostility and view one mistake as total failure.

3. *They constantly want something they don't have and are unhappy with what they do have.* Nothing satisfies them and nothing is enough, contributing to high levels of anxiety and stress and preventing them from trusting others.

4. *They rarely experience a sense of peace.* Instead, they unconsciously create and search for problems to upset them. They run the same emotional race over and over again and continually lament the same problem, even if it happened years ago.

5. *They attempt to avoid stress by controlling their world and the people in it.* They create a chaotic world that enables them to view their situations in the manner of their own choosing. They are rarely able to see themselves as controlling, because they are overwhelmed by their feelings of being victimized by others and by their situations.

By virtue of the pandemonium that surrounds them, people who live in chaos are unable to look inside themselves or to establish close, meaningful relationships. Their turmoil is unconsciously designed to serve that very purpose; it prevents them from seeing and having to deal with themselves and serves as a smoke screen, which hides them from others. Partners and spouses who stay with them are equally reluctant to be introspective or close, or they would never have chosen this type of partner to begin with. Their lover's constant emotional upheaval serves as their hiding place, which allows them to avoid having to see themselves, their insecurities, or their fears. For this reason, they unconsciously need their partner to stay in a state of chaos. Without it, they might be forced to look at themselves. Thus, they unconsciously contribute to and help perpetuate their spouse's chaos. The end result is a continual state of disharmony, pain, and confusion.

People who live this chaotic existence genuinely suffer, but, because of their own pain, they tend to be insensitive to the pain they cause others. From a clinical point of view, depending on its intensity, their behavior can become pathological in nature and result in their becoming totally emotionally paralyzed. To understand these individuals, it is necessary to view their behavior and emotions as a basic attempt to cope through controlling their world, albeit in a self-destructive manner. It is a highly nonconstructive means of coping. To alter this pattern, "people of chaos" have to muster up the courage to face life squarely. They need to realize that their problems, their frailties, and their humanness are not unique. The solution for them, as it is for every one of us, is "to go into self, in order to get out." They are rarely able to do so on their own and should be encouraged to seek professional help.

It is only by facing, accepting, and forgiving their fears of insufficiency, imperfection, and unlovability that they can eliminate their need for the upheaval and distress they create for themselves. Only by looking inside will they ever discover that their problems are not the result of others. The recognition that the chaos they experience is of their own making is the first step in the process of assuming responsibility for their plight. The second step in this process is recognizing that their self-generated turmoil serves two major purposes. The first is to separate or distance them from their inner pain, usually related to concerns over their adequacy. The second is to divert the attention from them by virtue of the smoke screen they create. In either case, their behavior does the opposite. It brings attention to them, does little to alleviate their anxieties, and provides no solution to their problems. This brings about the third step, which is for all human beings who wish to rid themselves of their fears to take control of themselves. This means that they must avoid becoming consumed with what others think or who they wish they were. Instead, they must accept who they are and be prepared to honestly share that person with everyone whose love they desire.

Let me give you an example. An individual tells his spouse how hurt he feels by the way he has been treated, and the response he receives is, "What makes you think you're the only one who hurts?" The normal reaction might be to become angry, to take flight, grab the car keys, and drive off or decide to see a lawyer about filing for divorce. But if he needs the chaos to continue, he might say, "You don't care. You're just like your mother. You only think about yourself." It's similar to throwing gasoline on a fire. If, however, he truly wants to establish a positive relationship, his response might be, "I understand that you may be hurting, too. But what I'm trying to tell you is that I love you. I am pained by the hurt we share, and I desperately need for you to hold me and reassure me that you care." To paraphrase from a famous quote, if people want to escape a chaotic way of life, they should ask not what their partner can do for them but what they can do for their partner and themselves. They can do this by clearing the air of the confusion they create to avoid seeing or being seen for the person they fear they are. In almost every instance, who you really are and what you genuinely feel is far more palatable than the defense you use to hide yourself.

The problems people experience interpersonally are usually only reflections of the fears they harbor within themselves. Their fears are manifested by particular behaviors, such as self-deceit, rationalization, and intellectualization, or smoke screens, such as anger, depression, helplessness, alcohol, drugs, gambling, or obesity. These problems only serve as the chaos that clouds their lives. When this explanation is provided to patients, the most common response is "Are you crazy? Why would I create pain for myself? I can't stand the stress. I hate being fat. I want to be liked," et cetera. The answer is not a difficult one. Pain of a self-inflicted nature is far easier to tolerate than pain stemming from a source over which you have little or no control.

I recall years ago, after stepping out of the shower, hearing my wife say, "Where in the world did you get that bruise?" I looked down and saw a large bruise on the inner part of my thigh. The blood vessels were broken, and my thigh was a vivid spectrum of purples. You would have thought that I would have known how or when the damage was sustained, but I didn't. Several days later, I remembered that I'd had dental work done earlier that week. In order to obscure the pain from the shot of Novocain I was about to receive, I had grabbed the inner part of my thigh and squeezed hard enough to direct my full attention to the pain I created and away from the pain I anticipated.

In the course of living our lives, many of us hide the pains we experienced in childhood by creating stress, chaos, and problems in our daily lives. The distraction we create must always be greater than the secret fears we harbor. The problem is that this solves nothing. The original pain is still there. Thus, the distraction—be it alcohol, drugs, upsets, bruises, or crises of any nature—needs to be continuous.

There is only one solution. *People need to run toward their fears, identify them, accept them and learn to live with them or in spite of them.* That isn't easily done. Each new insight, every step closer to your hidden truths, is accompanied by increased hurt. It's the very emotion most people were attempting to avoid in the first place. Getting in touch with one's own reality is an extremely painful process. It's similar to piercing a blister or removing a benign tumor. It hurts terribly, but there is no way of dealing with the problem and initiating the healing process without pain. Some individuals can accomplish this on their own, but the process usually requires professional help. If people of chaos commit themselves to the process, they can eventually exchange their confusion for clarity and begin to direct their efforts toward solving problems, rather than creating symptoms or smoke screens.

CHAPTER FOURTEEN

YOU'RE NOT TRAPPED

Oftentimes, it is difficult to see that the traps we find ourselves in are of our own making. By virtue of our words and deeds, we sometimes create situations wherein we feel ourselves the victim when we are really the perpetrator of our own crime.

Years ago, in the jungles of New Guinea, the natives hunted baboons both as a delicacy and to sell to zoos around the world. The method they used was to create a mixture of mashed banana and shaved coconut and place it in a hollowed-out coconut shell, over which they had built a slatted box. The box was constructed of thin strips of bamboo set closely together and then staked to the ground. The trap was an ingenious device. In order for the primate to reach the sweet gruel inside, it had to put its hand sideways between the slats. It could then reach into the bowl and grab a handful of the gruel. However, with its fist clenched around the food, it was impossible for the baboon to withdraw it through the narrow space between the bamboo slats. During the time the baboon grappled with the problem, a native would throw a net over it and capture it. So who trapped the baboon? Did the natives do it, or did the baboon trap itself? All it had to do was withdraw its hand the same way it had inserted it, but the baboon couldn't do it. Its sweet tooth drove it toward another goal, which trapped it.

Too often, human beings act in a similar fashion. I see it time and time again in therapy. Individuals who are married intellectually verbalize and declare their love for one another and their desire for a close, meaningful relationship with their partners. Yet, they act in ways that make achieving that goal impossible. Too frequently, they are trapped in a situation of their own making that is counterproductive to achieving the goals they desire.

Gordon and Janet were like that. Although they were two very bright, successful physicians, their home life seemed in constant turmoil. Gordon tended to hold his feelings in. He was a reserved, analytical, emotionally controlled person. In his mind's eye, he never got angry, but his anger was readily apparent to his wife and children. It didn't take the form of yelling and screaming. Instead, it manifested itself in isolation, silence, and preoccupation with reading. As Gordon told me, "I may get irritated, but I just say to myself, 'What the hell; it's not worth fighting about,' but I suppose it bothers me a little bit inside." Janet, on the other hand, wore her feelings on her sleeve. She was emotionally reactive, warm, and sensitive but also controlling and inflexible. She perpetually perceived herself to be the injured or victimized partner in an unhappy marital relationship.

If you were to spend an hour with Gordon and hear about his wife's lack of concern with domestic duties, her feelings of being overburdened by his and the children's desires, and her lack of interest in cooking, caring for the house, or any form of domestic activities, it would lead you to think, *What a wimp. How can he stay married to her? He works in a very successful group practice, earns a great deal of money, then comes home to cook the meals, pick up around the house, and tend to the lawn.* In his mind, there was no doubt whatsoever that he was, without any doubt, the injured party in their relationship. As he himself said, "Nothing I ever do is enough. Nothing I ever do makes her happy. If I meet one expectation, the bar only goes up a notch higher. She always wants just a little bit more than I'm giving at the time. I truly don't know how to please her." He was ready to throw in the towel, and after listening to him for one therapy session, I could hardly help but think that it was entirely reasonable for him to feel the way he did.

But Janet was at her wits' end, too. "Sure," she acknowledged, "I'm not a traditional housewife. But I have a job, and I earn a very good living. We can hire help for all the housework. Why do I have to do those things to prove that I care? Maybe he should look at himself. The kids and I live alone. Just ask him, 'What are the names of your children's teachers?' He can't name one. Ask him what size shoes his children wear. He won't know that, either. He's there, but he's not. In fact, he's no more there on an evening when he's home than when he's traveling out of town. He's lost in his own thoughts and his own world. The kids and I might as well be on a different planet. It certainly doesn't seem as though we are important to him. We're married, but we're just people who live together. We don't interact; we don't share emotions or feelings. I never know what he's thinking. I never know when he likes something or doesn't. Then when I complain—perhaps too much—he finally says something that indicates he cares or that we matter. But it just takes too much effort to get him to say one kind word or statement. I need more. I wouldn't care if he made half the money he makes, if there was a way to make him happy about me." When I put myself in Janet's position, I could hardly help but understand her feelings of loneliness too.

If you think, *They can't both be right, can they?* my answer is, "Why not?" They've been married fourteen years, have three children, two good careers, a lovely home, and all the toys that contribute to living life well, but they're both desperately unhappy. They have built a trap in which each of them feels entangled, without any way to escape. Similar to the baboons in New Guinea, neither was willing to let go.

When I tried to figure out how they had constructed that trap, I noticed a couple of important factors:

- The more you complain in any kind of relationship, the more fuel you heap on your own fire. Your complaints needn't be verbalized or directed toward the other person; they just need to be on your mind. You need only concentrate on them before going to bed or be preoccupied by them when you wake in the morning. Then, later during the day, you look for anything to support your position, to reaffirm your perception and justify the pain you feel.
- This self-affirmation then serves to reinforce your own discontent. It creates a state of disenchantment, irritation, and fault-finding, like clenching your fist even tighter in the trap.

Without necessarily expressing it in words, but behaviorally, through various unconscious actions, Gordon and Janet also sent a message to their kids. Gordon basically said, "Your mother is a lousy wife and a lousy parent. She doesn't care about you. She doesn't clean. She doesn't cook. She doesn't take care of the house. She could leave something stacked in a corner, and it would be there a week later. She's always unhappy. You can never please her. You don't have to love her because she's desperately lacking."

Similarly, Janet was saying, "We don't need your father. When he's here, he's not here at all. In fact, when he's gone on a business trip, things are better. We don't have to worry about his complaining, his nitpicking about leaving things around the house, his orders to organize and clean and stack and pick up articles that have been strewn in corners. It's more fun when he's gone. All he does is find fault. We don't matter to him, not you or me. He just thinks we're supposed to be happy as cooks and maids."

Neither parent would make those statements directly or consciously to their children. Yet, that was what was communicated in a myriad of ways almost every day of every year of the kids' lives. They were aghast when I asked them, "Do you realize what you're saying to your children? Is this what you meant to say?" They opened their mouths, but no words came out. When you look at the total picture, you become aware that Gordon's and Janet's actions and behaviors were designed to create distance and animosity. How different it might have been if each of them sought the closeness they both feared but desired. By virtue of acting out of fear, as opposed to their desire, they wound up constructing an emotional trap. It engulfed them in conflict and provided a model for their children that would perpetuate problems into the next generation.

How different it might have been if they were capable of speaking to each other from the heart about their feelings, their needs, and their wishes. In my head, I can almost hear what I imagine Janet might say, if she were capable of opening up and being vulnerable without being defensive, without critiquing or finding fault, without criticizing her husband. It might sound something like this: "Gordon, I love you very, very much. I admire you. I know you're a fine physician. I respect all of those things. I even know, in my head, that you love me and the children. I know that we matter, but I don't feel it and I need to. Whether you're aware of it or not, you married an emotionally needy, dependent person, someone who never got the love she needed or wanted as a child and is accustomed to not getting it now. But somewhere deep inside of me, I'm beginning to think I deserve more. I deserve someone who not only cares but can show it. I own up to the fact that I'm not a stereotypical housewife. But I care and love you. And I need to hear you build me up and tell me that I matter, that I'm important to you. Somehow, I feel if you could help to convince me that I'm important to someone, I wouldn't have to fight quite so hard. I wouldn't feel as though I were buying someone's love by picking up articles of clothing that have been strewn around the house, or by going in the kitchen and cooking a meal. Please help me with this problem."

I can envision Gordon saying, "Janet, I was equally hurt as a kid, but I don't wear my wounds openly like you. I hide it. I close up. I push people away. I don't let them see that they can get to me ever. Letting people know I care, making small talk, showing emotions, isn't my strong suit. But I do love you. I do want you and the kids. I didn't have a very good role model to emulate. All I ever got from my dad was rejection and orders, and my mom never made up for the harshness or his lack of involvement. She was too afraid not to support his actions. Sometimes my head knows what I have to do, but when it comes down to doing it, to showing the love I have, I'm paralyzed. I sit there, and I watch you and my dear children looking for something from me, and it's so hard, so very hard, to let you know what I feel inside. I believe I can do better than I do, and I'm asking you to love me and accept me even before I'm able to show it to you."

These are statements of care and vulnerability that reveal the person making them. They say, "I want a relationship. I want to give you love and get love in return." It is a different, more positive way of approaching a spouse, a partner, a friend, or even a business acquaintance. It is an approach that doesn't create conflict or cause emotional distress to your partner or your children. Nor does it create distance or animosity. Instead, it opens a door that allows you to put your toe in the crack and say, "Please let me in. I'm through putting my hand into a trap that prevents me from having the relationship with you that I truly want." Will it work? Yes. Can it happen in one day? No. Will you have to reread this chapter on numerous occasions to refresh your memory? Definitely. Is it worth it? Absolutely. I only hope that you will one day be able to turn my words into your actions. However, that can only happen if you begin to face and own your fears, take responsibility for your side of the relationship equation, and risk reaching out to your significant other (i.e., by becoming a winner).

CHAPTER FIFTEEN

YESTERDAY'S CURES AND TOMORROW'S PROBLEMS

O nce you've decided to put yourself into the equation, the way you go about doing it can be even more important. Give some thought to the fact that the behaviors and emotions that made it possible for you to "successfully" survive the first part of your life won't work quite as well during the second. For example, think about the following:

- *Dependency needs*—When you were a child, fear of being without your parents and the notion you couldn't make it on your own and needed protection and nurturing caused you to stick close to home and to defer to the adults who cared for you. When practiced during the second part of your life, these same behavioral patterns stifle performance, prevent independence, and restrict your ability to grow. Even more, they are no longer endearing behaviors. Although you may still perceive them as charming or cute, behind your back, people say, "I hope he/she eventually *grows up*."

- *Feelings of insecurity*—Everyone feels insecure sometimes, but in excess, insecurity causes you to engage with your world in a highly egocentric manner. If you're an insecure person, you rarely see others for who and what they are. Your primary interest is only how others perceive and feel about you. In your mind, you constantly ask, *Do they accept me? Do they care for me? Are they angry with me? Do they want me around? Am I saying the right thing? Am I smart enough or rich enough?* These concerns tend to color all of your interpersonal relations, so much so that you perceive every interaction and every circumstance only in terms of how it will affect you. This makes it difficult, if not impossible, to create healthy adult relationships.

- *Feelings of jealousy*—"My friend likes another friend better than me. The only recourse I have is to divide and conquer. To achieve this, I purchase each of their affections. I invite them, separately, to special events. I share secrets with each of them about the other, even going so far as to embellish the truth or lie." When you were a child, this behavior often enhanced relations; when you do this as an adult, it eventually destroys them.

- *Consumption with vanity*—Every hair has to be in place. Every article of clothing has to be the latest fashion and accompanied by a designer name. Later on in life, there often isn't as much hair as there used to be. Stylish clothing doesn't come in your new size, and you may not have the financial means to purchase it. However, even when there is an abundance of hair, you're still a size 2, and money isn't an issue, you fear others will discover that beneath the surface, there is only a shallow person whose feelings of inadequacy are hidden by appearances, clothing, or money.

- *Greed*—You may have learned early in life that success, financial accomplishments, and possessions are the means to a happy end. The more toys you've got—the bigger the house, car, or boat you own—the more successful you are and the more you will be loved and admired. Sometime later, you realize that all those things, though pleasant to have, aren't necessarily the road to happiness. Other factors, such as friends, relationships, love, and health become increasingly important. They more accurately reflect how rich you really are. Best of all, they're available to you if you make them your priority. They're also the essential ingredients that can make your life worth living.

- *The need for power*—In youth, the stronger you were, the more intimidating you were. The prettier or more physically developed you were, the more control you could exert over your peers. Later in life, it's not quite the same. There's nothing less powerful than an old, banged-up high-school quarterback who can only look to his past warrior image for his sense of self-worth. It's no different for the aging cheerleader whose sole claim to fame was based on form instead of substance. In both cases, time takes its toll and the truth hidden behind earlier coping behaviors becomes more apparent. One hopes, as you grow older, you'll choose your friends more wisely and realize that only those who really care will be there when you're down and out. Consequently, they're the ones you need to search out, no matter your or their outward appearance.

- *Desire for attention*—Individuals of this ilk come in many forms. They include the motor mouth, the whiner, the complainer, or the jokester. In junior high, they were entertaining. In high school, they began to lose their luster. By adulthood, they became annoying. A little of them goes a long way.

There are other categories you could add to this list, but, suffice to say, childish coping techniques should be restricted to childhood. When carried beyond that stage, they distract, rather than attract. Peculiarly, they don't necessarily interfere with success in the world. These individuals can do well in business and achieve fame, but their emotional relationships always suffer. That being the case, you might expect people to curtail these behaviors. Sadly, that doesn't often happen for two reasons:

1. If a pattern of behavior is successful early in life, it is generally habituated throughout life.
2. Most individuals aren't aware of the consequences of their behavior.

There is an old song that says it well: "Folks are dumb where I come from. They don't have very much learning. Still, they're happy as can be, doing what comes naturally."

There are many similarities between each of the previous coping techniques and the stereotypical warrior and wimp patterns of behavior. It can be blamed on a litany of factors: DNA, experience, role models, learned behavior, or survival techniques. No matter the motivating forces, these behaviors are no longer constructive when you reach adulthood. In fact, they can more accurately be considered destructive to interpersonal relationships, as well as the institution of marriage. Although these behaviors may have worked during your youth and the early stages of marriage, they are no longer viable. The statistics say it all: Fifty-odd percent of marriages fail.

In therapy, I frequently tell my patients, *"You can no longer behave normally. Behaving normally, doing what comes naturally, is what got you here in the first place."* You must learn to behave abnormally, atypically. It's not easy, but it is learnable. The first step is awareness, which, in itself, doesn't come naturally, because it can be painful and human beings naturally avoid pain. If you exhibit any of the previous behaviors, don't deny, rationalize, or discount them. Instead, pay them heed and change. If people you care for still act like children or teenagers, don't talk behind their back, criticize them, or laugh at them. Express your love for them by gently saying, "You have to grow up before you grow old." It's a message they need to hear, especially if it is packaged with concern for their well-being and seasoned with love. The problem is that the initial reaction most people have is, "I don't know how to behave differently." What you don't realize is that you really do know what to do. You even practice it in select situations, such as in your professional life at the office or when you interact with friends. Therefore, you need to reorganize your thoughts to find what's been missing. You don't lack the tools, just the awareness that you have them.

CHAPTER SIXTEEN

THE ORDEAL OF CHANGE

B y this time, you've heard me say, probably too many times, "change your behavior." However, of all the ordeals that you will face in a lifetime, there is probably none more difficult to achieve than attempting to alter your own behavior. You would think that knowing, alone, would be sufficient to motivate a person to change. But after watching people in therapy, it's apparent that knowing right from wrong, good from bad, appropriate from inappropriate, or constructive from destructive, isn't enough. Think about it. How many people do you know who are overweight, despise their body image, and repeatedly make resolutions to go on a diet but never do? They know their weight will result in hypertension, heart disease, kidney problems, circulatory problems, and premature death, but it doesn't seem to matter. Similarly, how many people do you know who smoke, even though the package tells them that it is injurious to their health? Every day, the literature reinforces the notion that smoking not only causes cancer but is associated with a myriad of other diseases. Nevertheless, they persist in buying cigarettes. They may even say, "I have to stop smoking," but it doesn't translate into behavior. The same can be said for people who drink to excess, take drugs, gamble, are addicted to pornography, or engage in the physical or emotional abuse of their spouse or children. Most of them know their behavior is unacceptable. After every episode, they're remorseful. Still, their behavior continues. Saying it's an addiction is only providing a definition. It is not an excuse, a justification, or a solution.

Ironically, more often than not, human beings need to be hit over the head to wake them up and to motivate them to initiate changes they always wanted to make but were too fearful or lacked the confidence to actualize. Often, it takes a heart attack to get someone on a diet. It might take cancer to cause someone to stop smoking. One or two divorces might finally make people recognize that their behavior contributed to the situation they're in and that they desperately need to look at themselves.

It is useless to make excuses, to blame others, or to plead ignorance. You need to take responsibility for yourself in order to become the person you truly want to be. In the long run, for change to occur, it must come about not because others are pushing or motivating you, but because deep down inside, you want to be thin or stop smoking, drinking, gambling, taking drugs, mistreating others, or staying in dead-end jobs or relationships with people you believe take advantage of you.

Otto, a man whose children I saw in therapy, was a prime example of someone who needed a catastrophe to initiate change. He was a basically well-intentioned individual; he loved his family but dealt with them in a highly self-righteous, authoritarian manner. He restricted, demeaned, and subordinated his spouse and children, all of whom were frightened and intimidated by him. In spite of that, each of them strongly desired his love, approval, and attention, but he didn't know how to give it. For him, demonstrative feelings only reflected weakness. Otto was the classic example of a warrior.

Throughout the time I saw his children, Otto periodically visited me. His manner was always abrupt. His words lacked emotion, and he was critical of others. It was difficult to hear him out without feeling that you hadn't quite lived up to his expectations. Despite several attempts to help him face the negative impact of his actions, his self-righteous defenses prevented him from seeing his reality. As a result, he curtailed his appointments and called every other week to discuss his children's behavior. To be truthful, it came as a welcome surprise when the calls ceased for a period of almost six weeks. During that time, his children were at summer camp and I went on vacation. I had little information about what was happening at their home. Then one weekend, he called again, but something was different. He asked how I was and whether I had enjoyed my vacation. He seemed far more animated and responsive than I had ever perceived him to be. He was more emotional and the anger that usually accompanied his conversations was noticeably absent.

He said, "I thought it appropriate to call and let you know what's happening with me. I guess you noticed I haven't called for about six weeks. I've had a bout of surgery. My doctor discovered a tumor during a routine examination, and, to make a long story short, I have melanoma. I'm not sure yet what kind. I have no idea what's going to happen. But no matter what the future holds, I want to live the present differently. I'm trying to be positive about things, and I want to tell you a funny story involving an associate of mine. He called and told me about a friend of his whose father was diagnosed with cancer and told that he only had a short period of time to live. As a result, he decided to fulfill his fondest dream—to go to Africa, along with everyone in his family and several select friends. He spent a tremendous amount of money on one of the most wonderful trips that any of them had ever been on. That was twenty-six years ago. He's been griping about all the money he spent ever since! But I thought in case you were of the same mind-set, I ought to call and say that I'd like to go with you."

Then Otto broke out into laughter. I was talking to a different man. I thought how sad it was that he needed a catastrophic event to cause him to grow and alter his behavior. On one hand, I felt sorry for him. On the other, I was glad.

Unfortunately, sometimes even a heart attack, cancer, divorce, or repeated involvement in dead-end relationships isn't sufficient to motivate change. Take the example of Melissa, a thirty-four-year-old, very attractive, bright professional who found it almost impossible to become the person she wanted to be. Instead, her actions were controlled by inner feelings of insecurity and inadequacy, stemming from being raised in a home where family tradition and emotional support were all but absent. As a result, she desperately longed for a meaning-ful, close relationship with someone who would care for, love, and support her. Her longing, however, was a concept built on fantasy and wishful thinking, because she never really expe-rienced love. She had no idea what it consisted of. She knew the dream. She knew what it was that she wanted and desired, but like most people, she behaviorally clung to and searched for what was familiar. Consequently, she repeatedly became involved with men who, over time, provided the same empty emotional relationship that she experienced as a child.

In the end, she always felt used and unappreciated, both very familiar emotions. Still, she was unable to extradite herself from these relations. In her mind's eye, if she lost the man she had, there would be nobody to fill the void. She couldn't make herself believe that anyone of real substance would love, nurture, or want her. Because of this, she stayed in at least two relationships long after she knew they weren't providing her with what she wanted. She tolerated behavior she perceived as unacceptable and stayed angry with herself for her inability to change. She was unable to leave until her pain, depression, and feelings of unworthiness became so acute that she felt she could no longer survive emotionally.

At the same time, it appeared as though she deliberately increased her own discomfort to the point that it would give her the courage to leave. She was like a person who first has to gain sufficient weight to reach a point where it is so unacceptable to him or her that it provides the initiative to go on the diet he or she spoke about ten pounds earlier.

From the outside looking in, the picture appears absurd. If you know what you want, are certain it would be beneficial to you, and hate yourself because of your inaction, you need to do something. But you don't. Instead, you stay frozen in place, despite the fact that you make repeated promises to yourself to initiate a change. Time and time again, you say, "I'll do it tonight," "I'll start this weekend," "After the holidays," or "When the kids' finals are over." But the deadlines come and go and you're still in the same place you were weeks, months, or years ago. It doesn't seem to make sense, yet thousands of people find themselves facing the same dilemma. The details may differ, but the emotional dynamics are essentially the same. It doesn't matter whether you are searching for a sales job but are reluctant to cold-call; want to start a diet and exercise but love food; desire a divorce but are afraid of hurting your children and spouse; are looking for a raise but are afraid to ask for it; need to escape an abusive relationship; or have to make any one of a thousand different decisions—it's difficult to alter habituated behaviors. Think of it as though you were a novice trapeze artist, standing on a high platform at one end of a tent. Your goal is to reach a platform on the other side of the tent. Your partner hangs by his feet and swings toward you with his arms outstretched. Your job is to swing out on your trapeze, let go, do a flip in the air, and grasp his hands as you fall. There is one problem: once you let go of your trapeze, you have nothing to hold onto until you reach his outstretched hands. It doesn't seem absurd that you stand frozen on your platform or swing back and forth, gaining momentum for your jump, but can't seem to let go and fly out into the void. It makes a lot of sense; fear of the unknown itself can be a very strong motivator, but acting out of your fear makes your life a living hell.

Years ago, a group of psychologists did a study entitled "Learned Helplessness." They constructed a box four feet wide by ten feet long with solid sides five feet high. In the center, they placed a partition three feet high, thus creating two four-by-five compartments. In one compartment, they placed an iron grid attached to an electrical charge. They randomly selected a large group of adolescent dogs and began their study. They would take a dog, put him into the side with the grid, and sound a bell. Several moments later, they would send an electric charge to the grid. Without deviation, when the electrical charge hit the grid, the dog yelped and jumped over the partition to the other compartment. It was almost one-shot learning. It showed that an animal automatically avoids pain and hurt. It's a natural aversion behavior. Then, one by one, they placed the dogs into the compartment with the grid. This time, however, it was covered by a thick piece of Lucite. They then rang the bell, which was followed several moments later by an electrical charge. The dogs yelped, barked, bit, defecated, urinated, or curled up in the corner compliantly, awaiting the charge that they learned would follow the bell. After approximately twenty trials with each dog, they removed the Lucite cover. Once again, they placed the dogs into the grid side of the box and rang the bell, indicating that the dogs would soon be shocked. Each of the dogs knew that there was no cover. Each of the dogs had previously been shocked and jumped over the partition, but do you know what the dogs did? They barked, bit, urinated, defecated, and crawled off in the corner and yelped, resigned to the fact that they were going to be shocked. Not one of the dogs jumped over the partition. They had learned to be helpless, despite the fact that they were free to leave the noxious situation they were in. The smartest dog, with the help of the trainers, took two hundred trials before it learned to jump over the partition.

If we think of this in terms of the pain people experience early in their lives, the helplessness that they learn, and the wimp behavior or warrior stance they later demonstrate in life, it makes sense. We can all become accustomed to painful situations, abusive partnerships, and dead-end jobs, because we see no light at the end of the tunnel and feel we deserve nothing better.

You might say, "Well, that's dogs, not people." Let me tell you a story that a friend of mine told me years ago. He was a CIA agent who had been traveling in Russia during the Cold War. One day, he found himself waiting for a train at a railroad station in central Russia in the middle of winter. The station was freezing. There was a crack in the wall and the cold Russian air was seeping into the waiting room. The men and women waiting in the station with him all sat in their parkas with their hats and gloves on, tolerating the cold. At one point, he got up and moved several suitcases in front of the crack, and after a period of time, the station warmed up to the point that many people took off their parkas, hats, and gloves. One group of men even started playing cards. Sometime later, a train arrived and the man who owned the suitcases my friend had put against the wall picked them up and left to catch his train. The room began to get cold again, and the people put on their parkas, hats, and gloves and stopped their card game. My friend found this confusing. It was so obvious all they had to do was move some other suitcases in front of the opening. He asked me if I could explain this behavior. I told him about the dogs and learned helplessness and suggested that human beings often learn a state of helplessness. They become resigned to disappointment, hurt, failure, and even to abuse. Though they complain bitterly and resolve time and time again to change their behavior, they remain in the same place, too frightened to try something new, not believing that if they do, they could succeed or that they deserve any better than life has already dealt them.

Change is extremely difficult, but there are lessons to be learned from the previous examples. You can live your life without ever changing. People often remain in situations that cause them pain. The reward is that they needn't look at their lack of courage because they blame others for their situations.

Despite your resolve and your desire for something new, nothing in your life will ever change unless you convert your wishes into actions. More often than not, however, you reluctantly stay with what you know and what is familiar. Why? Primarily because you are afraid of change and frightened to live your life the way you desire, as a thin, sober, self-controlled, loveable, independent, happily married, or successful human being. So you remain where you are, despite how suffocating it may feel. Change, when it does occur, only comes as a result of catastrophic, life-threatening events or blinding flashes of the obvious. It rarely occurs because of positive motivation and conviction stemming from the belief that, "I needn't live my life controlled by my emotions. I can act in accordance with my wishes." Of course, this should be everyone's goal. It may well be your goal, but too many times, your behavior belies your convictions. To alter that, use the following guidelines to aid you in the difficult process:

1. You need to ask yourself two questions: One, "What do I want?" and two, "Where do I want to go?" You may even have to write them down and answer them every day. Your response to these questions can then serve as a guide to the direction you need to follow.

2. You have to be aware that change doesn't take place with one big step. You first have to crawl and then walk before you finally run toward what you desire.

3. You must act, in spite of your fears, your feelings of insufficiency, and your reluctance to fail. Your eventual success won't come about because those feelings went away but because you tried and failed a sufficient number of times to learn to succeed. You always learn more from your mistakes than your accomplishments.

4. You must remember that progress only comes about as a result of forward thinking, but it almost always involves taking three steps forward and two steps back. Although those two steps back may be interpreted as a failure, they are very necessary because you will learn from your failures and benefit from your mistakes and because you will never experience success unless you have first allowed yourself to experience failure.

5. You must not be disheartened when your first attempts to change result in you going to an extreme. For example, the passive, compliant people first act angry and hostile before they level off. The pattern that change takes is similar to the behavior of a pendulum on a cuckoo clock. You start it by positioning the pendulum at one extreme and letting it go, causing it to swing to the opposite extreme. Then you wait for it to level out. Human beings react in the same manner.

6. Finally, you need to force yourself to take the first step in the right direction. Thereafter, your body will follow.

I hope I've provided you with the impetus to risk change, to figuratively let go of that trapeze and fly to where you can grow. It's frightening and challenging, but it also promotes growth and is tremendously rewarding.

WHAT YOU NEED TO DO

To put it simply, if people want emotionally healthy relationships, they have to be emotionally healthy themselves—in other words, they have to be winners, as opposed to warriors or wimps. That's the reason I have always objected to the term "*marriage counselor.*" I don't believe therapists can counsel marriages. Unfortunately, that's what many individuals desire, because it's a great deal easier to look at and deal with a broken relationship or a spouse you perceive as flawed than it is to view yourself honestly.

That's not to say a therapist can't help both you and your partner to better communicate with one another. But if both of you are emotionally damaged and only search for help to alter your behavior, you are bound to wind up with a broken marriage. The adage is true: people with problems search out people with problems, establish relationships and marriages with problems, and raise problem children. In my opinion, marriage counseling, as most people think of it, only results in temporarily Scotch-taping together individuals who, when the tape dries out or cracks, either break up or stay together feeling unfulfilled. These individuals continue to hide behind their role as warriors who unconsciously punish their partners for what they see in them that they can't accept in themselves or wimps who feel abused and helpless.

The following section of *Warrior, Wimp, or Winner* provides guidelines for becoming whole, healthy human beings who feel self-sufficient, value themselves, accept their shortcomings, and are capable of creating healthy relationships in spite of them. These guidelines aren't sacred or carved in stone. Emulate the examples that you feel apply to you, and reconsider whether the remaining rules might aid you in your future adjustment before you discard them. Use those that apply to you as directions for becoming the healthy person you've always wanted to be. Make them the first steps you follow in order to become a winner and to create a positive relationship with another positive human being.

CHAPTER SEVENTEEN

BEHAVE ABNORMALLY

M ore times than I can count, I have been asked, "What kind of problems do you see in therapy?" For the most part, my answer has been, "Normal ones," which usually puzzles the inquirers. They say something to the effect of, "No, I mean seriously, what problems do people have?" Well, they feel depressed about their lives and their situations; they're unhappy in their marriages, dissatisfied with their jobs, and disillusioned with God, religion, or the government and no longer believe in the "Great American Dream"; they feel lonely, inadequate, and unlovable. They behave out of guilt and responsibility, and because of that, they tend to hate themselves for not having the courage to take the risk of speaking out. They feel too fat or, on rare occasions, too thin, too short, too tall, too poor, and too weak. Some even feel too fortunate because they have everything they could possibly ask for and none of it has any meaning. Need I go any further?

What I call "normal" is what many people think of as abnormal. For a moment, consider the following thoughts: there are millions of people in our country who are taking antidepressant and anti-anxiety medication on a daily basis; there are probably even more who are self-medicating with alcohol, nicotine, carbohydrates, sugar, pot, cocaine, designer drugs like ecstasy and LSD, and barbiturates like heroin; 50 percent of marriages fail; and consequently, half of our children come from broken homes. Several years ago, the rate of unwed motherhood began to rise. Children ranging from age twelve and up are experimenting with sexual behavior. There are an ever-increasing number of homeless people in, of all places, the United States of America, one of the richest countries in the world. Uncontrolled rage and anger is beginning to account for a large number of senseless shootings on our highways, in our schools, and at our homes.

These facts constitute the norm. They are the normal feelings and behaviors present in our society and in a majority of the individuals I see in therapy. To their credit, those in therapy are searching for answers to these problems. Far too many other individuals elect, consciously or unconsciously, either to deny or accept them and live out their lives unhappily or settle for just existing.

Aside from the social and psychological comment these considerations evoke, the point I want to make is that going to therapy shouldn't help you to be or to act "normal." Quite the contrary, people don't need help in that direction; they do all too well on their own. Take Gino, for example. He was brought up in a traditional Italian home. His matriarch of a mother loved him totally—he was her little boy—but her love was emotionally expensive. It was available if he prostituted himself emotionally, discounted his own feelings, and allowed her to control him. Internally, he was filled with anger and resentment for the price he paid for her love, but he dared not risk expressing these feelings, lest she reject him entirely. Consequently, he denied his feelings and lived his life blind to them. All the while, he played the role of "the good son" in his relationship with his mother. Later in life, his wife became the recipient of his rage. In their interactions, he squelched any behavior he viewed in her as controlling or critical and could only rarely lower his emotional guard. Warrior behavior was "normal" for Gino, but it was also destructive to the possibility that he could ever experience a healthy relationship with any woman. Before that occurs, he has to recognize the source of his anger and deal with that issue directly.

In a similar fashion, Paula, the quintessential wimp, desperately hung on to the hope that Steve would live up to his promises of marriage. After all they had been through over the previous five years, she secretly felt he "owed it" to her. Couldn't he see how she stuck with him through all the problems, the breakups, and the disappointments? Who else would have been so loyal?

The answer she didn't want to hear was, "Any other dependent, emotionally needy woman who was accustomed to playing the role of 'victim.'" She was angered by my response. It was as though she felt she should receive an Oscar for the part she had played. I suggested that her only reward was the security she felt.

She objected to that observation as well and screamed indignantly, "What security do you think I get?"

My response was, "You married your excuse. You get to blame your difficulties on him, and you avoid having to take the risk of rejection that might come from attempting to set limits or boundaries. Moreover, you get to stay in a familiar situation, one you have experienced since childhood. Your relationship with Steve is no different from growing up with an abusive father, whose love you still long for, and a superficial mother who coddled you and said all the right words but never protected you or gave you the emotional nurturing you needed."

In both cases, it may seem as though I'm attributing Gino's and Paula's problems to their parents. I'm really not. The purpose behind examining your early life experiences is not to blame parents but to understand and explain your own behavior. It is not to justify, but to account for why you are the way you are today. In no way am I looking for people to punish their parents for what took place twenty, thirty, or sometimes forty years earlier. Instead, I hope my clients understand that the behavior they demonstrate today, which they may even find fault with and criticize, is normal for them and doesn't occur by accident. What they must realize is that if what was "normal" has proven to be ineffective or destructive, they need to learn and adopt new "abnormal" patterns of behavior.

One particularly illustrative example can be seen in the history provided by Roger. He was a soft-spoken, passive individual—a wimp—who came to therapy after discovering his wife was involved with one of his coworkers. Roger's father was a successful physician who hid behind his profession and had a charming sense of humor. At home, he was different. He was a large hulk of a man with a booming voice. Even more, he was an alcoholic and was often intellectually and physically abusive. In contrast, Roger's mother was a cold, undemonstrative, extremely bright individual, who, in spite of her intelligence, was incapable of providing emotional nurturing or protection for herself or her son. It takes little effort to imagine Roger as a small boy, cowed by his father's fury, frightened for himself physically and feeling trapped, without anyone to protect him or anyplace to go. No wonder he unconsciously chose not to speak up unless directly spoken to for fear of being criticized or depreciated.

This behavior continued throughout his life. As a result, he had few friends in high school and never dated. He was too frightened to reach out, lest he be rejected. His adult relations were totally governed by his childhood fears. It was apparent that as long as his "normal" behavior persisted, Roger would remain a frightened child. When he came to therapy, he felt depressed and totally beaten down. He felt as though he had no choices. If he wished to grow emotionally and behaviorally, he had no choice but to overcome these fears, speak up, and set limits. Experience had taught him assertive action on his part only resulted in pain and rejection. What he had to learn was that, intellectually, he was no longer a child and the adult, thinking facet of his being had to first comfort the scared child inside him and then encourage that child to behave as an adult, in spite of his fears.

Sadly, in all three instances, my patients, in varying degrees, clung to what was familiar. Almost everyone does. People cling to what they know or what they experience in their early years. It serves as a form of security, as evidenced by the flawed axiom I have heard repeatedly throughout my life, "It is better to serve the devil you know than the devil you don't." Pragmatically, it would appear that familiarity, security, and normality are one and the same. The problem is that most people are accustomed to thinking of "normal" as positive. That just isn't so. Let us suppose that an individual learned as a child to respond to any form of stress or frustration with violent behavior. Later in life, when frustrated with his children, his spouse, or his boss, it should not be surprising that he behaves violently. Violence was "normal" for him, but it is not a positive behavior. What Gino, Paula, and Roger have to realize is that what they learned as a child became familiar, no matter how noxious it may have been. Years later, they demonstrate the same behavior because it is normal for them. However, in order to grow, they need to make their abnormal their new normal.

> That's why therapy should be seen as a process designed to teach people abnormal behavior. It suggests that they need to accept who and what they are, change what they cannot accept, and learn to recognize and live in peace with what they do not necessarily like in themselves but realize they are incapable of changing. They can't change who they are inside or how they feel, but they can and must alter how they react if it's destructive to their lives.

To that end, many individuals are becoming increasingly open to searching for alternative ways to deal with what I am describing as their "normal behavior." They are questioning their old ways of reacting, learning new techniques for rearing children, taking courses in philosophy, becoming more involved with religion, and entering therapy. None of these endeavors are intended to threaten or negate their inner child.

He or she will always remain the same and harbor the same feelings and fears. It's their inner adult that needs to mature and take responsibility for their future behavior. The two of them need not be in competition. Instead, the goal of therapy is to integrate them and help individuals find value in every facet of their lives. Emotional growth consists of assimilating what people have learned and forming it into a harmonious totality that enables them to live happily with a minimum of conflict or pain. It requires them to develop a manual override for habitual behavioral patterns. Over time, the new behavior can become more the rule than the exception. However, you should know that, with the advent of any perceived sign of intense pain or criticism, regressive behavior can, and frequently does, occur. On good days, you will catch yourself before you react on the basis of your childish emotions. On bad days, you may respond impulsively, but you will generally recognize the error of your ways more quickly and are then far more likely to make amends for your reactions.

Consistent with the goal of learning abnormal behavior, individuals first need to conduct a personal audit to determine what is "normal" behavior for them. Second, they must judge, as objectively as possible, the acceptability of their behavior on the basis of their own standards. One rule of thumb that might apply is, "If individuals can't discuss it out loud, display it openly in public, or share it with pride with their spouse, parents, siblings, friends, and coworkers, they need to reconsider whether their behavior is truly acceptable. Lastly, it is essential that they alter those behaviors they deem unacceptable. This involves opening themselves up to new ideas and alternative behaviors and committing to a personal resolution to risk emotional pain and to grow intellectually. How can they go about that? By running toward their fears.

CHAPTER EIGHTEEN

RUN TOWARD YOUR FEARS

I t wasn't the end of the world, but it was nearly the end of their relationship. Charlie finally agreed to go to the doctor. It was the third time he had felt dizzy and lost his balance while climbing the stairs of the courthouse. His girlfriend and his daughter were both extremely concerned about him. So was he, but, consistent with his macho male attitude, he wasn't about to admit that to anyone, not even himself. After all, warriors are strong, impervious to illness, and never need anyone.

Nevertheless, he and his girlfriend, Cheryl, agreed to meet at the courthouse the morning of his doctor's appointment, so they could go to the doctor's office together. She arrived early and waited ten to fifteen minutes. When Charlie didn't show, she second-guessed herself and thought maybe he had meant they should meet in the parking garage. Minutes after she left, he arrived. When they finally got together, he was irate because she hadn't listened to his instructions. She was defensive and angry. After all, she was there before him, and if he were the tiniest bit considerate, he would have been on time. Their morning was off to a bad start.

By the time they got to his car, their conflict had escalated. She asked him, "Do you really want me to go to the doctor with you?"

"Why?" he retorted.

"Well, you're huffing and puffing and angry, and, you know, if you don't want me to go, then I won't."

"Well, I don't care if you go or not. It's up to you. If you want to go, you can. If you don't want to go, you don't have to. I'm a big boy. I can make it to the doctor alone."

"That isn't fair or civil," Cheryl said. "I was trying to help you, and, in the process, I got what I always get—only criticism. So, just tell me: do you want me to go?"

"I don't care if you go or not, but it's late so if you're going to go, get in the car."

With that, they both got in the car and drove to the doctor's office for his examination. After a brief examination, the doctor said he would have to schedule a series of tests to understand what was causing Charlie's problems.

As they left the office, Charlie suggested lunch, but Cheryl indicated she wasn't hungry. He dropped her off at her office, and they avoided each other for the remainder of the day. That night, she arrived home to a sullen, non-communicative, angry partner, who spoke in monosyllables. She responded in kind. Following a silent dinner, she took a sleeping pill and went to sleep, despite the fact that he had the radio playing in the bedroom, the TV blaring in the living room, and noise "everywhere I turned."

The next morning, I saw her in therapy. She found it difficult to understand what had happened. She questioned why she was involved with him and wondered if the relationship was going anywhere. She was upset about the way she had been treated and the fact that she could never speak with him without him yelling, screaming, and talking over her. She said that, before she had taken the sleeping pill, she had tried to discuss the problem with him, but he became furious about her having to rehash dirt and stir up old problems. To her way of thinking, things were hopeless, and she wondered if, perhaps, it wasn't time to end the relationship entirely. Finally, in total frustration, she had lost it. She began screaming, yelling, and waving her arms, whereupon he chastised her for being too emotional. With that, she took the pill to escape the situation.

For Cheryl, things had reached a new low. There just didn't seem any way out. For me, I was hearing a story that I had heard thousands of times before. In my opinion, the situation wasn't half as bad as she imagined. The argument was predictable, and the solution was equally simple. This type of interaction occurs time and time again, in millions of relationships, without individuals really looking at themselves, their behavior, and the motivations underlying their reactions.

Cheryl needed to look at herself. She had to ask why she reacted the way she did and to understand her part in creating a mountain out of a molehill. On one hand, there was no need for the situation to grow so out of control. It would have taken so little understanding on her part to cope with it in a healthier manner. She was a very bright, capable professional, but she was totally lacking in her ability to deal with issues of an emotional nature. It is not surprising that when I suggested this, she became extremely defensive and angry.

It is strange that we human beings can accept that we aren't capable of solving a complex mathematical problem, answering a question about biochemistry, or comprehending a formula applicable to nuclear fission—we're able to say, "Well, that's not something I have any training in"—yet, when someone suggests that our wherewithal to cope emotionally isn't fully developed, we perceive it as an insult or a criticism. It is almost as though we have the notion that just by virtue of being human, we should inherently have total knowledge about living. But understanding emotions and having an awareness of human interactions are just as much learned abilities as solving problems in calculus. Without adequate training or education, you can be just as ignorant about emotions as any other area. However, once you become aware of your own lack of knowledge, you can correct it, if you so desire. This training should have come in childhood, but therapy is available. When you are responsive to it, you can develop expertise in this area, just as you can in any other area of learning.

Had Cheryl had that training, she would have experienced little difficulty in dealing with Charlie's behavior. It was kindergarten emotion. Charlie was scared. He didn't know what to expect at the doctor's office. Not only could he not admit his fear, he was unable to ask for help. As a result, he responded out of fear. For him, Cheryl's not being there at the prescribed time was rejection. Her implying he had miscommunicated was, in his eyes, defensive. Put together, it meant she really didn't care. To compound matters, even asking whether he wanted her to accompany him was asking him to beg, to admit he was weak and needed help. Even on a good day, he found it difficult to own any of those feelings or emotions. If she had really wanted to go, she wouldn't have asked. It was one more reinforcement of his childhood feelings—that people didn't care and didn't love him and he didn't matter.

Without any doubt, Cheryl wasn't sensitive to Charlie's behavior. This does not suggest that Charlie's actions or reactions were justifiable. They weren't. Nevertheless, had Cheryl understood where he was coming from, her reactions probably would have been significantly different. It probably wouldn't have altered his behavior, but over time and, with understanding, unacceptable behavior becomes more palatable or at least less upsetting. Unfortunately, Cheryl behaved out of her own dependent, fearful, emotionally needy orientation. All she saw was someone who was critical, found fault, and acted in an abrasive way. It certainly appeared he didn't want her to accompany him. After all, anyone who did would have been far more appreciative or, at least, minimally inviting. As a result, she wasn't sure she wanted to go because she wasn't sure she was wanted. Her asking, "Do you want me to come with you?" reflected her way of searching for reassurance of his love. The problem is that fearful people (which was exactly what Charlie was at that moment) aren't able to reassure themselves, much less anyone else. To make matters worse, solutions are impossible when both individuals are frightened or feel inadequate.

As is usually the case in situations of this type, Cheryl lost sight of Charlie, his problem, and his feelings. She could only see things through her own eyes, which were filtered by her own emotional needs. In this instance, Cheryl had little awareness of her own shortsightedness. She was totally involved with her own immature fears and desires.

What she needed to look at was an analogy between her situation with Charlie and the hypothetical example of someone whose cherished pet dog runs out into the middle of the street and gets hit by a passing car. With overwhelming concern, the dog's owner rushes over to see how badly the dog is injured, and as he or she reaches out, the dog, blinded by pain and fear, only sees something else coming at it, no different from the bumper of a car. With whatever strength it possesses, the dog snaps and bites in an attempt to protect itself. The kneejerk reaction the owner might exhibit would be to retreat or yell, "The hell with you! Die!" Of course, that's not the appropriate response. Instead, the owner might carefully place the dog in a blanket, roll it up slowly to avoid being bitten again or further injuring the animal, and rush it to a vet. Almost every pet owner knows that. Unfortunately, not all loving partners know that about their spouses. Too often, when they snap and bite, they figuratively kick them and shout, "Die!" or, as with Cheryl, retreat, totally consumed with the rejection and hurt they experienced. What Charlie needed, despite his inappropriate behavior, was to be gently rolled in a protective blanket of words, touches, and looks and then rushed to the doctor's office.

What Charlie and Cheryl did was run from their fears. Their behavior was normal. Threatened and scared people run; it's either fight or flight. If something is out there that can hurt you, it seems appropriate either to get away from it or kill it. Unfortunately, that does little to resolve the problem. How far do you have to run to feel safe? How many threats do you have to hear before you are no longer frightened?

There is no answer to either question, but there is an alternative behavior: run toward your fears. Unfortunately, few people take that road. It means facing up to your fear, something we weren't trained to do. Instead, we avoid those things that are potentially threatening or hurtful. We build walls between us and them. The mortar and bricks people use are varied. We become promiscuous, stay angry, retreat from life, trade our fifty-year-old partners in for two twenty-five-year-olds, act compulsively, or hide behind work and children. But we do not face our fears.

In the case of Charlie and Cheryl, the end result was two emotionally insecure individuals looking to one another for the support neither was able to provide at that moment. Charlie wanted a mother, someone who would know his pain, not rub it in, and provide him with support. Cheryl was looking for a parent—a strong father figure who would love her, protect her, and reassure her she was wanted and needed. Their problem was each was searching for adult support, but neither was an adult emotionally; they were both children, looking for what they were unable to give.

Let me give you a pragmatic example of how you might go about running toward the things you fear.

George is a very successful physician. He is the oldest of seven children who were raised in low-income housing. He was abused physically by his father and never protected by his mother, who stood by and let it happen. His reaction was to do what he had to do to make it: to be strong and never let himself be in a position where someone could hurt him or where he would need someone to protect him. On the outside, he achieved that goal. Emotionally, however, he was still the needy little boy. He married and was divorced three times from weak, dependent women—wimps—whom he chose because they needed him and wouldn't leave him. He thought they would be appreciative of him, but that didn't prove to be the case. Why? Because, more often than not, dependent people resent those they depend on. After his third divorce, he found himself consumed with rage. His dreams were filled with thoughts of punishments he wanted to inflict on the most recent ex-wife. It consumed him night and day.

"After all I did for her, she had the gall to have an affair right out in the open, where all my friends and acquaintances could see. I have a right to my anger!" he shouted during a therapy session. Sure he did, but he was paying a terrible price for it. He couldn't sleep, eat, or work. The only thing it did for him was help him to avoid the inner hurt, the feelings that he couldn't be loved, and his fear that he wasn't good enough for anybody. He was totally involved in running from his fears.

George's only alternative was to change the direction of his energies. He had to admit his fears to himself first and then to her. Periodically, she would call him to see if there was a way of reconciling. On those occasions, he was generally rude or verbally abusive. What he needed to be was honest. He needed to say to her, "I want you to know that whatever I did wrong, it wasn't because I didn't care. I loved you, and you hurt me. I'm not invincible. I realize that now. But I also know I don't want to talk to you or be friends with you. It hurts too much, and I don't want to continue being hurt and angry. I want to get on with living my life in a healthier fashion." You see, only by running *toward* his fears could he get in touch with them, grasp them, and then let them go. When you run *from* fears, they are always there somewhere in your life and you have to keep running.

Sadly, this pattern of behavior is all too common. It stems from reacting emotionally instead of intellectually, which prevents you from focusing on your own fears and insecurities. Although lashing out from fear is not a unique response, it is in no way acceptable behavior for anyone. Quite the contrary. The next time you find yourself in this type of situation, you need to remember Charlie, Cheryl, and George and learn from their mistakes.

1. You have to recognize that it is no sin to be a human being who is inexperienced in loving. But it may be a sin not to try to improve the way you love.

2. You need to see that it is permissible, even necessary, and, perhaps, far more courageous to express and ask for the help and support you need from a loved one than to hide behind a defensive mask of machismo, criticism, and anger, the classic weapons of warriors and the last resort for wimps.

3. You must remember that when people are drunk, on drugs, hysterical with anger, or blinded by fear and emotionally upset, you cannot listen to their words or react to their behavior. When you do, it says more about you than it does them, because your reactions are more reflective of where you're coming from than what is being done to you. Responding to immature behavior in kind only points out your own insecurities, fears, and neediness.

4. You must resolve that you will try to act not out of your emotional child's needs but in spite of them. You must allow the adult in you to govern your actions and speech. The motto you must adhere to is a simple one: *Run toward your fears, not away from them.*

CHAPTER NINETEEN

DON'T BE A VICTIM

There comes a time when you reach a crossroad in life. It's when you've traveled further in your past than you're going to go in the future. This event usually takes place later for men than women, the reason being that men tend to have feelings of immortality that suggest they will live forever and conquer every adversary and are immune to the consequences of their actions. But they too eventually encounter that crossroad. No matter when it happens to you, I hope it will wake you to the fact it is time to take an accounting, to determine whether you're satisfied with where you've been, or if you want to alter where you're headed.

That crossroad is different for everyone. It can be the loss of a parent, spouse, or friend; being laid off from a job; the kids leaving home; a serious illness; a divorce; or the realization that your emotional life needs a major overhaul.

For me, it occurs every time I have to go to a funeral. It causes me to consider my own mortality seriously. It's odd, but the older I get, the faster time seems to pass. In fact, I must be getting very old, because time seems to be flying by. No sooner do I make my New Year's resolution to make my life more meaningful during the next twelve months than I find the year has passed and I'm still struggling with the same resolutions. Once again, it becomes apparent I need to examine my lack of action and not only reconfirm my previous resolutions but commit to actualizing them.

I suspect that's equally true for everyone who shares my perception that time is passing faster and each year you live brings you one step closer to the end of your time. Time becomes much more precious. Not only do you not have a lot of it to waste, but your actions and interactions with others begin to take on far greater significance, all because you recognize that there are some very important things you still want to do and a lot less time in which to do them. Those goals will differ for each of us, but the realization that "life is short" is the same for every one of us. It is, therefore, important that you start today to decide just what it is you want to do with whatever time you have left.

Ask yourself, *How many more mountains do I want to climb? How many more relationships do I want to discard or repair? How many more dollars do I need to make? How many more degrees do I want to obtain? How many new homes do I have to build? How many new dresses, rings, bracelets, or necklaces do I need?* There is nothing wrong with these milestones. I am for anything that truly makes you happy, fills your life with joy, and gives you a sense of meaning, worthiness, and accomplishment: plastic surgery, buying a new dress, going to the beauty parlor, finding the perfect set of new golf clubs, buying the second home you've always wanted, or taking that trip you promised yourself you'd go on before you die.

What you should avoid is filling the time you have left with misery, anger, vengeance, conflict, petty grievances, or problems of your own making. As I noted earlier in this book, the vast majority of the time, our difficulties are of our own making. Whether you are consciously aware of it or not, you choose your demeanor, your tone of voice, and your opinions, as well as the intensity of your anger and the length of time you stay upset. More often than not, you even create the difficulties you experience in life, and then you lament what life has dealt out to you. Somehow, it's always easier to play the victim than to be proactive, look at where you are and what's facing you, and say, "How am I going to deal with this?" instead of "Why did this have to happen to me?" or "Woe is me; I always get the short end of the stick."

Let me give you an example.

When I first met Jenny, it was apparent that she was depressed. She described her world as "filled with endless conflicts, sleepless nights, an inability to focus at work, and an absence of joy." She was disappointed in her marriage, but it was her second time around and she couldn't "bear the thought of another failure." At the same time, she stated that her first marriage really shouldn't count; she had been young, in her first year of college, and so in love that she didn't listen to or hear what everyone told her. Less than six months after the wedding, he began staying out with the boys, going fishing and hunting on the weekends, and expressing little desire for sex. When she complained, he would fly into a fury and threaten her physically. By the end of the first year, he periodically hit her because of her "constant whining and bickering." Despite her feelings of shame and embarrassment, she finally told her parents and filed for a divorce with their support and a heavy dose of pressure.

Jenny later graduated from college, moved to Houston, and began teaching math in high school. In the evenings, she attended graduate school and eventually became a CPA. About the same time, she met Gary, her second husband. Despite two previous marriages, he seemed an absolute gem in comparison to her former spouse. He had a good job, earned a comfortable living, and liked working around the house. He was constantly painting and fixing things, finding one project after another. Before too long, she became an active participant in these activities. Her jobs were primarily related to the lawn, the flower beds, and the landscaping because "his allergies didn't permit him to work outside." Later, his "bad back" forced her to become his helpmate whenever heavy lifting was involved. Eventually, she found herself physically and emotionally drowning in the lawn work, his carpentry projects, her own full-time job, all of the household responsibilities, and caring for his myriad of physical aches and pains. When she finally had the courage to suggest she needed help around the house, he told her, "That's woman's work, and a man doesn't do it." Meanwhile, his expectations and demands on her increased in direct relation to her professional success and salary. The more money she brought home, the more she was assured she was lacking as a person and failing in her "wifely responsibilities." Ironically, she never questioned his criticism. She was as much the dutiful wife as she was or had been the dutiful daughter as a child. Gary's sense of emotional insecurity and resulting need to devalue Jenny—his warrior mentality—dovetailed perfectly with her emotional neediness and her willingness to capitulate and play the wimp. Both Gary and Jenny saw themselves as victims. He was saddled with this whining, disgruntled wife, and she was trapped, once again, in a marriage with an emotionally abusive husband.

In spite of their complaints, they both stayed, because their emotional needs neurotically meshed. She could live out the rest of her life as the daughter who was never good enough and who needed to try harder if she really wanted to be loved. He could stay the perpetual asthmatic child who required constant care and indulgence in order to make up for the suffering he experienced.

Or take the example of the absolutely beautiful twenty-four-year old young lady who recently came to therapy because she had been raped by her stepfather twenty years earlier. As is, unfortunately, often the case after sexual abuse during childhood, she later became involved in numerous promiscuous relationships and three long-term, so-called "loving relationships" with married men. In each one, she was used and abused, both physically and emotionally. On the rare occasions when her boyfriend returned her love and became potentially available to her, her interest rapidly waned, and the relationship subsequently ended. Her fear of emotional pain dictated her behavior. She could not bear to care and to be hurt again. Her victim status, however, much like those of Jenny and Gary, was not an accident. She set it up. It served to protect her from ever totally loving a man and getting hurt again and to punish her for the guilt almost all rape victims wrongly feel.

In a similar fashion, I will always recall a woman talking to me about years and years of family birthday parties where her children would joyfully get to sit next to daddy in the seat of honor. Because of the jealousies this created among the siblings, she always sat where she thought a buffer might be needed. She never thought, *Where do I want to sit?*

As the kids grew up, got married, and had kids, their kids also had to be included at the table. Fortunately, it was always large enough to accommodate all of them. Eventually, however, that also changed. In her continuing effort to please, she thought of a new plan: the little kids would all sit at a little kids' table. The kids, however, didn't want to sit at the little table. They wanted to be with the adults. Lest even they be disappointed, she set up a plan that left her sitting with a distant relative at a little table while everybody else sat at the big table. As she related the tale, it was evident she felt unimportant and estranged from the family.

I asked, "Who put you at that little table? Who is it who said, 'It doesn't matter where I sit; I'll just fit in, be the buffer. Everybody else's pleasure is more important than mine'?"

Her reply was, "Well, my husband never said he wanted me next to him." Her voice and her story made me sad for her, even though I knew she wasn't a victim; she was a volunteer.

Her story brings to mind still another example, related to me by a very depressed male patient about his seventy-eight-year-old mother who "came to life" after his father's death. In the midst of the man's worst despair, he called his mother and said, "What are you doing on such a lovely day?"

She said, "Oh, I'm outside washing the car."

My God, he thought, *seventy-eight years old and she's out washing the car while I'm in here feeling sorry for myself.*

Then she asked, "Could you possibly get me some tickets to the Astros?"

He said, "Sure, but what do you want them for?"

"The ladies in the bowling league want to go to an Astros game."

He called up one of the large oil service companies he dealt with that was always offering him tickets and asked for nine of the best tickets available to the Astros. In less than an hour, they called back and said, "You've got 'em for an afternoon game, along with parking tickets."

He called his mother back. "Tell me, Mom, you had all us kids, four boys, and all those years when we went with Dad to the baseball, football, and basketball games; how come you never went with us?"

Her answer was simply, "Nobody ever asked me." But then again, I am sure she never made it known it was something she wanted.

In the end, the facts in each of these examples are of little consequence, but the realization, on the part of each individual, that he or she actively engaged in playing the victim is of major importance. To most observers, the behavior was readily apparent. The "victims," however, tend to perceive themselves as trapped and helpless. In their eyes, the world holds no choices, only orders and demands. Victims rarely have a life of their own. The center of their world is never within themselves. They live in a world dictated by their victimizers, and their identities are determined by the approval or disapproval they experience in their interaction with their significant others. In a convoluted sense, although they accept no responsibility for the outcome of events in their relationships, they tend to feel, "If only I had behaved differently, the people around me wouldn't be mad at me." They worry about things getting done; bills being paid, home repairs being made, and meals being prepared. They expect nothing, feel hurt, and resent the fact that "nothing" is exactly what they get. They play the martyr, blame others for their emotional plight in life, and take no risks. They just suffer in accordance with a pattern of behavior they experienced and learned as a child.

Their marriages and interpersonal relationships are filled with the same arguments, power struggles, and pathological interactions they promised themselves they would never expose their children to. Although the situations they stay in are familiar to them, they still cause them pain. The payoff, once again, is they get to blame others for the problems they experience. They remain blind to the psychodynamics they experienced as a child and elect to perpetuate a fantasy childhood, free of conflict or pain and requiring no introspective investigation. On the other hand, they are bitter and feel victimized by their early childhood experiences and view their spouses as no different from their parents or siblings who mistreated them. Even worse, they then set their spouses up in order to actualize their own expectations and prove they're right: others do abuse them.

Take the example of Joan, whose husband had just arrived home from a three-day business trip. During his absence, Joan had car trouble, the dog got sick and was still at the vet's, and their daughter called from college to say she needed their help moving in to her new apartment that weekend. She added, "By the way, who should I call about my car's sunroof? It flew off as I was driving on the freeway."

Within the first fifteen minutes of his return, Joan dumped all of these problems in her husband's lap. His response was to rant and rave.

"Why can't she get her friends to help her? She's always carting them around. Probably one of them loosened the sunroof. They don't come off on their own."

Before he could finish, Joan jumped in. "I don't need you to jump on me the minute you walk in. You always come home and start screaming. I'm the one who gets to stay home and face the problems. You're never home when there are problems, and when I try to tell you about them, you shoot the messenger." Then she turned and walked out of the room.

This interaction reminds me of a cartoon I saw years ago. It depicted a king shooting arrows across an empty field. At the other side of the field was a squire holding a large target. The squire raced around with the target, positioning it so the arrows would hit the bull's-eye. Many people live their lives that way. They paint emotional targets on their chests and jump in front of as many arrows as possible to ensure that they become the victim.

Although Joan didn't know it, subconsciously, she played a bull's-eye perfectly. She had choices, however. She could have elected to be the sympathetic partner who said, "I know how you feel. I reacted the same way after getting all the calls. Don't worry; we can deal with all of it together."

The solution doesn't come about with a flick of a switch. People don't change like that. Once again, it is a case of three steps forward and two steps back. The process involves small steps and equally small realizations, the first and foremost of which is the awareness that you aren't trapped or helpless and that you do have choices, although they may not be readily apparent to you. Your choices, however, are not free. You pay a price in life. Whenever you are too frightened to take risks, lack the courage to bet on yourself, or hesitate to speak up honestly because of the consequences, you avoid a fight but hate yourself. When you remain indecisive and choose to live life as a victim, you pay a very high price: you lose your identity and deplete any sense of dignity you may have possessed. The second realization is that you need to develop a rational self-interest. It isn't that others aren't important, but they can no longer serve as the center of your universe. Instead, you discover a centeredness within yourself and you realize you can't spend the rest of your life concentrating on what your family or your spouse is going to do or how your children are going to react to you. Nor can or should you live your life worried about the boss liking or not liking you. What you have to do is your job, and you have to do a great job. That's all that really matters.

It all begins with the resolve that you will never again sit at the little table or buffer everybody at the big table because you don't matter; you are through being the only one to sacrifice, and if you want to go to a baseball, football, or basketball game, you'll say so. You realize it's time to cut the emotional umbilical cord to the past and to live your own life, especially if it leads you toward washing your own car on a pretty day at the age of seventy-eight.

Rid yourself of any bull's-eyes, and reach for the goodness surrounding you, which you may have been blind to for most of your lifetime.

But you don't get there by accident. You get there with purpose and by making the decision you no longer want to be a victim. Recognize that you have been a volunteer to misery all your life and then resolve to volunteer for all the good things life and the world have to offer. With each step, the victim in you will disappear, and you will become more the person you want to be.

> If you've lived life as a warrior, it was to fight and/or compensate. If you've lived the life of a wimp, it was to rationalize and capitulate. But if you choose to become a winner, you will live according to what your heart and brain dictate.

One added benefit is that your life won't pass by as rapidly, because you will be taking the time to savor it.

CHAPTER TWENTY

LITTLE THINGS MEAN A LOT

When people hear me say, "If a relationship is worth having, it must be worth fighting for," their initial thought is that I'm saying people need to fight with their partner. That isn't true. The fight is not with their partner. It is, first and foremost, a struggle with themselves to overcome their fears of confrontation and rejection. They must learn they cannot become compliant or accept what is unacceptable to them. They must also develop the insight to recognize what they truly want (not as easy a task as you might think) and find the courage to speak up regarding their wishes. Their success in dealing with these issues will not necessarily guarantee that the relationship they desire will materialize, but it will mitigate the anger they direct at themselves and their fear and resentment of others. As a result, they will find themselves in a healthier place than they ever have before. They will feel a sense of inner peace stemming from the assurance that they are able to choose the direction they want to take when they come face-to-face with the emotional crossroads in their lives. That means they no longer have to control or to crawl—to choose between being a warrior or a wimp.

Unfortunately, we often find it difficult to recognize when we've reached a crossroad or impasse in our lives. We're so accustomed to overlooking or denying potentially controversial or inflammatory situations that we're blind to them. Let me tell you about one classic incident from my own life.

It was one of those events you could easily overlook, and I probably would have if the checkout line had been moving along at its usual pace. Instead, the person ahead of me was bickering over the price of an item she felt she had been overcharged for or that had been marked incorrectly. Consequently, I had time to observe the attractive couple in line behind me. They were in their late twenties or, at most, their early thirties. He was a tall, slender, good-looking young man. She was an attractive young lady, whose facial expressions seemed far more serious than you might expect for someone in a supermarket line. She was totally engrossed in arranging the items in her basket for checkout when I overheard her husband say to her, "Would you like some ice cream?"

Without hesitation, she responded with an emphatic, "No."

"Well, I just thought we might get some ice cream," he answered.

"No. We don't need it. Why? Do you want some?"

"Well, no, not if you don't," he said.

"Well, it's really not good for me. You know that. Anyway, I don't think I should have any." With that, she went back to rearranging the items in her basket.

"Well, if you don't want any, I don't want it either."

Then I did something that surprised me. I turned, looked directly at her, and said, "You know, he really does want ice cream."

There was a noticeable pause, followed by, "Well, I don't want any, but if you must, get something." With that, he raced off to the frozen-food section like an excited kid and returned in a matter of seconds with a stack of chocolate mint ice cream sandwiches, which she immediately rejected by adamantly shaking her head from side to side.

"Those are definitely something I won't eat."

"But they're 90 percent fat free; it says right here."

"It's something I wouldn't eat," she said with deliberation.

Once again, he hurried off to the frozen-food section. This time, he returned with something she deemed acceptable.

As I left the store, I could not help but think, *Here is a divorce in the making. No doubt they'll forget today. They'll take their groceries home and the incident will be filed away as one of those little things that never mattered.* It is, however, those little things, more than any of the big events in life, that undermine and destroy relationships, before, during, and after marriage. It really wasn't a case of having the ice cream. That wasn't the crucial issue. He was saying to her, in a multitude of ways, "This is what I'd like." She failed to hear him. She never even considered what he was saying. When I intervened in their exchange, what I really wanted to shout to her was, "Miss, your husband wants some ice cream. Does that matter to you at all? He isn't asking if you want any. He is saying to you 'I would like some' and you are so preoccupied with your organization and your obsessive need to control your world, that you are totally deaf to his words. Make no mistake, he'll get over this; he'll forget about it much more quickly than I will, but it will stay with him. It will act like a drop of water on a rock, water that drips and drips and collects until it finally carves the rock into a shape of its own creation. Probably because he learned very early in life not to think about what he deserves. Sadly, he doesn't realize that. Instead, he'll think he's the nice guy and you're the witch." What he needed to hear was, "If you don't alter your behavior today, and learn to speak up for yourself, you'll live with growing resentment that, over the years, will very likely be evidenced by passive-aggressive behavior that will hurt her on the outside, but tear you up emotionally on the inside, to the point that your relationship will never be repairable."

It's a case of one more wimp, one more warrior.

I wish I could say their interaction was an exception to the rule and that incidences of this type are few and far between. But that would be a lie. They are common to all too many of us, and they take their toll on all of our relationships. Each incident acts like a seed that germinates anger and resentment, which, years later, causes husbands and wives to doubt or question whether they truly love their spouse or whether they even want their marriage. In most cases, they only know they feel unloved, unimportant, and hungry for someone to love them. They rarely realize that, in reality, they desire someone who will care for them more than they care for themselves. It is far easier for them to point a finger at their partner than it is to own up to the feelings of self-degradation they harbor within because they lack the courage to stand up and risk the rejection of the person whose love they desire. As a result, they are unable to say, "I'll be back in a moment. I want some ice cream for dessert." Instead, they utter, "If you don't want any, I don't either."

I tend to believe that the young lady in the supermarket probably loves her husband, but she certainly isn't sensitive to him. She has no idea ice cream might one day wind up being an itemized grievance in a divorce case. Then again, neither does he. You might ask, "How could she when he hasn't fully apprised her of the fact?" The answer is easy. What she probably thinks is that they love one another, they care for one another, they're shopping together, and they're cooperating in their domestic activities. Were she more aware of her husband, instead of being preoccupied with self, the reorganization of her basket, and maintaining control of her figure, her marriage might be healthier. It's evident that her warrior behavior is destructive to her relationship.

But what about the young man? Where is he coming from? How frightened must he be? How needy and unloved must he feel? And how long has he felt this way? If he had a backbone, if he was willing to stand up for himself or had learned to do so as a child, he might have said to her, "I want ice cream! Don't eat any if you don't want to, but it's something I've got a hankering for and it needs to be satisfied."

Unfortunately, these individuals were on different wavelengths. They were far more involved in their own emotional survival than they were with one another. I can almost close my eyes and visualize him saying to her, years from now, "I'm angry with you, and I don't know why. I can't pinpoint it or blame it on anything of any significance. Yet, I feel distance from you, resentment for you, and sexually unresponsive toward you."

You would have to give him credit if he were able to verbalize these feelings. Most wimps don't. Instead, they express their unconscious feelings passive-aggressively or indirectly. They argue over other issues that seem important at that moment but are really inconsequential. It seems almost absurd or childish to say to a spouse, "I'm mad at you because, three months ago"—or thirty years ago—"you didn't let me buy ice cream." On the surface, it doesn't appear to make a great deal of sense. It certainly sounds immature, but inside, where we collect pain and resentment, these "ice cream" exchanges are anything but unimportant. They are stored and erroneously processed into full-fledged resentment, even hatred. They later wind up as justification for staying out late, drinking, spending time with the boys or girls, losing sexual interest, having an extramarital relationship, or hiding behind books, television, children, work, or hobbies. After all, the only other alternative is to look inside and recognize that the person you are really angry at is yourself.

There is no simple way to resolve this issue, nor any one incident or person to blame. However, one thing is for sure: it has nothing to do with ice cream. It has more to do with the two individuals involved. I suspect if you were able to look into their backgrounds, you would probably find the young lady had a mother who was all backbone, who took the warrior role and controlled her world. Similarly, I suspect the young man's home environment also consisted of a passive, easily led father and a mother who took charge and made sure things ran well. That is almost a certainty, because most people learn "loving" from their mothers. They then interact with their spouse in the same way they interacted with their mother, rather than on the basis of their conscious wishes or desires. It is a pattern that gets repeated over and over again and stands in the way of establishing a successful, loving relationship or marriage.

To achieve this end requires breaking very old, habituated behaviors that manifest themselves with great speed and frequency, without conscious thought or awareness. The propensity to act this way never changes, but our behavior can if we open our eyes and take sole responsibility for the part we play in our interactions with others. The solution involves a simple five-step process. It is one which anyone can undertake, regardless of the behavior of his or her partner or spouse. At times, you may find it far easier, even more desirable, to resist the steps involved by hiding behind the circumstances of a given situation. However, if you commit to this process, you will later learn that facts are inconsequential. They are only justifications we use to rationalize the position we've taken in our conflict with our partner.

1. To begin the process of controlling or altering your own behavior, no matter the nature of the conflict, you need to totally forget your partner or anyone else who may be involved. You must focus entirely on yourself and ask the following question: "What do I want?" You've heard me request that you ask that question before. It's important for you to know. But don't be surprised if you find it difficult to answer. Few people really know. They typically say, "I want to be happy," but are unable to go beyond that response. If you find you fall into that category, modify the question by asking, "What is it that will truly make me happy with myself in the long term?" It is immediately apparent that a new car, a larger home, or sudden wealth isn't the answer. After several months, the new car smell is gone and the newer models make it obsolete and the larger home will eventually require

a fresh paint job, a new roof, or plumbing repairs. The sudden wealth would certainly solve a multitude of immediate problems, but the long-term experiences of many lottery winners and the fact that a large number of my patients who have no money problems are nevertheless in therapy would seem to be testimony to the fact that money, in itself, is not the answer to this question. You need to search deeper inside yourself for another answer. It may surprise you that, more often than not, the answer is not a tangible one. Let me give you a hint: it could be to accept and love yourself.

2. After you find an answer you feel satisfied with, you will be ready for the second step. Make it your goal and commit to achieving it. The commitment itself is not something complex or difficult, it is merely a decision, involving the resolve to adhere to and give value and precedence to whatever it takes to achieve that end. This means, given the decision between a free trip to Las Vegas and staying home with a spouse recuperating from surgery, you have no difficulty in deciding your behavior. This will, of course, depend on whether you have first decided and then committed to becoming a professional gambler or establishing a loving, meaningful, long-term relationship with a spouse as the avenue that will eventually bring you happiness.

3. Step number three not only requires that you then act in accordance with your commitment but also stresses the need to investigate and determine the steps necessary to reach your goal. If you determine that happiness will only come about as a result of your being thin,

you will have little trouble refusing a serving of mashed potatoes and brown gravy; pasta with a mushroom, cheese, and cream fettuccini; or a large slice of cheese cake. With regard to the decision between staying home with a recuperating spouse or a free trip to Las Vegas, the behavior you choose should be equally easy. It really isn't a question of right or wrong. You might well debate the Las Vegas example in terms of leaving a spouse with relatives and professional health-care providers so you can get a few needed days of rest and recuperation. You might argue that, given several days of rest, you would be a more patient, considerate care-giver. Conversely, it is entirely possible that by not going, your covert resentment would interfere with your help-fulness in the future. Your spouse may even insist you take advantage of the opportunity. At the same time, if you decide to go, others may question your decision or view it as selfish and uncaring. It is, however, not for others to decide. The decision is yours and yours alone. First and foremost, you are the one who must live with it the rest of your life. Consequently, you must ensure your behavior is consistent with what you decide will bring you the long-term contentment you are search-ing for. Before every decision or action, you must ask yourself, "Will this bring me the inner harmony that I desire? Will it enable me to live my life with less conflict or stress? Will it make me a winner?" Achieving your goal requires a congruence between what you say, think, feel, want, and do. This congruence won't be perfect, but the amount of overlap will determine the degree to which you will eventually experience harmony within yourself. Simplistically, all you need to do is question whether each individual decision you make is consistent with your overall commitment. If it isn't, you must discontinue it, discard it, or alter the goal you're committed to.

4. The fourth step involves setting limits or boundaries beyond which you will not be manipulated by others or permit yourself to venture. It is an emotional insurance policy of sorts, which ensures you do not prostitute yourself, your values, or your convictions. This step is not an easy one. It requires that you censor yourself and your actions. Whenever you are in doubt, you must ask yourself two questions: "Twenty-four hours from now, will I be proud of this behavior?" and "Can I honestly tell others what I did?" If the answer to either question is no, you need to change your behavior because your purpose in life should be to eliminate or mitigate your feelings of fear, conflict, and guilt. This censoring process will help to make your decisions in life clear. The hard part will then be forcing yourself to do what you know to be right. In every instance, the conflict will consist of a struggle between your intellectual and your emotional selves. It is a struggle you will encounter throughout the remainder of your life. No one can really help you with this one. Only you can determine whether you will live life in accordance with the impulsive, childish directives of the five-, six-, or seven-year-old emotional child inside you or under the control of the intellectual adult residing in you, the one who knows right from wrong, good

from bad, moral from immoral and what will bring you angst or pleasure in the future.

5. The fifth and last step is simple. It consists of never forgetting that it may be the last straw that breaks the camel's back, but your problems are the result of a long stream of accumulated actions (or inactions) and pain associated with them. A warrior or a wimp isn't formed overnight. That being the case, the truth is apparent. Little things mean a lot, and the things you say or don't say now (or the ice cream you buy or don't buy today) will have serious consequences in your future.

CHAPTER TWENTY-ONE

DARE TO BE SELFISH

Few of us were told that we needed to be selfish in our interactions with others. I recall my mother instructing me as a child to share my cookie, candy, or pretzel with a friend. Her specific words were: "Break it in half, and give the biggest piece to your friend." That never made sense to me, but to this day, no one can break a cookie in half more evenly than I. What does that have to do with learning to be a winner? You'll understand after hearing about a very special therapy session.

Gus was there with Mickie, his possible future wife. She was attractive, tall, intelligent, and personable. But, then again, so were his three previous fiancées—a testimony to Gus's good taste. This time, however, Gus was more intent on developing a permanent relationship, getting married, and having a home and a family. That was apparent because, for the first time in all the years I had known him, he was able to say the word *marriage* without whispering or stuttering. During the session, Mickie noted how thrilled she was with a conversation that had taken place between them the night before. In the past, it could have developed into an argument that would have lasted for days. With pride, she said, "This time, I said what I really felt. I had the courage to tell him what I wanted. Next Wednesday, he's scheduled to leave on a ski trip to Colorado with four of his best friends and return Sunday night. That's perfectly all right. I understand that his friend Jay is getting married and this is the last time the four single guys can make a long weekend of it. There's only one problem. Thursday is the one-year anniversary of the day we first met. It's a very special time to me, and though I don't resent him going, I really wanted to be with him on Thursday to celebrate that occasion. Well, I had the courage to ask him if he would consider the possibility of not leaving for the ski trip until Friday morning so we could celebrate together on Thursday night."

I looked at Gus to gauge his response or reaction to her statement.

He said, "It was no problem. I mean, I thought maybe we could celebrate Tuesday and then I could leave on Wednesday night. I even suggested the possibility of us celebrating it the next weekend. But once I understood how absolutely important it was to her, it made me happy to think I could please her and be with her. It was difficult for a moment, though, because I felt that I was caught between my friend and my partner. If I did what Jay wanted, she'd be unhappy. If I did what she wanted, Jay would be unhappy. I had to decide which one I was going to please. Hands down, I love her, so the answer was obvious."

Before I continue to describe the therapy session, I'll ask you to stop for a moment and think what you would have done in the same situation. Whom would you have pleased? Should

Gus have agreed so readily? Did he owe something more to his friend who was getting married? Or was he negligent in not remembering that the following Thursday was the anniversary of meeting Mickie one year earlier? What was the right thing for him to do?

In therapy, I frequently find myself saying there is no right or wrong. Your feelings have to be taken into consideration. Stop trying to be perfect or to do "the right thing." Do what you feel is best for you. In this instance, however, there was a right thing to do, and that was for Gus to recognize, first and foremost, that his reaction to Mickie's request was wrong. His problem had little or nothing to do with whether he satisfied his soon-to-be wife or his soon-to-be-married friend. Gus saw himself as having to decide between the two of them. What he failed to see was there was a third party he had to deal with. He had to ask himself, not "What does Mickie or Jay want?" but "What do *I* want? What do I really want to do?"

When I said that to Gus, he looked dumbfounded. His mouth dropped open. He stared out almost blindly at the two of us, and you could literally see the wheels turning in his head. Then he said, "I know, in ways, I was supposed to understand this before, but I have never had it so vividly displayed to me. I can see it perfectly clear. I never ever think to ask that question. *What do I want?* I haven't really asked that question of myself throughout most of my life, at least not when I interact with people I love. Instead, I concentrate on doing whatever pleases someone else. I'm afraid if I really ask that question, I'll be selfish."

Gus told us that, years ago, his father had told him, "Before you do anything, you have to think about the other person and where they're coming from." His father's favorite saying was,

"To really understand another person's situation, you have to walk a mile in their moccasins."

"I always thought that was such a good thought," Gus said. "But I'm beginning to think that he forgot to tell me that, before you can walk in someone else's moccasins, you have to be able to walk upright in your own. As crazy as it sounds, I'm afraid of what other people will think. I don't want Mickie or Jay to think I don't care or that I'm not a good person" (the perfect wimp).

In many ways, Gus had discovered the key that would open up his understanding of what I mean when I say to every one of my patients, "I want you to learn to be selfish. To look out for yourself. To adopt a *rational self-interest*, which will influence how you act and behave and the kind of decisions you make." It is the biggest step most of us will ever take in our lives. It doesn't mean we will cease to consider the feelings of others, nor does it mean we will always make sure we get the biggest piece for ourselves. It just means we need to make ourselves a part of the equation when making choices and determining behaviors.

Far too many of us go through life negating ourselves. When we do this, our identity is nullified and our perceptions, accurate or not, of the expectations of others serves to influence who and what we are and do. This does not mean we always appear the same on the surface. Some of us, the wimps, are compliant and chameleon-like. Others, the warriors, are totally selfish.

If you're a wimp, your behavior stems from your conscious fear that you'll be rejected or abandoned because you're not good enough. If you're a warrior, your behavior is primarily a smoke screen. Your authoritative, unbending, rigid attitude is designed to compensate for your own similar feelings of weakness and desire for love.

Behavior genuinely stemming from a rational self-interest takes into consideration the thoughts and desires of others, but when your own thoughts and desires differ, you're free to express them and follow them. Thus, you're able to air your opinions with sensitivity and awareness of how they may affect someone else but not alter them to avoid upsetting others. You aren't responsible for how they react. You're only responsible for how you act.

In therapy, I told Gus, "If you originally decided that you wanted to go for the extended weekend with your friends because it had been planned months before, your response to Mickie might have been, 'I love you to death. I recognize how important this is, and I'm sorry to say that I never even thought about the one-year anniversary of our first meeting. It doesn't mean I don't care. Nor does it mean that your desires and feelings aren't important to me. However, I know one thing for certain. Although part of me wants to please you and stay, if I do, I'm going to feel guilty about not leaving early for this weekend trip with the guys. Long-term, however, I know I'll resent you because I'm weak and allow you to control me. Alternatively, I could go out to celebrate on Thursday night and the next day scramble like mad to pack, catch a flight, and get out to Colorado to spend two days with the guys. In the end, I will have cheated you, I will have cheated them, and I will have cheated me. I don't want to do that. I want to go with the guys this weekend and make next weekend very special for both of us. I'm sure there will be other times when we won't be able to make things work perfectly or will choose to celebrate events on a different day. But we will still be able to make the time we spend together very special and make each other aware of how much we love one another. I hope you understand."

Before Gus could respond, Mickie said, "If he had said that, it's all I would have had to hear. It really wasn't the day that was so important; it was probably my way of asking him to appease my fear that he didn't love me. I needed the reassurance of his love more than I needed him to demonstrate it by doing what I wanted."

Unfortunately, Gus behaved in accordance with the way he learned early in life to deal with situations in which he saw himself "trapped." He clammed up, kept his feelings inside, and agreed to stay with her. In the long run, this could only serve to escalate her fears and doubts concerning his love.

The story doesn't end there. After our session, they arrived home to spend an evening together. She made dinner; he went and got his mail. As he looked through the letters, he saw a card, obviously written by a woman and an invitation that said, "Mr. Gus Jones and Guest." Without *consciously* thinking it through, he placed it behind a picture frame on the shelf by his chair.

When I questioned his behavior, he said, "I didn't want her to get upset because some girl from the past had sent me a card. After all, I haven't been out with anyone else in a year. Also, why should I let her see an invitation to 'Mr. Jones and Guest'? I did once before, and she was hurt and angry at the sender for not inviting her as an individual."

But Gus wasn't quick enough. Mickie saw him hide the letter and questioned his motivation. An argument ensued. He apologized and explained he had totally forgotten the lesson he had learned earlier in the day. He went on to say that his behavior was designed to protect her, to keep her happy, to avoid upsetting her. He went so far as to say, "I should have just said, 'Hey, there's a card here from so-and-so. She's having a party, so put it down on our calendar.'"

His good intentions only reinforced his "wimp" behavior. They certainly didn't reassure Mickie. Instead, they proved to be only one more indication that he could not be trusted. His behavior only increased her doubts concerning his love. Before he realized it, she put her shoes on and stalked out of the house. He stood there, watching her go, almost glad she was leaving and, at the same time, confused with regard to how he might have acted differently.

Note that he totally forgot to ask, "What do I want?" Once again, he saw himself caught between the devil and the deep blue sea. He spent most of that night going over the situation in a number of different ways. He finally recognized, "I am exhausted from overplaying this game. I don't want to go through the rest of my life this way. From now on, I'm just going to ask 'What do I want?'" He never bothered to call her to apologize any further or to plead with her to forgive him. He called for another therapy appointment the next morning and, after relating the story, said, "You know, I really love this lady. I'm not mad at her. I'm not angry. For the first time in my life, I feel liberated. I know it sounds crazy, but I'm free to love her and she's free to do what she wants to do. She has to make her own decisions. I also recognize something else. From now on, I'm going to make myself a part of the equation. I have a right to do that. You know what else I have a right to? To be human.

To make mistakes and to still be loved. I feel worthy of it. And, you know, I recognize that I lied to her. It's no wonder she can't trust me. I was living a lie. I rarely considered me. I only gave people what I thought they wanted. Now they can know me; they can take me or leave me, and I can be who I am."

Gus had listened well and learned fast. But there was one problem. He had experienced what I've referred to as the "pendulum clock syndrome." It is a common occurrence, which no one is immune to. It is usually the first perceptible step in the process of growing. Invariably, when an individual commits to an act of change, there is an equally intense act of change in the opposite direction. Thus, for example, when an aggressive individual determines that he needs to alter his behavior, he generally becomes as passive as he initially was aggressive. Similarly, when an individual who has, throughout his life, given little consideration to self, realizes that a change of attitude is in order, he becomes full of himself, just as Gus did, by not at least calling her. It's going from wimp to warrior status in one step.

Usually, however, this is only a temporary reaction. The pendulum finds a happy medium, and so did Gus. He called to reassure her once again that he loved her. He was able to strike a balance between a healthy interest in self and an appropriate consideration for others.

It can be the same for every one of you. Once you recognize that you have a right to be in the equation and what you want counts, you are liberated. You are free to love. You don't have to control others because you are no longer fearful of being rejected or abandoned. Other people can have their reactions, and you don't have to resent them. Nor will you feel like a martyr. You will no longer have a need to hold on to any resentment, because you've stopped giving away the "biggest half of your cookie." It will make you free to love, without fear that you're controlled or manipulated. Once again, it isn't easy to do. It's a difficult step to take. Be forewarned that you will never achieve a state where you always believe that there is a world out there that you belong in, one in which you are of importance and where you feel worthy of being accepted and loved. But if you can put yourself in the equation 75 to 80 percent of the time, you will have carved out a large portion of life to satisfy your emotional needs and allow yourself to choose how you wish to act in the future. It will make you a winner, a person who behaves with a rational self-interest.

CHAPTER TWENTY-TWO

SET LIMITS

I n the world of love, there are few rules we can live by, yet there is one that proves itself true time and again: *For any relationship to work, you have got to be able to set limits.*

Sounds simple enough, doesn't it? Still, every day, I see people in my practice who put up with all manner of indignities, inconveniences, and injustices just so they won't have to set limits on how they're treated and risk rejection.

Marge is a classic example. For months, her boyfriend had been acting strangely. He was "busy" on Friday and Saturday nights. He spent increasingly more time with the boys from the office, and twice when she was at his apartment, he had "odd" phone calls, which he attributed to wrong numbers or old friends. Once, she smelled what she thought was perfume in his beard, but she couldn't be sure. She was afraid to accuse him but unable to live with her suspicions.

One evening after he picked her up for a date an hour late, she shouted, "I won't put up with other women in your life!

Do it again, and you'll be sorry!" The words came out without warning or conscious thought. She was even more surprised by her anger than he was. Unfortunately, it wasn't a case of courage but emotional impulsiveness.

"Don't threaten me. I'll do what I please," he replied.

"It isn't fair, and you'll regret it." But the fact is, he didn't seem to regret it and Marge, who thought, *For the first time, I've set a limit,* had only made a benign threat.

Marge is like most of us. So often, when we think we're setting limits, we're not. As one patient said, "I have no trouble setting limits. I set them over and over again. It's just that I can't stick to them." In her case, she was only making accusations, threats, and demands. They weren't limits, because *you can't set limits on another person. You can only set them on yourself.* A limit is not a threat, a demand, or an ultimatum. A limit is a solemn, faithful promise to yourself of what you will and will not live with.

> To differentiate between the two, you must realize that threats, demands, and ultimatums are desperate attempts to change others or to prove to yourself you are loved by them. They imply: "Do this and I will know you love me." In contrast, limits are statements indicating, "If I do this, I'll love myself."

Months later, Marge finally set a limit for herself. It was then that her empty threats and idle demands became courageous promises he had to deal with if he intended to sustain a relationship with her. She risked rejection, but she also found herself. In retrospect, she risked very little and gained a lot. If her partner couldn't live monogamously before marriage, he very likely wouldn't live any differently afterward. Still, it's frightening to set limits. There is always uncertainty about the response you'll receive, but at least there will be no doubt about where you stand.

Unfortunately, life doesn't present us with guarantees. You don't always win, even if you're right. Therefore, it always has to come down to, "Which way can I best live with myself?"

I'm sure you can see that the difficulty setting limits is directly related to self-confidence. People who stay in relationships with partners who show little concern for them have a poor sense of self-worth and feel unworthy of anything better. Any hope that time will change things is a fantasy, which, long term, results in an emotional dilemma. On one hand, they are grateful for whatever or whomever they settle for in life. On the other hand, they are dissatisfied, even disgusted, with how little they value themselves. By not setting limits or standing up for themselves, they lose nothing, give up nothing…and gain nothing. They settle for a safe life.

Consider the alternatives: to dream, take risks, stand up for yourself, and run toward the things you fear. Why? Because the gnawing inner rage that many of us harbor toward ourselves is gone as soon as you make a decision to set limits. The need to be bitter at either yourself for your lack of courage to do what you believe or toward your employer, friend, spouse, or lover because you see him or her controlling you also disappears. In its place, perhaps for the first time in your life, a comforting peace of mind emerges. Finally, you know there will be an end to a way of life you detested. At last, you can behave out of strength rather than weakness—*because you are finally free to do as you desire.* You can respect yourself. You can feel worthwhile.

You no longer need to run or hide. You will have a feeling of emotional liberation and freedom because you no longer perceive yourself as a victim. It is essential, however, that you take care to ensure your declaration of independence is not a benign threat, a bluff, or a compensating action that has you jumping from the frying pan into the fire. Your goal has to be to become a winner, not to convert a wimp into a warrior.

Stewart is a perfect example. After twenty years, he left his marriage for Tracy, whom he called "the love of my life." It took every ounce of courage he could muster up to permanently leave his wife and daughter. Although he had thought of divorcing for years, the impetus that Tracy provided had never been there before. It wasn't that his wife was a bad person. In fact, she was extremely bright and quite attractive. Moreover, they rarely fought, probably because he just went along with her wishes. The primary bone of contention between the two of them was her devotion to her career. She left early every morning, came home late in the evening, and frequently went in on weekends. In his eyes, her job was more important to her than her home, her child, or her husband.

That wasn't the case with Tracy. To the contrary, Stewart was her whole life. She demonstrated that consistently. It fed an emptiness in him that had been there since childhood. No one before had ever made him feel a priority. She catered to him, both emotionally and physically. It was everything he had craved throughout his life. As a result, her every wish became his command. No desire, no matter how small or large, went unnoticed or unfulfilled. It wasn't that the desire or need to please was something new to him. It was just that this was the first time he felt his giving behavior was rewarded.

To understand where Stewart was coming from, you need to know that, as a youth, he constantly strove to please, but nothing he did ever seemed to fully garner his mother's approval. She was as involved with and attached to his older brother as his wife was to her career. No wonder he left her to live with Tracy. She was everything he'd ever dreamed of. Therefore, he could ill afford to lose her. Consequently, when she complained his divorce was progressing too slowly, he told his attorney his first wife could have everything in order to speed up the process. When Tracy admired a gold necklace in a jewelry store, it became hers. He bought a new car for Tracy's son. He bought a Caribbean cruise for her entire family. There was no end to the lengths he was willing to go to please her and keep her love.

But there was one very serious problem. Stewart could no more financially afford to satisfy her dreams than he could emotionally risk denying them. Finally, he tapped the well too often and too deeply. He was financially drained, up to his neck in debt, and frightened to tell Tracy the truth about his circumstances. He resorted to writing several large bad checks and was arrested for fraud.

Throughout his ordeal, Stewart attributed his actions to his love for Tracy. I'm sure he believed that to be true, but it is difficult to view his behavior as a reflection of true love. It seems more indicative of emotional neediness, dependency, and poor judgment.

The extremes to which Stewart went may make his situation seem uncommon, but over the years, I have observed the same behavioral pattern on countless occasions. These "good guys and gals" aren't bad people, but their behavior frequently results in bad consequences. Unlike Stewart, they rarely wind up in jail, but they almost always have unhappy relationships, which they tolerate, or marriages that end in divorce. The primary reasons are that they feel themselves a martyr, behave contrary to their own desires, and then cling to subconscious resentment. They are people who assume excessive responsibility for, and react primarily to, the feelings of others. They are emotionally needy individuals who find it almost impossible to disappoint or hurt someone they care for and avoid conflict at any cost. As a result, they are unable to straightforwardly express or communicate their own opinions, needs, or desires in a healthy manner and fail to establish limits or boundaries for their children, spouse, friends, and employees. For the most part, others only learn about their anger or dissatisfaction after a catastrophic event, when the "good guys" or "good gals" finally reach their breaking point. All of which perfectly describes a wimp.

When warriors get into relationships with wimps, both of them act out of fear. Their outward behaviors may appear different, but both are attempting to avoid emotional pain and rejection. Wimps attempt to ensure they don't get hurt by purchasing love, warriors by denying they need love. It is noteworthy that, for these individuals, abandonment can consist of any form of rejection, be it disapproval, conflict, or even the slightest difference of opinion. For the most part, warriors and wimps are out of touch with their own dynamics. It is the consequence of concentrating, throughout their lives, on the behavior of others and then determining their sense of worth and lovability on the basis of how they treat them. Warriors and wimps don't know where they're coming from, where they want to go, or what they want. The way they behave is similar to how children who are afraid that they can't survive without someone loving them act. Their fears and feelings of inadequacy run so deep that they are willing either to prostitute themselves or abuse someone else. It's the opposite of the way love is demonstrated by a healthy adult whose affections are given freely of his or her own accord, without fear of rejection or abandonment.

Several good rules of thumb are:

1. To the degree you can't trust yourself to be honest with those you love, they can't trust your love for them.

2. The extent to which you feel driven to please others and to make them happy is the extent to which you eventually harbor hidden fears and resentments that you can't openly express.

3. Conversely, healthy adult love involves the wherewithal to give your love, to honestly express your opinions, to set limits, to deny requests, and to communicate your shortcomings, your fears, and your grievances.

4. It's only when you can be you, without being defensive, controlling, or hostile that you can genuinely love.

5. You need to learn to say *no* first in order to be able to genuinely say *yes* to a partner and to living and loving.

CHAPTER TWENTY-THREE

CHOOSE LIBERATION OVER REBELLION

C harlie came into my office with a sheepish grin on his face, and I knew he had been up to his usual shenanigans. Charlie is married, has two children, and commands considerable respect from those who know him professionally. However, people who deal with him personally see him quite differently. Their image is that of an adolescent who flaunts the rules and does things his own way, sometimes with blind disregard for others. This is not because he wishes to hurt them but because he is short-sighted and lives primarily for immediate pleasure, rather than long-term happiness. Sounds like a warrior to me.

Charlie looked at me mischievously as he sat sipping coffee and baiting me to ask about the newest crisis in his life. He is an individual who thrives on controversy and is the quintessential example of a person of chaos. He needs his world to be in turmoil. He busies himself putting out fires so that he has no time to breathe easy or to look in a mirror. His coping technique isn't necessarily atypical. Many of us, without realizing it, juggle our affairs the same way. We create smoke screens that keep us so preoccupied we live life blind to our own feelings and emotions and the impact our behavior has on others, but Charlie does it to a degree that shames most others.

Charlie finally said, "Well, are you going to ask?"

"Sure, why not? What's new?"

"She caught me," he said. "She found this number in my shirt pocket and called it, and when a girl answered, she hung up. She even drove by the girl's apartment to see what she looked like. I told her it was just the name of someone I met on an airplane who talked to me about the possibility of employment and I just neglected to take the name out of my shirt pocket."

"Quick thinking," I said. "Do you think she believed you?"

"Not entirely. You know she's always accusing me of something."

"Not without reason."

"But I think I managed to convince her that this is an innocent situation," he said.

Nevertheless, I asked Charlie, "Based on our conversations over the past several months, I wonder if I might ask you a rhetorical question? You needn't answer it immediately, just think about it. What are you trying to achieve? You're an extremely bright, capable individual. You have the world in the palm of your hand, and yet you need to live on the edge. You need to keep the pot boiling. In the process, you wind up hurting your wife, the women you get involved with, your children, and, although you may not realize it, yourself."

"I know my behavior is somewhat self-destructive," he said. "But I love the excitement. I can't stay interested in just one thing or one person. I get bored."

"But what's the motivation underlying all this? What do you think might have led you to this lifestyle, and what's the payoff?"

"Simple," he replied. "Freedom. I've got that figured out. After the first couple of months in therapy, I could see that I wasn't about to let Helen control me the way Mom controlled Dad. He was totally emasculated. I doubt if he ever did anything he really wanted. He had to check in with her, report where he was going, and got griped at all the time. I vowed back then I'd never let that happen to me. I loved that guy, but I've come to realize I didn't respect him. I thought so many times, *If only just once he'd pop her in the mouth, maybe she'd stop all that carping at him and the rest of us as well.* That's what it all boils down to: liberation."

"No," I said, "I don't think so. I'm sure from your side of the fence, it seems like that. To me, it seems more like rebellion. Forty-two years old and you're still rebelling. Still trying to break the umbilical cord."

Charlie is not alone. He has lots of company. Marie, for example, is her mother's chosen child. Marie's divorce is almost final, but she thanks God every day that she has her mother to lean on. "She is like a sister to me, and I can't think of anyone I'd rather be with." Her soon-to-be-ex-husband and two grown children will testify to that statement. The price Marie pays for the role of the chosen child is one of blind obedience and a sense of total responsibility for her mother's emotional and physical well-being. The degree of servitude she displays toward her mother is almost equivalent to the amount of resentment she harbors toward any expectations or demands made upon her by her husband or children. For her, the only rebellion from her mother she can afford is to act out in her marriage.

Then there is Mark, a fifty-nine-year-old patient whose relationships at work have never been successful. On almost every job, he starts with a flash. His attendance and performance exceed expectation. Typically, his salary and position are immediately elevated. Before long, however, he becomes disappointed with his superiors and dissatisfied with the company. His performance suffers, and eventually, he quits or is fired. It is the same pattern he demonstrated throughout childhood, in high school, and in college. It is a passive-aggressive form of self-destructive behavior, which he developed early in life. It was the only means he had of dealing with a demanding, critical mother figure, who constantly referred to him as "my little man," and a stern father whose love and acceptance he sought but never obtained. It is no surprise that years later he is still a "little" man. Despite his intellect and abilities, he is emotionally unable to escape or grow. Instead, he is a "flash in the pan" and eventually a disappointment to every surrogate parent he collects in life.

What Charlie, Marie, and Mark fail to realize is that there is a big difference between rebelling and liberation. You are "liberated" by standing up on your own two feet, speaking out honestly, dealing forthrightly with people, and letting them know where you're coming from and what your boundaries are without anger or hostility. It is tantamount to cutting the umbilical cord. In contrast, "rebellion" is equivalent to stretching the umbilical cord but leaving it intact. As a result, you stay a child emotionally. No matter your age, you always feel controlled.

To the extent you feel that control, you can ill afford to give in, capitulate, or say "yes" without the fear of losing your own false sense of freedom and independence. Consequently, you remain tethered to your emotional past. Every time you call your parents or visit their home, you revert to being a rebellious youth (a warrior) or a compliant kid (a wimp). You never feel free to love openly from your heart or to live your own life without a hidden agenda. I hope, whether you are male or female, young or old, that every one of you who is able to see yourself as figuratively or literally tied to your past will eventually recognize that no one is keeping you there. *You are not trapped; you only feel you are.*

As long as the umbilical cord remains intact, all of your endeavors to pull away or to find yourself will be for naught because the process you utilize to achieve independence will be rebellious in nature and will only serve to exacerbate the problem. In the end, you will still feel tied down and trapped. All rebellion does is put increased pressure on the situation and the individuals involved. It does not allow you to deal straightforwardly with any issues. It contributes to feelings of anxiety, frustration, and anger, which will, consciously or not, contaminate your interactions with others. Think how much better it would be to make a clean, honest break with your past—to cut the cord.

To that end, there is no substitute for running toward and through the things you fear and dealing with them directly, with love and honesty. This takes courage and requires that you be able to distinguish between honesty and hostility. The only similarity between the two is they both begin with the same letter, but all too often, they seem to go together. Far too many people are only able to be honest when they're angry. On those occasions, they are prone to say things like, "There are a few things I've been meaning to tell you for the last ten or twenty years."

My question is: Why did they wait so long?

You can only change this reaction when you see that you are the one who traps yourself. The solution to most of your problems is, more often than not, inside you. Dealing with these problems requires you to look at yourself apart from others or from your situation. In that context, as a lone entity, you may be able to discover what it is that you as an individual want and what is best for you. You can then expend the energy necessary to actualize it. This separation isn't necessarily a physical act, such as disowning parents, getting a divorce, or quitting a job. It involves coming to grips with who and what you are and what you really feel about yourself and asking yourself, "What will it take to make me feel good about myself on the inside, not for an hour or a week, but for the rest of my life?"

This is not the kind of freedom Charlie talked about, which depended on hurting the people around him, but the wherewithal to live "free" with yourself. It is no small task. It is a process that you must practice throughout the rest of your life, taking one small step, one day at a time. This process necessitates that you be honest with yourself and with others. It permits moments of weakness and always rewards corrective behavior. You may recall the delight you felt with yourself every time in the past when you set a limit, spoke up, or honestly expressed your thoughts. It made you feel warm inside and pleased with yourself from the tip of your toes to the top of your head. You didn't feel angry or resentful, just good to be free of your fears. The procedure enables you to divest yourself of long-standing pain and grievances and lightens the emotional burden that drags you down and curtails your emotional growth.

CHAPTER TWENTY-FOUR

TELL THEM WHO YOU ARE

I was listening while a husband and wife argued back and forth in a manner that was obviously very familiar to them. I am sure the same interaction had taken place on numerous occasions before that session. I am equally sure that the issues were never fully resolved. Both of them were trapped in their own point of view, so much so that each had difficulty hearing what the other was trying to say. It was sad because, in between their attempts to have their partner see the errors of his or her ways, there were countless oblique statements testifying to their love for one another, for their desire to establish a loving relationship, and even to their commitment to their marriage. As I listened, the sadness that struck me most of all was realizing this argument, or at least parts of it, could have taken place in any home, between any two spouses, with the same results.

The story was that Jim's father was ill in the hospital. By the time the argument took place, his condition had been upgraded somewhat, and, for all intents and purposes, the doctors had reassured the family he would very likely recover. There was still a lot of healing needed, but he was no longer critical. The tubes and hoses were still attached, but he was responsive and alert and the physical signs were all positive. Nevertheless, Jim was still emotionally distraught. Throughout his life, his relationship with his father had been full of conflict. He had always strived to get his father's understanding and acceptance, which was verbalized but never with enough authenticity to satisfy Jim's feelings of insecurity and doubts about himself. At that point in time, Jim desperately felt a need for his wife's support and understanding. However, his capacity to ask for help was severely limited because he lived his life continuously working never to appear weak or vulnerable. It was his primary defense against his fears of rejection. Rather than reveal himself as the dependent, helpless person he felt himself to be, he gave the impression of a haughty, controlling individual who felt entitled to whatever he demanded.

Tiffany, on the other hand, was the emotionally freer partner in the relationship. She was demonstrative; her feelings were far more accessible and included depth, warmth, and sensitivity. She was also the more hostile of the two and could, after a couple of drinks, become quite caustic verbally. However, without the effects of alcohol, she was a passive-aggressive individual. It was an art she had perfected early in childhood as a result of her dealings with a very loving but highly manipulative mother.

Jim was the first to speak.

"If my partner's parent was in the hospital, I'd be calling all the time. I'd be checking all the time. I'd be wondering what was going on. How could I help? What could I do to make things easier? But all I got from you was one call. That's all. It was like you were only checking in to see how he was doing or what his progress was. My friends called all the time. They were sensitive to how I felt and how worried I was. Not you. You obviously didn't care."

Note Jim's attempts to manipulate through guilt. It was the same as Tiffany's mother.

Tiffany's answer was, "But that's not my world. I'm different from you. You call your parents four times a day. I call my mother every other week, and sometimes that's too much. In fact, it got to the point where she used to call me and check how I was doing, knowing that I wasn't going to call her. Now even that's stopped, because she knows when I want to talk to her, I'll call her. But don't give Dr. Ed the notion that I don't care. When we were together, I asked how things were and you said your dad was doing fine that day."

"No, I didn't," he said. "I never said 'fine.' I said 'okay.'"

"Well, fine and okay are the same to me."

"Well, they're not to me. There is a big difference between fine and okay. He was still in the hospital, with tubes coming out of him. It's just that they told us he was going to live. But then what else did you do? You went off to Dallas to visit your friend."

"Well, after I heard he was fine…"

"Not fine! '*Okay*'!" he shouted.

"Well, either way, I decided since you were going to be at the hospital all weekend, I might as well go. Then, when you called me when I was in the car and forty miles out of town, you were angry. You were angry because I left; you were angry because I wasn't home. You seem to forget that I asked you if it was okay if I went."

"Well, at that time, it was okay. I didn't want you to stay out of pity. If I had to ask you to stay, you could just go."

"Well, I didn't know what to do. You were so angry I didn't want to be home. I did ask if you wanted me to turn back, and you didn't tell me anything about how you felt or what you wanted."

"I already told you, by then, I was so angry I didn't want you home."

'No, what you wanted was for me to go so you could be angry," she retorted.

"Well, I'll tell you now what I wanted. I wanted you to be considerate. I wanted you to be compassionate, to be close, to be there to support me."

"Then why didn't you tell me what you needed was for me to come home?"

"I already told you the answer to that. If you were already on your way, you might as well go. But then, not only did you go, but you didn't call me for two days. You didn't call me when you got there; you didn't call me till the next day."

"Of course not. I knew when I got there if I called, all you'd do is yell and tell me how selfish I was for going. Why would I call to talk to somebody who was just going to dump on me? I didn't need that. Remember? You told me, 'Don't come home.'"

"Well, I shouldn't have had to ask. You should have known after I called you to turn around and come home. And, anyway, if you really cared, you wouldn't have gone in the first place. Even if you'd come home after I called, it wouldn't have meant a thing. Because when you have to ask for something, it isn't worth having."

I kept listening, but I noted that Jim had it absolutely backward: *if something is worth having, it's definitely worth asking for.*

"So, what you're saying is I couldn't have won either way. If I'd come home, you would've been mad because I left and you would have punished me with your silence and if I didn't, you'd be mad because I didn't come home."

"Yeah, you could've won. If you'd never left or come home without my asking. If you did it on your own."

"Well, maybe that's the problem. Maybe I can't ever be what you want. I can't be perfect. And you know something? I'm not a mind reader. I don't know what you want all the time."

Tiffany was absolutely on target. She doesn't know what he wants, not only because he doesn't tell her, but because most of her energy goes into what she perceives as defending herself. "Well," Jim said, "maybe you should. I think about what people I love want. I think about what they need. And I try to do it for them even before they ask."

"Well, just because you do it, doesn't mean I can. We're different. Why can't you love me even though we're different? I come over to you, and I put my arms around you. I kiss you on the top of your head. Don't you think I want you to do the same thing to me? But you never do."

"That's not so. I show you a great deal of love."

"That's not true. If you really want to look at it, go back to January. We had sex New Year's Eve, and it was the greatest. By the fifteenth, we hadn't had sex again. That's when I started counting," Tiffany said. "I said to myself, 'I'll be darned if I'll initiate sex with him. I want to see how long it will take before he wants me the way I want him.' Finally, by February, I was so angry I told you about it. But I'll bet a year could have passed before you would have wanted anything. So you can say I don't do what you want? Well, you don't do what I want, either."

"Sex is different," Jim said. "It's not necessarily an emotional thing. An emotional thing is when you need somebody's support because your parent's in the hospital, and she doesn't even recognize it. And then when you don't initiate sex, is that your way of saying you love me, you care for me? The real issue is I spent the whole weekend alone and feeling terrible. I was worried about my father, and you and had no one to support me. How do you think I felt? And then having you not even call me."

Although they didn't reach a solution during that session, they did share their feelings in a relatively calm, civil manner. It was a new experience for both of them. That alone constituted a very significant first step, even though their progress wasn't apparent to them until the next appointment.

When they first entered my office, they were far more cordial and seemed anxious to talk about their issues. It was evident that they had heard more than each other's words during the first session. Perhaps they recognized they had both been saying the same thing. It was apparent these two people loved each other very much, even though neither was really capable of stating it directly or willing to ask the other for it. It was far easier to say, "You don't care. You lack courtesy and sensitivity," or "You should know what I need without me having to ask."

We all need to be able to request what we need or desire openly, but you can't do that unless you first know what you really need or want. That requires you to look inside yourself, not outward toward your partner, and as I said earlier, that's difficult to do. It is much safer to hold onto anger and to view your stress or discontent as being caused by your partner. Jim and Tiffany were just beginning to learn that living safely isn't emotionally healthy. They still had a long way to go, but they had taken a very positive first step. Tiffany spoke first this time.

"He rarely asks me to do anything, and when he does, half the time before I can get to it, he does it. And he can do it twice as good as me. Sometimes, I feel that he doesn't trust me to get anything done right. Instead, he just seems to want to give me a test that he's sure I can't pass and then inform me just how dumb I am. I don't know if he's plain mean or if he has to put me down in his own mind in order to keep me. It's sad, because I know we love each other, but I also know we're different people."

At times, Jim and Tiffany appeared to want different things, but they were really after the same thing: love and concern. They simply hadn't learned to ask for it in a way that the other person could understand.

"Since we've been married," Tiffany said, "I've asked for him to be sensitive to my physical needs, but he doesn't seem to hear me."

"Well," Jim interjected, "I've asked for you to show affection and concern the way I do since we've been married and you don't hear me either."

"Did you ever think about the way you ask me? You do it in a convoluted manner, just like with the hospital, Jim. You say, 'Do you want to go to the hospital with me?' and my question is, 'Do you want me to go? If you want me to, ask me and I'll go.' If you want to know the truth, I don't want to go to the hospital. I had enough of hospitals when my own father died. I don't like looking at someone with tubes up their nose and near death. It really affects me. At the same time, I love you and I would have gone with you."

"You're making a mountain out of a molehill."

"No, I'm just trying to say to you that maybe there's a better way of asking. And I'll even accept the fact that maybe there's a better way that I need to respond."

I sat there marveling at the new form of communication. It was radically different from their "normal" exchanges. There was a major change, but for that change to materialize, Jim and Tiffany first had to recognize what was normal for one of them wasn't necessarily normal for the other, that you can't get mad at an individual just for being different or disagreeing. Instead, you have to recognize and respect that difference. When you do, you usually discover the differences are only skin deep. Underneath, people in intimate relationships are usually very similar. Getting mad at the differences doesn't help. You don't get mad at your cat because it can't bark. You may try, unsuccessfully, to teach it to bark. It may even try to learn, but you cannot get mad at it because it can't.

What Jim and Tiffany did in the past was punish each other by turning away, causing both of them to become so defensive that they were totally incapable of looking at their own behavior. Both were bound and determined to perceive themselves as the injured party. They would become so morose and bitter that they felt forced to estrange themselves from each other. They blamed one another and saw themselves as helpless and victimized, even though neither one was helpless or a victim, except in his or her own eyes.

To have an emotionally healthy marriage, human beings have to:

1. Take responsibility for themselves
2. Take risks
3. Ask for what they want and know what it is they're asking for, because too many times, people's words don't tell the whole story

Every human being lives in his or her own unique world, with his or her own needs, his or her own pain, his or her own disappointment, and his or her own way of expressing them. Although some individuals may appear to have a greater sensitivity, awareness, or capacity to read another person, that doesn't necessarily mean that they're the "good" person or that they care more. It may even mean they're more sensitive, more alert to disappointment or the emotions of others because they are so desperately in need of love. Their sensitivity is not a badge of honor but an indication of their own feelings of neediness and isolation.

Overcoming whatever shortcomings or handicaps you brought into your relationship requires that you take full responsibility for your own actions and reactions. Of course, it helps when both people have the same goals and recognize that a marriage, a relationship, or a union isn't built by one person alone. You do respond to and react to one another, but too often, your responses and actions are based on faulty perceptions and erroneous interpretations. That being the case, when you interact, you have to tread slowly. You have to be prepared to back down, to count to ten before you overreact, and to put some space between yourself and whatever problems you may be facing. At that point, you can look at the problem again from a distance and determine if it's yours or your partner's. If it's yours, you need to alter your behavior. If it's your partner's, you cannot get angry at it. You have to respect it and try to be there to help him or her recognize and deal with it. How do you go about that? By creating open, honest communications that will allow you to see yourself and recognize that you can only change yourself, not anyone else.

I'd like to share with you the inscription on the tombstone of an Anglican bishop in Westminster Abbey in London:

> *When I was young and free and my imagination had no limits, I dreamed of changing the world. As I grew older and wiser, I discovered the world would not change. So I shortened my sights somewhat and decided to change only my country. But it, too, seemed immovable. As I grew into my twilight years, in one last desperate attempt, I settled for changing only my family, those closest to me. But, alas, they would have none of it. And now I realize, as I lie on my deathbed, if I had only changed myself first, then, by example, I might have changed my family. From their inspiration and encouragement I would then have been able to better my country. And who knows? I may have even changed the world.*

In relationships, we shouldn't have to be mind readers. It would be wonderful if each of us had a crystal ball that told us exactly where our lover, spouse, or partner was coming from, but we don't. The best we can hope for is that we learn to be a mind reader insofar as our own mind is concerned. That would at least enable us to accurately convey to others where we're coming from, where we want to go, and what we need. Even more, it would cure half the problems in our marriages or relations: our own.

CHAPTER TWENTY-FIVE

HAVE THE COURAGE TO FACE YOUR OWN TRUTHS

There is a problem most men and women share, whether they're wimps or warriors: a desperate need for attention and love. That need is as important to their emotional survival as food, air, and water are to their physical well-being. You might ask, if we share this need, why is it a problem? Because, early in life, too few people learn that they have a right to ask for it. In fact, they probably learn the opposite. If you admit to needing love, you're either weak or dependent and therefore not deserving of it. This is especially true for men, who, early in life, develop their own unique behavior patterns to elicit the emotional care they want without revealing their need for it.

Cliff was one of those people. He thought his world was near-perfect. He was financially successful. His marriage, although not without some problems, was, in his own words, "All that anyone could ask for." Two of his children had already graduated from great universities, and one of them had married. A third had dropped out of college but immediately went to work in the family business and seemed to be doing quite well.

Then, suddenly, the bottom fell out. His single daughter announced she was pregnant and informed the family that the father was a young man Cliff had forbidden her to see. Next, his major client, who was also a personal friend, declared bankruptcy while still owing Cliff a very large sum of money. To make matters even worse, a former employee sued the company. She claimed she had been fired because of her age and that she had been emotionally abused in an attempt to get her to quit. When it seemed nothing more could possibly go wrong, Cliff's wife issued an ultimatum: "Either you go with me for marital counseling, or I want you to move out."

Cliff thought, *This isn't the way I've lived my life. I've always dotted my i's and crossed my t's. I've worked hard to make sure there were no loose ends. Now, everything seems to be falling apart.*

What Cliff didn't realize was that his rigid behaviors were the very reason everything was in shambles. For one thing, his efforts to control his family and those around him were excessive. For another, he was blind to his need to control. He couldn't comprehend that a benign dictator is still a dictator and, no matter how generous you may be, there is no acceptable price you can pay to control someone. When you deprive others of their freedom, they wind up resenting you. It doesn't matter whether your intentions are good, your choices are ones they would have made on their own, or that you saved them from making a serious, life-altering mistake. They might appreciate you for all of those reasons, but their resentment will still persist.

The best example of these behaviors is one I learned in my first psychology class. The professor spoke about the correlation between having the opportunity to make choices and developing a healthy sense of self-esteem. He said one way to test the impact of a perceived loss of this freedom was to follow people—your roommate, partner, or spouse—around and anticipate their actions. Then, before they have a chance to act upon them, instruct them to do what you anticipated. I hurried home and found my wife busily engaged in cooking dinner. As she reached for the salt, I quickly stated, "Add some more salt." When she reached for a wooden spoon, I suggested that the pot might need stirring, lest the contents stick. Needless to say, it didn't take long for me to get a rise out of her.

All of which brings me back to Cliff. Despite his rough exterior, Cliff cared. People really mattered to him. He wanted and needed them to love and care for him. Because of that, he went out of his way for them. He was sensitive to their feelings and acted in ways he believed would bring them pleasure or garner their love. For that reason, Cliff found it extremely difficult to accept the notion he was in any way a controlling individual. In that respect, he was no different from overprotective parents who won't allow their children to participate in any activity or sport in which they might be injured. Their need to protect is not for the child. It stems from the parents' need to control their environment, those they love, and the world, all to lessen their own anxiety. It is no different than parents who "help" their children do their homework so they won't fail. They are blind to the fact that their so-called "loving behavior" only serves, long term, to emotionally cripple the child. No child ever felt better about him- or herself for getting an "A" on a paper his or her parents wrote.

The behavior may be well-intended, but the primary motivation does not stem from a concern for others. In Cliff's case, it was, instead, a reflection of his desperate need for love and his doubt that he was worthy of it. Because of his fear of rejection, he manipulated those around him but took few risks, because he controlled them. In the long run, by limiting his emotional exposure to pain, he was limiting his gains and never got the opportunity to know if he would have been loved solely on the basis of who he was, instead of what he did.

Cliff's mother had died early in his childhood, and two unloving stepmothers and a father who was gone three months at a time contributed to his underlying belief that he must have been unworthy of affection. If not, he wondered, wouldn't someone have been there to support, nurture, and love him? In order to survive emotionally, Cliff, the child, unconsciously resolved never to depend on, or put his trust in, anyone again. The mantra he learned to live by was, "If you need something done, do it yourself." Accordingly, when it seemed his world was falling apart, he did what he had always done. He pushed others away, sought his own counsel, and attempted to control as many other facets of his life as possible. Controlling others made him feel less helpless, but it also served to heighten every feeling of resentment in his wife, children, and friends. The result was to mitigate their willingness to support him in his time of need.

If you think Cliff's behavior seems contrary to what he needed, you're right. Nevertheless, every one of us has probably demonstrated the very same behavior at least once in our lives. Think about it. On how many occasions has someone asked you what was wrong, only to hear you answer, "Nothing,

I'm fine"? How often have you yelled at your spouse, "Leave me alone! I don't need your help!" when, in fact, what you desperately wanted was his or her support? How many times have you threatened to leave, to file for divorce, or said, "I wish I was dead," in order to elicit his or her loving reassurance of his or her care for you?

What you wanted to hear your partner say was, "Sorry, you're stuck with me, because I love you and all your crazy behavior isn't going to push me away. I'm going to be here for you night and day for the rest of my life." A spouse who is mature and emotionally healthy enough to be capable of that response in the heat of the moment is rare.

Cliff's behavior was no different from hungry teenagers who run from the dinner table, slam the door of their bedroom, and anxiously wait for their parents to beg them to come back and eat. It doesn't always work. Often, those around you fail to hear what you are really asking for. Instead, they take your words literally and react out of their own insecurities, causing both of you to be disappointed and estranged from one another.

There is a simple solution to this common problem, but it's extremely difficult to act on. How many times have you heard that? It requires that you ask, out loud, for what you honestly need in order for you to feel better. As I've repeatedly suggested, that's hard to do, particularly if you're a warrior or a wimp. It's also difficult to do because, at that moment, you are either unaware of what you truly want or need or are so caught up in your own pain and disappointment that you are reluctant to drop your defenses and risk even greater pain. You are too embarrassed to reveal how weak you feel. In the end, pouting, running away, or anger seem to be more viable solutions.

But none of those behaviors ever results in a satisfactory solution. The next time you find yourself in a situation where you desperately want love, support, or nurturing, recognize that your old behavioral patterns don't work. Getting mad and sleeping on the sofa, all the while hoping your partner will seek you out and reassure you of his or her love, doesn't work.

What you need to do is take a deep breath and say, "I'm sorry for what I said and how I acted. I'm hurting inside, rightly or wrongly, and what I desperately need to know is that you love and care for me and that you'll be here for me whether I fail or succeed. I desperately need you to assure me I'm worth loving in spite of my weakness, my fears, and my inappropriate behaviors."

Again, it is a simple solution, but before you can actualize it, you need to gain the courage to face your own truths, to be emotionally vulnerable, and to risk the rejection you fear. You need to know that there is no shame in wanting someone to love you despite your shortcomings; more often than not, they are only shortcomings in your eyes. Nor do you need to feel shame over having feelings of weakness or inadequacy. All of us are imperfect, and all of us harbor the same wish to be loved for who we are. That desire isn't unique to one person. It holds true at any age, for any person, of any gender.

CHAPTER TWENTY-SIX

TELL THE WORLD YOU MATTER

Betsy was severely hurt as a child, but you would never know it. Everything about her, from the time she was a little girl until she came to see me, forty-four years later, spoke to her happiness. To know her for a short time was to learn that she rarely complained, gathered large groups of individuals around her as friends, and tended to see the glass half full, rather than half empty. Her relationships were void of conflict because she acquiesced and agreed with others, rather than face controversy or hostility. Those were the ways she'd coped all her life, by displaying all the characteristics of a wimp.

You can understand why it came as a total surprise to her husband, Bill, the day she looked at him and said, in the gentlest of tones, "I want a divorce. I no longer want to be married to you, and I want it as soon as possible." At first, Bill thought something must be physically wrong with Betsy.

Then he began to suspect there might be another man in her life. She wouldn't just end a nineteen-year marriage for no apparent reason.

He did recall that, on several occasions, she had stated they should see a marriage counselor, but those requests were few and far between. For the most part, at least from his viewpoint, everything was fine. They rarely argued. Their lives were financially comfortable. They would never be filthy rich, but early in their marriage, they had started saving for their retirement and their daughter's college education. They had a beautiful home and were pretty much free of debt. It didn't make sense. He was completely dumbfounded.

Initially, he attempted to resort to his usual way of dealing with controversy—talk loud, carry a big stick, threaten, and intimidate, like any other warrior. Over the years, he had only had to assume this role sparingly, because it took little for Betsy to acquiesce. But it didn't work this time. As a last resort, he begged that they go to therapy. She agreed but stated adamantly that nothing would change her mind. She was unwilling to bend anymore. She feared that if she did, it would be the end of her. She would lose whatever sense of strength and resolve she had finally managed to build up.

During their first session, Bill listed all the reasons why they shouldn't divorce. Several times, he almost succumbed to anger but quickly tempered it, because it was pretty evident that it would only reinforce her decision to leave. Throughout the session, Betsy responded with monosyllabic answers. I suggested it would be appropriate for me to see each of them alone at a later date, and Betsy readily agreed.

During her first individual session, Betsy opened up and poured out her feelings. She was upset with Bill, and she provided a litany of reasons. He never listened to her; he always did things his way; he drank too much; he periodically gambled to excess; he wasn't assertive enough; he didn't work as hard as she would like him to; he was more involved with his mother and their daughter than he was with her; and so on.

Betsy went on to say that she and Bill had never been on a vacation together. Every occasion included his mother, to whom he catered. She described his mother as a fragile little lady who was in absolute control of her son. Early in their marriage, for instance, she and Bill had agreed they would alternate Christmas, Thanksgiving, and Easter visits between their families. But after a dozen years, a pattern became evident. Those years when they were ready to leave town to visit her family, Bill's mother would become deathly ill, incapacitated, and in severe need of help. On several occasions, she required hospitalization, and in every instance, their plans had to be changed.

Mother, she continued, had a key to their home, which she used freely, with little regard for their privacy or any activities they had planned. Bill's comment was that she was old and that after she died, Betsy's time would come. Betsy went along with this arrangement for nineteen years before she finally erupted. "I want a divorce," she told me. "I'm tired of playing third fiddle, and I want to know that I matter."

I attempted to make it evident to Betsy that, prior to getting a divorce, it seemed at least minimally fair that she tell Bill why she was so upset. I also felt it was important she learn to verbalize her emotions, particularly those of anger. I further indicated that, even if she was adamant that nothing would change, she still had to learn to alter her own behavior. Otherwise, every future marriage would only result in the same scenario—she would continually acquiesce, would resent her partner, and would eventually decide the marriage had to end. She assured me she could not imagine being married again, to any man. I told her that history had a tendency to repeat itself and that she would likely wind up acquiescing to and then resenting her daughter, just as she had her husband, her mother-in-law, and her parents. Several days later, Betsy succinctly described to Bill the source of her discontent.

To my surprise and, I believe, to Betsy's, Bill heard her. He understood her reasoning and acknowledged its credibility. He also heard me when I said the manner in which he interacted with his mother was no different from the way Betsy related to him. I suggested there might be more hostility present inside him than he realized, and it was manifested by control and lack of sensitivity to even the minimal complaints Betsy had made throughout the nineteen years they were married. It was his way of assuring himself that no other person would ever control him the way his mother did.

Bill and Betsy kept coming to sessions. Bill responded positively and more rapidly than is normally the case for therapy patients. There was one problem, however. The more he changed, the more loving comments he made, the more he demonstrated his love and concern for his wife, the greater the estrangement between them.

Finally, Bill told Betsy, "I've tried to listen. I really know that what you and Dr. Ed told me is true, and I want this relationship. But I don't believe there's any hope. The more I try, the further away you get and the less responsive you are. If this is the best it will ever be, we need to split everything up and go our separate ways."

A silence followed, and then Betsy began to cry hysterically. When her sobs subsided, she said, "It's not that I don't care. I know you've tried. So much so that now I think you're totally neglecting your mother and I feel responsible. I think she's hurt, and even though I'm hurt by all her behavior, I know she's old and I hate to see her suffer." It was good bullshit but not real. Then she continued, "You're exactly the way I always hoped you would be. You're the kind, caring person that I loved when we first dated. But after we married, you changed. All your love went to our daughter and your mother. All I got was leftovers. I felt that I didn't matter. I love who you are now, but I don't trust it. I'm afraid that if I give in and let my feelings out, you'll change. Everything will go back to the way it was before, and I won't have the courage to stand up for me again. So, I'll wind up staying, unhappy and resentful, for the rest of my life. What assurance do I have that this isn't just a way to manipulate me and to get me back in line again?"

Bill was flabbergasted. It seemed evident that he wanted her; he was telling her and doing things to prove it, and she just distanced herself even more. It angered him, but I intervened and tried to show him the distrust wasn't of him and that it wasn't an unusual reaction. The battle most people experience in life is not with others; it's with themselves—it's learning how to have the courage of their convictions; to behave in accordance with what they know is best; to stand up for themselves, their values, and their principles; and to feel they matter and have a right to be loved and nurtured. He needed to see that Betsy was closer to him now than ever before in their marriage. The paradox most people fail to understand is that the more you feel, the more you fear. Thus, the more loving he became, the further she moved away because she was becoming more frightened. What she needed now was not ultimatums but reassurance.

It's the same for all of us. If we want to live life in a manner that gives us a sense of well-being about ourselves, we have to learn to speak up. Not to *stand up to others*, but to *stand up for ourselves*, by expressing our views and setting boundaries. What it boils down to is not a case of giving ultimatums to our partner or spouse, friends, or business associates but of proving to ourselves that we have the integrity and the strength to stand up for what we believe.

Again, success in standing up, having integrity, and setting limits comes about after a lifetime of successful battles with ourselves. It requires that we consistently act in a way that exemplifies the feelings and emotions within us. Only after years of struggle will some of us ever discover we have won the war over ourselves.

CHAPTER TWENTY-SEVEN

ACCEPT THE UNACCEPTABLE

Pam sat expressionless in a chair in my office. She had a vague, faraway look in her eyes. She appeared pensive, forlorn, and somehow resigned to her emotional state. Her recent wedding and wonderful honeymoon hadn't changed a thing. She thought it would; it did, for a brief period of time, but now that everything had settled down and returned to normal, she realized she still felt the same way she had since childhood. It was hard for her to put it into words, but, essentially, she said it felt as though her emotions were covered by a heavy, damp blanket. Sometimes, it was difficult for her to breathe; she often felt as if she didn't have enough energy to make even casual conversation, and laughter seemed all but impossible.

Pam said, "It's always been this way. I remember, in high school, thinking that if only Jimmy Peterson would date me, I'd be okay. Later, I was certain being accepted at LSU, pledging the right sorority, finding a good job, and finally being married to a wonderful guy would do it. But nothing really helped. I'm still insecure. I feel inadequate, too frightened to take risks, lacking in confidence, and ugly. Not only on the outside, but inside. I don't know what to do anymore. I've prayed, I've cursed, and I've blamed others—my husband, parents, teachers, bosses, the fickle finger of fate, even God. I just want to feel good inside, but I don't know what it takes to get there."

Pam isn't alone. There are probably countless others who have had the same thoughts and made the same requests of a higher power. It usually goes something like this.

God, just this one time, if you make it possible for me to:

> *get a car from my parents on my birthday*
> *get a date*
> *find a new job*
> *get a higher salary*
> *have my book published*
> *win the lottery…*
> *then I'll never, ever ask you for another thing the rest of my life.*

How many of us have had at least one of those thoughts and promised God we'd never ask him for another thing? And how many of us went back on that promise, because even after we got the car, the date, the job, and the raise, we still didn't feel okay? I don't know about you, but I have my hand raised. I suspect many of you do, as well. If that's the case, then the question you desperately need to ask is, "What does it take to be okay?"

In Pam's case, you might initially think all she needs to do is feel more secure, more adequate, and less frightened to take risks; increase her level of confidence; and no longer feel ugly inside. That's a pretty tall order. I don't really believe she, or for that matter anyone, can do all that. Let's face it. She did not come by those feelings by accident. Either she has a chemical imbalance or her emotional experiences in childhood contributed to her developing a very negative self-image.

It is no different for the rest of us. Our childhoods may have varied, but in their own way, they each affected how we perceive ourselves, what we see ourselves being entitled to, and the degree to which we can accept love from others. These basic feelings, once imprinted on our hard drives, never change, at least not on the inside. They become as much a part of who and what we are as the color of our eyes and our height. Therapy can't change them, and while positive thinking might obscure them, our hearts will always know. Throughout our lives, during moments of anxiety, these ugly feelings will come to the surface and haunt us once again.

That being the case, we have no alternative but to learn to face them, accept them, and live with them. Even more important, we need to learn not to judge them, or ourselves, because they are part of us.

All of which reminds me of a group therapy session I conducted some years ago. One person leaned forward in his chair so that he could look directly at his wife, who was squirming rather uncomfortably in her chair as a result of a question I had posed to her. It was obvious that she couldn't or didn't want to deal with it. When he finally caught her eye, he said, with a sneer on his face, "What are you, a coward? Look at the way you're fidgeting. For crying out loud, just answer the man!"

It was totally out of character for this man. It was more representative of the man he had been when he initially walked into therapy almost a year earlier. I looked at him and asked, "Do you realize how hostile and demeaning your question sounded? The tone of your voice, your body language, and the expression on your face showed more hostility than I've seen in you for a long time. What's triggering it?"

Suddenly, he found himself on the hot seat. After hemming and hawing, he apologized for his behavior and said, "I looked over at her, and I couldn't stand the sight of her groveling, being frightened like that." He paused and then added, "Probably because that's the way I've been all my life, at least on the inside. I never let anyone know. That's what my anger was for, to cover up my cowardice."

I then turned to her and said, "Do you want to answer his question? Are you a coward? There may be some truth to his question, because most of us marry who we are."

Even as I spoke, I thought to myself, *Am I a coward?* His question had obviously had an impact on me, as well. My immediate answer was "no." After all, I was the man who spent a good deal of his life traveling off the beaten path, skydiving, and trying all types of potentially dangerous activities.

But I was also the man who had recently waited only two days before calling an agent regarding a manuscript I had submitted. I had mulled every consequence associated with calling. I wondered if it would influence her opinion one way or another or if it would portray me as the anxious, insecure individual I am when it comes to my ability to write.

Were there other instances where my actions were mitigated by my fears and insecurities? Of course. So the answer was, "Yes, I'm a coward." I can add that to the multiple other characteristics I find distasteful in myself. But there's little I can do to change them. They were hardwired into me by the time I was five or six. Now, I have no other alternative but to accept them, face them, and behave in spite of them, rather than because of them.

It's the same for everyone. We are who we are, and we must learn to accept and love ourselves, just as Pam needed to be able to say, "This is me. I am a person who lacks confidence, feels inadequate, and sees myself as ugly. I don't like being that person, but it's who I am. It's the only person I have, so I guess I'm stuck with her. Consequently, I'm no longer going to waste my emotional energy trying to change or hide her. I'm going to show her to the world and say, 'You have to love me with all my shortcomings. If you can't accept me, tell me, because I'm going to look for someone else who can.'"

I couldn't help but believe that the real Pam would have no difficulty being loved by most everyone, particularly when she was able to be up front and honest. By virtue of those qualities, I also believed her confidence would increase and her sense of inadequacy and ugliness would decrease. There would still be occasions when the old Pam rose to the surface and, for a short time, pulled her down. But these instances were not likely to devastate her because she would have learned to face and accept herself and to share her feelings with others in her world. Most important, she would have come to love herself.

You can do the same, as long as you remember that:

The acceptance by you
of the inadequacies, insecurities, fears, and ugliness you
perceive in you
is the only way to truly actualize you.

CHAPTER TWENTY-EIGHT

LEARN TO FLOAT

E veryone has problems. There's no way to live in this world without problems or without feeling inadequate and experiencing anxiety. If we have children, we are bound to experience concern, fear, and frustration because of them. If we live long enough, we're bound to deal with some form of illness or physical impairment and/or experience the loss of someone dear to us. Fortunately, the key to living well isn't whether we have problems; it's how we cope with them.

Therefore, we have to ask ourselves: "What is my primary means of coping? Which defense mechanisms do I use when faced with problems? Do I yell? Become angry or critical? Do I push others away or ask for their help? Do I overeat, drink to excess, or submerge myself in work, children, or new projects? Do I become engrossed in my problems, take to bed, feel sick, become excessively concerned with my appearance or completely let myself go, or begin buying things I don't need?"

Once we recognize what we do, it is equally important that we determine the degree to which we do it. Defense mechanisms are always the result of excess: far too much or far too little. For example, a person has a minor car accident or is late for an appointment. Does he or she become hysterical and fall to pieces, paralyzed with anxiety? Or does the person barely respond and act as though nothing happened? Both reactions are pathological because they're extremes.

So, we need to ask ourselves: "What do I do to excess?" It will help us not only to recognize our defense mechanisms but to decide if we want to use them in a positive manner, as warning flags that indicate we're in trouble. To illustrate, early in life, my coping techniques were fat, funny, and fast. Thus, whenever I realize I'm gaining too much weight, telling too many jokes, or becoming hyperactive, I ask myself, "What's bothering me?" My first two answers may find me lying to myself—the truth hurts, after all. To be emotionally healthy, however, I know I have to keep searching; it's only when I genuinely know what's broken that I can fix it.

I've come to realize that there is no way to live life without occasionally experiencing conflicting needs or desires, which can cause us to feel overwhelmed or frightened to death; in our attempt to save ourselves, we often allow our defense mechanisms to become detrimental. For example, an occasional drink isn't necessarily an issue. But when used excessively, this defense becomes problematic. It may aid us in dealing with our immediate fears, but long-term, the price we pay is to become alcoholic and depressed. It can be the same with drugs, food, sleep, work, kids, anger, and acquiescence. Anything to excess is pathological.

There is another alternative: *instead of fighting or fleeing, learn to float.* Let me provide an example of the value of floating. It's a lesson I learned that's so simple, I wondered why I had never thought of it before. (Probably it's because we're blind to those things that are most obvious.)

Some time ago, I decided to upgrade my television and stereo system. Although the equipment was there and working, I thought it could be drastically improved. I called someone who assured me it was an easy task and that he could keep it within budget. It turned out, of course, that I needed additional equipment. Eventually, shipping boxes and new instruction manuals began to fill my living room.

When the installation was finally done, the system didn't work at all. When I turned the TV on, the satellite sent the message "weak signal." If I had a picture, I had no sound. If I had sound, I had no picture. The stereo system was a total mess.

The failure of the project began to threaten my entire sense of well-being. My initial budget had tripled, I had half the performance I had started with, and I felt frustrated and dumb.

Finally, the man I had hired told me, "The problem is the satellite. You need to call them." It took all the restraint I had not to put my hands around his neck. Instead, I called the satellite provider. Have you ever tried to talk to an automated telephone system? The line was busy for hours. I finally gave up, set my alarm clock for 2:00 a.m., and called then. Surprisingly, a live person answered! I described the problem and told him about the "weak signal" messages the TV was displaying. He proceeded to go through a set of instructions, which I followed to no avail. Three hours later, he said to me, "We can't fix it."

My reaction was immediate and hysterical. "Don't panic," he said. "Go in the back and pull all the plugs." Five minutes later, he said, "Plug everything in again." Then we went through the same procedure we had tried earlier. Lo and behold, the TV worked! I wanted to jump up and down like a child and shout, "It works! The TV works!"

Then I thought about having the same problem with my computer. Because I'm a certified computer idiot, I have frequently managed to freeze up my computer. That used to paralyze me, but I've become adept at shutting the computer off—despite all the warnings that I could lose information or delete the changes I wasn't even aware I had made—and rebooting it, which somehow allows it to reconfigure. Why? I'll never know.

Several days after the incident with my satellite provider, the thought came to me that, occasionally, I can be a certified idiot about *myself*. However, I had discovered the remedy: pull the plug temporarily, and float. That's exactly what we can do when we find ourselves overwhelmed by conflict, anxiety, and emotionally paralyzing frustration. All we need to do is pull the mental plugs so we can reboot later. What that means is we need to put some distance between ourselves and our problems. We could go exercise, sleep, take a bath, attend a yoga class, meditate, take a coffee break, or call a friend. We can do whatever works for us, as long as we recognize that we can't fix everything all at once. We may want to, and society may support that notion, but it doesn't work in the long run.

I still don't understand why things get better after you pull the plug, but I know that they do. It works for computers and satellite dishes, and it can work for each of us, because human beings are far more capable of restoring themselves, of solving their problems and reconfiguring, than any man-made piece of equipment.

It's really pretty simple. Instead of fighting or fleeing, float. When things become overwhelming and we feel paralyzed, anxious, or confused, we have to separate ourselves from the problem, shut ourselves down for a while, and know that, after a break, we'll be far better able to resolve what's troubling us.

EVERYTHING IN A NUTSHELL

B y now, we know the rules for becoming a winner: stand up, speak out, accept ourselves, develop a rational self-interest, and take control of ourselves. The goal is to create a healthy, whole person, inside and out. It's the only way to come to peace with who we are or to get to experience the meaningful relationships we have always dreamed of. Essentially, when it comes to long-term relationships, we always get who we are. That explains why warriors invariably look for wimps they can control, and wimps search for warriors to control them. Their emotional dynamics are exactly the same, even if their means of coping are precisely opposite. I should add that, similarly, every winner winds up with a winner.

Section 4 reinforces the notion that positive solutions are possible. It describes why so many long-term relationships and marriages don't work and what can be done to make ours the one we always longed for but may have doubted was possible. In our quest for that relationship, it helps to keep in mind that anything to excess is pathological. Thus, if we are too angry, too nice, too giving, too much of a martyr, too controlling, too inflexible, too frightened, or too unwilling to look at ourselves, our relationship or marriage is bound to be too much as well.

It can also be helpful to reserve the option to seek help beyond what this book can offer. Doing so isn't a sign of weakness. In fact, thinking we don't need help can be like saying, "I'm going to do brain surgery on myself." It's rarely successful. We sometimes need an objective, outside source to help us see our forest through our trees, a person who can show us where we are and what we have to do to grow and to become the winner we all are inside.

CHAPTER TWENTY-NINE

WHY RELATIONSHIPS DON'T WORK

There are, of course, myriad reasons why relationships don't work. The complaints I've heard from so many of my patients are numerous, and by the time they come to my office, a third party is generally involved. Nevertheless, the people and their problems generally fall into one of five categories:

1. People who blame their partners for all their problems but can't leave because they still care for—not love—their spouses and don't want to hurt them or their children.

2. People who assume all the blame for the problems but maintain they can't or won't change because that's the way they are. All the while, they adhere to their conviction that there is nothing left to work on. For them, the marriage is all but dead and buried, but they still stay.

3. Couples who go through the *motions* but never the *emotions*—Their relationships and marriages are strong in form but extremely weak in substance. They survive, they look good, but they only tolerate each other. They experience little joy but much disappointment and have frequent daydreams regarding what might have been.

4. Individuals and couples who go through their lives blindly—Unless their spouse slaps them across the head with a two-by-four in the form of an affair or filing for divorce, they see no problem. Everything is satisfactory for them. Despite countless conflicts, requests for attention, poor treatment, abuse, excessive drinking, drug use, and financial problems, the blind spouse keeps his or her eyes closed because he or she doesn't want to deal with his or her own realities or any form of confrontation.

5. People who can't recognize the patterns in their own emotional lives—Many people divorce their spouse not once but many times. Sometimes, two or three divorces later, they realize that the common denominator in each marriage was them. All their criticisms of their former spouses may, in fact, have been accurate, but they are the one who repeatedly and consistently chose those flawed spouses.

In each of the five categories, one common thread exists: spouses aren't always on the same page at the same time. Instead, they're engaged in a war, be it confrontational or silent, which neither realizes has been going on for generations before them. No matter who plays the wimp or warrior, the gender war prevents them both from hearing or seeing what each needs, is saying, or is hurt by. Their defenses have been honed over centuries, and the general consensus seems to be that men and women are so different that never the twain shall meet. But that isn't entirely accurate. To be sure, men and women differ neurologically, psychologically, and emotionally, but, in most ways, their dynamics are very much alike. They both want to be loved and feel safe from emotional harm. They're equally fearful of being rejected or abandoned. Most people, no matter which paradigm they use to cope with their situations, are blind to the role they play in determining the course their relationships follow.

I believe that inside, underneath the public image, all of us know if our marriages are in trouble and into which of these five categories we fall. There are, however, some necessary precautions that we may take. Before we act impulsively, we must open our eyes and really look at where we're coming from, what we're doing, and where we want to go. We must recognize that every day that goes by, we get a day older and if we don't do anything about the feelings inside us, they won't get better tomorrow. Thus, it's essential that we say to ourselves, "I have a choice. I can close my eyes, make believe everything is fine, argue all the time, and become consumed with other activities, such as work, sports, the Internet, addictive behaviors, household duties, and kids' and grandchildren's events, or pursue my own interests and take separate vacations.

None of those are constructive, but it may well be a bargain we're willing to make because it's the most we expect from life. We are the only ones who can make that decision for ourselves. However, if we see ourselves constantly complaining, unhappy, physically sick too much of the time, filled with despair, tearful, or excessively angry, we need to open our eyes and ask ourselves, "Is this where I want to be two, three, or four years from now?" Then we must exercise our right to choose between leaving, tolerating, or repairing ourselves and our situation. It is a positive alternative to blaming someone else, feeling trapped, and hiding from our own truths. To do so will require us to be, insofar as possible, introspectively honest with ourselves. That's difficult. Whether we a warrior or a wimp, a part of us will want to protect ourselves from the pain we will experience in the process.

To help us in this endeavor, we might need to put on blinders to avoid any distractions that could easily come about, such as what our partner does, the way our partner acts, and why our partner is to blame for our actions. It doesn't matter if his or her behavior is truly noxious; to cope with problems that exist inside us, we need to look at the role we play, how we got there, why we got there, and whether we want to continue being there.

Once again, you need to know that you do have other alternatives. You can choose to run from the relationship and get into another equally bad relationship; you can leave and resolve never to get involved again with anyone; you can play the victim; or you can face the situation you're in by taking full responsibility for your own behavior.

The first step is to decide what it is you truly want and go for it. In effect, you need to outline and affirm your goals, your intentions, and your desires. If need be, write them down. Keep them in front of you constantly. Ask yourself, with every action, interaction, and reaction, "Will this get me what I claim I want?" If the answer is "no," curtail the behavior. But if the behavior persists, believe it, because, more often than not, your behavior tells you what you really want, not your words. If you discover that you're lying to yourself, you need to change what you say you want or alter what you're doing. If these steps fail to get you the results you want, you can then decide what your next step will be.

What you have to realize is that most human beings live lies and have hidden agendas that direct or govern their actions without them being consciously aware of their own motives. For example, I cannot begin to count the number of single patients I have seen over the years who have come to me in tears, angry about the hand that life has dealt them. Each of them in his or her own way, at that point in time, seemed to have given up. They were all sure that nothing existed for them out in the world and that their chances for emotional happiness, a good relationship, or a satisfying and meaningful marriage were slim to none. The reasons? "I make bad choices. Every time I get involved with someone, no matter what he appears to be in the beginning, he turns out to be a loser, a jerk, abusive, takes advantage of me, or never lives up to my expectations."

There may be a lot of losers out there, but repeatedly making the same poor choices can only be blamed on the losers for so long. You have to ask, "Is it their fault, or is it mine?"

Still others have come in and said, "The only good spouses are married, dead, or gay."

Well, that just isn't so. There are good ones out there. One of the questions you have to ask yourself is, "How many of them am I looking for anyway?" You only want one, and that one is potentially available.

There is another significant group of individuals I have seen. Those who have divorced or broken up but remain, for all intents and purposes, "married." They may even marry someone, but emotionally, they remain in their old relationship.

Thus, years later, they are still doing battle with their ex, bemoaning their bad marriage and divorce, and blaming their former partner for their own anxieties and stress. They haven't moved on or created a new life. More important, they're clinging to old slights.

They're frightened to go out and risk getting hurt again, rightfully so in most instances, because they don't know how to love without being disappointed. They hide behind various excuses. They claim they want somebody, but they're so picky that nobody ever lives up to their expectations. They tell you how lonely they are and how they suffer, but they don't genuinely make themselves available. The end result is that they lament their loneliness, but do very little to change it. They don't open any doors. They don't invite people in, and they don't go out. Again, they see that they may go through the *motions* but not the *emotions* necessary to establish a new, healthy relationship. It's almost as though they're waiting for a miracle—for Mr. or Mrs. Right to knock on their door and say, "Hello, I've been looking for you all my life."

There are also those who are angry, so angry that when you see them, they are abrasive and abrupt. They seem to be actively in the process of pushing others away from them, of alienating and estranging themselves, and then they wonder why no one approaches them or is interested in them.

Last, there are those who are out of shape, obese, even unkempt, and yet do little to enhance all the good qualities they have. When someone suggests that if they lost weight or put themselves in a different package, they'd market better, they react negatively. Their attitude is defensive. "If someone can't love me for who I am, then I don't want them. I'm not going to play games. I'm going to tell it how it is. Someone has to love me fat, and if they don't, why should I try to be someone I'm not to get them?"

My usual response is, "For the same reasons that you get a college education. If you want a job that pays more, you generally have to have an advanced degree." If you meet someone who wants a job that requires a college degree but refuses to get it, what would you say to him or her? I think back years ago to a patient of mine who only wanted to be a policeman on the Houston police force. At that time, there was a minimum height requirement of five feet six inches. He was five four and a half, and there was no way he could stretch an inch and a half. No matter what he did or what his father, a politician, did, or how much influence his father's friends wielded, he was too short. When I suggested that, possibly, he unconsciously didn't want that job, he just wanted to complain and gripe about how unfair life was; he quit therapy.

Four years later, he came back again, to "give me another chance." When I asked what he was doing, his answer was he was still trying to get on the Houston police department. He thought they were about to change the height requirement! You know, during those four years, he could have become a constable. He might have gotten into a smaller police department in a Houston suburb. He could have considered becoming a private detective or a process server, anything that was available. But he didn't. He stayed unemployed and unhappy.

If you discover that you are living a lie, staying with the status quo, or claiming you want a relationship or a marriage yet failing, it's time for you to dig deeper into yourself. You have to learn to do something new or different and determine what you can change in yourself, not in your partner or the world at large. Invariably, when you try to change the world, you achieve nothing. Remember, you can't change the world or your community, family, or kids. But if you change yourself, it may influence one person. That one person might influence another person, and he or she might influence several others. Eventually, your life could prove meaningful and influential, but only if you initiate a change in your behavior.

If you are involved in an affair with a married person, for example, and maintain that you want to get married, you aren't telling the truth.

If your life is so totally consumed by your children or your work that you're unable to devote sufficient time and effort to your spouse and you expect him or her to take second place, you really don't want a healthy relationship. The activities you use to avoid it may be socially acceptable, even politically correct, but they don't get you what you claim you want. The only result is, your children wind up losing another parent and live with you in a broken home.

It is exactly the same for the many single people I have seen whose homes are filled with cat litter boxes. They are lonely, but their lives are totally preoccupied with the care of Kitty 1, Kitty 2, and Kitty 3. They are hiding behind their pets.

It's not that these behaviors, per se, are necessarily bad or wrong; it's just that they don't help you get what you claim you want.

In contrast, the rewards you can obtain from a positive, loving relationship are endless and unbelievably comforting, physically and emotionally. Statistically, if nothing else, we know the health of men (and now women) who are married long term is far better than that of single people, and married couples rate themselves as happier.

CHAPTER THIRTY

EASY SOLUTIONS ARE ATTAINABLE

I opened the door to the waiting room to hear Cindy saying, "Pick up your litter, and put it in the trash."

For just a moment, Bob's body flinched. He snarled, "I know what to do with it," and placed the items in the waste basket beside the couch. Then he hurriedly walked down the hallway, ten feet ahead of me and his wife, and entered the open door to my office. By the time I arrived, he was slouched down in one of the swivel chairs. It looked like the wheels in his head were churning.

Cindy took the seat opposite him and launched into a monologue. "I want you to know I'm still furious over what you said this morning. After our talk last night, I assumed you finally accepted that I'm not a morning person. I agreed to try to change, but I can't just wake up and start talking; it takes me a while. Yet, what did you say first thing this morning? 'Are you competent to talk now?' What in the world did you mean by am I competent? Do you think I'm stupid or retarded? I think I clearly explained I'm not a morning person."

Bob acted as though he had been totally blindsided. "For crying out loud, why didn't you say something this morning? I never know what's going on inside you, except that, eventually, you'll wind up taking potshots at me. And by the way, don't think you're the victim. What about me? When do you start showing me some concern? Every time something comes up about my mother, what do I hear from you? 'I feel so sorry for her. She's trying to have a relationship with you, and you don't allow her to get close. I think she's sorry for the way she treated you and she's trying to make up for it.' I never hear you say, 'I know how badly she treated you. I understand why you're reluctant to believe or trust her. Being grounded all year because your grades weren't up to her expectations was too severe. Being locked in a closet if you acted out was abusive. You have a right to be angry and distrustful of her.' Not to mention you talking to me as though I'm a child in the waiting room. I'm beginning to think you're no different than her."

Cindy's eyes opened wide, and she said, "But that isn't what I meant. I was just trying to tell you that she cares."

"Well, I wasn't trying to say you were retarded, either. That wasn't what I meant. I love you. But I want to be sure you love me."

"I do," she whispered, "but sometimes I'm afraid you'll wind up treating me the way you treat your mother."

So, there you have it. Two people angry with one another both behave on the basis of their own feelings of inadequacy and overreact to one another. I felt it was fortunate that the incident occurred while they were in my office; otherwise, their misunderstanding could have escalated into a full-blown war. Indeed, it was close enough. Instead, they not only resolved the conflict but also learned from it.

But these interactions are not unique to Bob and Cindy. They take place every day in countless homes around the world. They are rarely dealt with or resolved and tend to run their course until some other event obscures the original conflict. But the feelings associated with this type of interaction never fully go away. They're stored in the unconscious, along with myriad other resentments that are left to ferment.

On the positive side, Cindy and Bob's interaction shows these conflicts can be easily dealt with, but only if both of the individuals are willing and able to look inside for the solution to their problems, instead of blaming their partner. When you are able to be introspective, you usually discover that you react out of two motivating forces. The first is how you view yourself. An example that readily comes to my mind is how I felt in graduate school. I was frightened and insecure, possibly even a little paranoid. As a result, if I saw two professors talking as I walked down the corridor, my first thought was, *They're probably talking about me.* My second thought was, *They don't think I'll make it.* Those assumptions had nothing to do with them. It was my fear talking, and the greater my fear, the louder it sounded. Truth be known, they probably never noticed me and couldn't have cared less.

The second motivating force is how you perceive your partner's actions or words. This is directly related to the amount of trust you have that your partner or spouse really loves you. Ironically, this also connects back to fears and self-image. The way you view yourself is generally the major factor determining the extent to which you truly believe you're worthy of love and can accept the love of your partner.

When you feel positive about yourself, there are few things your partner can say to cause you to overreact or to become hysterical or defensive. Conversely, when you perceive yourself as insufficient and inadequate, everything your partner says will be viewed as critical and demeaning.

Cindy, for example, struggled through her education and saw herself as lacking in intellect. Because of her severe ADHD-related symptoms, she overreacted to Bob's decision to use the word *competent*. Needless to say, it was a poor choice of words on Bob's part, because it hit her in a very sensitive area.

Recall, however, that Bob was angry as well. Throughout his entire life, he felt treated like a little child by his mother. He never saw her as supportive, loving, or encouraging. It's no surprise that he would view his wife in a similar fashion, and if her words in the waiting room were an example, his perception was at least partially accurate.

Many people with a poor self-image question the motives of their partner and are distrustful of their love. Doubt, disbelief, and suspicion permeate their intimate relationships. They often use "testing behavior," the purpose of which is to determine if their partner really cares. At the same time, they create situations to prove they don't. The end result: everyone is hurt and feels rejected and unloved. The payoff is being able to say, "I knew it all along; you really don't care."

Obviously, behavior of this type is self-destructive. It usually results from an excessive need for love and reassurance, which warriors and wimps are reluctant to reveal, sometimes even to themselves. They perpetuate it because it provides an excuse for playing it safe emotionally. It justifies a lack of vulnerability, which would make them feel even weaker and, in their mind, even less deserving of the love they desire. It is a curious paradox that results in both partners being prevented from becoming winners.

Let me add that, in the midst of conflict, solutions are rarely visible, yet they're surprisingly attainable if you avoid directing your attention to the other person and learn to be painfully honest with yourself. How do you go about doing that? First, you must introspectively ask yourself, "What is it I really want? Will my present behavior get me what I want?" If not, stop it. At that point, you will be ready to take a second step, one that requires a great deal of courage but is generally well rewarded. Instead of playing games to see if your partner loves you, instead of trying to prove he or she doesn't or finding fault with him or her, you need to be vulnerable.

In this case, vulnerability means that you open up and, if you're Cindy, say, "Bob, what I need to know is that I matter. When you use the word *incompetent*, I feel that you have absolutely no regard for me, that I'm not worthwhile, that I don't matter, and it hurts, because I already feel that way. I desperately need reassurance that you don't really feel that way about me."

Those are difficult words to verbalize, just as it would be difficult for Bob to say, "I snarled at you when you told me to throw out my trash, because I felt that you were treating me like a little kid, that you were finding fault with me, and that I wasn't living up to your expectations. As crazy as it sounds, the next thing I expected was to be locked away. That's scary and frightening to me. What I need is someone who respects me, sees me as an adult, cares for me, and lets me know it. Because I love you, I especially want to feel my love returned by you."

The solution is simple: look inward, be real, be honest, and be vulnerable. But, in the heat of battle, simple solutions often prove invisible to the eye of confirmed warriors and wimps. Remember that warriors and wimps are notorious for their reluctance to openly reveal who they are and what they think or feel. The next time you find yourself overreacting or attacking, be sure your behavior isn't a result of the way you feel inside or the way you see yourself. Then muster up every bit of courage you have and take the steps necessary to achieve an "easy solution." How? By remembering that *you are not trapped.*

CHAPTER THIRTY-ONE

MAKE YOUR LOSSES YOUR GAINS

In the course of a lifetime, all of us will inevitably experience loss of one type or another. It will manifest itself in various shapes and forms, from the death of a loved one, the termination of a job, the end of a romance, a divorce, or major changes in residence to the loss of possessions, youth, physical prowess, or even health. It is not a case of whether or not these losses will occur. They will. That is a certainty. The real question is how best to cope with them.

Remember, *"When life closes a door, it also opens a window."* Over the years, I have observed people countless times, because of their fear or reluctance to be hurt again, become so overwhelmed by the closing of a door they are unable to see the open window. In fact, if and when it is open, they slam it shut rather than look out to see what else the world might have in store for them. Their reactions are not accidental. There are reasons for their behavior. Early in life, everyone develops coping mechanisms to deal with loss, failure, and depression. Years later, the learned patterns of behavior still persist. They become reinforced, habituated patterns, which automatically come into play at the first hint of possible emotional pain.

Too often, however, reactions learned in childhood are not beneficial to adults, nor are they effective means of resolving adult situations. Nevertheless, people continue to repeat them because they are unaware that there are better ways of coping with their problems.

The mind is a remarkably malleable organ though, and we can learn new methods of reacting to any type of adversity. All that is required is a little guidance, which can be derived from examples of the way others have dealt with adversity and some basic rules. The stories of Richard and Jean, two of my patients, may prove helpful in this regard.

Richard was employed by the same energy company for approximately fourteen years. Eight years ago, he came to therapy because of health problems that had no physical basis. Despite repeated physical examinations, numerous consultations with specialists, a series of tests, including MRIs and EKGs, and three changes in primary-care physicians, no one could explain his malaise, occasional dizziness, and stomach pain. After several sessions, during which he listed all of his medical problems, he reluctantly agreed to discuss his personal history.

He described growing up in an emotionally sterile home where verbal communication and demonstrations of affection were totally absent. His mother was a beaten-down human being who seemed resigned to her lot in life. She had long since given up any attempt to fight back or stand up for herself. In contrast, his father was a self-contained, stern authoritarian who was critical of everybody and everything. He was caustic—a quintessential warrior. Everyone in the family tiptoed around him, attempting to avoid his ire.

Early on, Richard, the youngest of three children, learned the consequences of stepping out of line by watching his older siblings. As a result, the coping skills he learned consisted primarily of walking a straight line, playing the "good child"—the fearful, compliant youngster who would keep his feelings and his dissatisfaction entirely to himself. He became a spectator in life, rarely a participant. He hid his thoughts in fantasy and blamed others for his not having the opportunity to gain the recognition he desperately desired.

He loathed his job, resented his superiors, and hated getting up every morning, but he was too frightened to quit. In therapy, he slowly became aware of the dissatisfaction within him. As he did, his medical complaints subsided and even disappeared. His anxieties about his work and life, however, increased. It is not an unusual occurrence. Typically, the better you get, the more you feel, the more you know, and the more you hurt. Richard's overt stress was only a symptom of his long-term problems, though.

Awareness of his dissatisfaction with his lifelong pattern of behavior led him to face those behaviors, but Richard was too frightened to consider the possibility that he could change himself or his situation. Instead, he continued to perceive himself as trapped. He chose to go on antidepressants, which had to be changed every three or four months when they no longer held his depression in check. At the same time, he discontinued his therapy appointments because he saw them as only contributing to his increasing anxiety.

That was six years ago. Only recently did he return to therapy. The precipitating reason was that he and two hundred of his fellow employees were laid off. He was consumed with anger and unable to sleep. His tolerance for frustrating situations was at an all-time low. As he put it, "I saw myself acting just like my father, and I couldn't let that happen."

Over the next few months of sessions, Richard began a complete about-face. Figuratively speaking, he slowly discovered the open window, and perhaps for the first time in his life, he began to breathe the fresh air it offered. He felt free, liberated from a pattern of life he abhorred, and saw the world as a challenge that offered future promise. He was no longer trapped by his fears or reluctant to assert himself because of his lack of confidence. He seemed to experience an inner sense of strength that he never knew he had. Even more, he was excited about getting up each morning to face a new day and new opportunities. He even took the first steps toward starting his own company. Surprisingly, he experienced a level of support, interest, and encouragement from others that he had never received from his parents. There were, of course, numerous tense and fearful moments, but overall, life was good and filled with hope. There was a bright light at the end of what had been a very long tunnel.

When I first met Jean, she was on her second marriage, her third career, and her thousandth diet. Both her husbands were attorneys. The first was extremely successful, but he was a workaholic. The second was the opposite. He was a straight shooter but self-defeating and satisfied with a minimal level of success.

Despite the differences in outward appearance, both husbands had many characteristics in common, two of which are of primary importance. First, both felt inadequate and insecure. One compensated by immersing himself in his work; the other avoided the risk of failure by not betting on himself at all. The second characteristic was that neither was truly capable of maintaining a meaningful relationship with anyone. They were too egocentrically concerned with their own plight. Consequently, neither marriage provided Jean the love she craved. She felt as unloved as an adult as she had as a child.

Her father was a man who also felt emotionally inadequate. He and her mother ran a small dry-goods store, which was open seven days a week, from dawn to dusk. Mother constantly complained that her sisters had married better than she had and that their husbands were far more successful than hers. The love of her life and the object of almost all the affections was Jean's brother, who was nine years older. Jean was jealous of him all her life and frequently described him as "the love of Mother's life" and "the golden child."

Jean was quite bright in her own right. She had had three consecutive successful careers: first as a teacher, then as a social worker, and finally as an attorney, but none of them filled the emotional hole she carried inside. She yearned for her mother's love and recognition. Despite the fact that she became her mother's caretaker, legal advisor, and the child to call in case of an emergency, she never achieved the divine status of her brother.

In her marriage, life was no different. She had almost all the responsibility for their finances, meals, home, and social life. She overlooked her first husband's lack of emotional involvement, his disdain for the closeness she desired, and the affairs she suspected him of having. She held little respect for her second spouse. Although she was dissatisfied, she could not bring herself to admit her real feelings. Just like Richard, who was consumed with his physical problems, she focused on her weight.

No matter what diet she went on or how many times she resolved to get thin, it was to no avail. In reality, she could ill afford to lose her hiding place. It wasn't palatable, but seventy or eighty extra pounds of weight served as an effective screen to hide behind. It obscured her disappointment with her husbands and her inability to admit that she had erred in both cases. She also realized that she was still hurting from the first divorce. To make matters worse, she was scared of leaving her second marriage because she doubted that anyone else would love her. So she stayed, feeling trapped and resentful and manifesting her feelings through increased weight.

Then, her second husband asked for a divorce, told her he had found an apartment, and moved out. Sometime later, she discovered that he had been having affairs, too. She was filled with rage. She wanted revenge. She wished him ill health and declared her intent to financially bring him to his knees. Her anger consumed her. As she said, "I feel like I'm yesterday's garbage left out for the trash man. I'm terrified of the future and feel terribly alone. I don't know what to do next."

Over time, Jean had several additional epiphanies. She came to see that she was free of someone she had been unhappy with for a prolonged period of time. New friends suddenly surfaced to support her, more than she had ever imagined she had. She discovered wishing him ill did her little good and she no longer needed anger to hide behind. She could finally admit and accept that she had made a poor choice.

She also knew she would never again settle, even if she had to live her life alone. She was through buying love from anyone and even fantasized that, just possibly, someone out there might love her for who and what she was. Even more, she suddenly turned around and saw that she had lost a tremendous amount of weight. She said, "It's a hell of a diet. I wouldn't recommend it to anyone, but the end result is wonderful. I haven't had much of an appetite. Most of the time, I'm too excited about the future to eat. It's like I'm living in a new world."

She had essentially followed the same emotional path as Richard. Both had lived a lie for a large portion of their lives. They had governed their actions primarily out of fear and attempted to deal with their stresses by utilizing old coping techniques they learned in childhood. When faced with emotional pain, their initial reactions were anger directed outward, instead of inward. However, when they came to own their responsibilities for the past, their anger dissipated. They were no longer concerned about the company or the ex-husband's behavior. They understood that "the best revenge is living well." These are the lessons everyone has to learn.

The path to happiness isn't always straight. After disappointment, death, divorce, or financial upset, the future is scary and uncertain. You will definitely feel insecure and come to realize that there are no guarantees in life. Depending on the nature of the loss, you will, to some degree, blame yourself and feel rejected, dispensable, unworthy, guilty, and inadequate. These are all normal emotions, which you have a right to feel or experience, but you cannot allow them to direct your behavior. You have to get a new life. That requires you to take small baby steps.

You must learn it is okay to ask for help. It's not a sign of weakness, and even if it were, after a loss, you are entitled to feel weak and to solicit help.

When you find yourself in a situation like Richard's or Jean's, start by making a list you can post on your refrigerator of whom to call when you feel lonely, whom to get in touch with when you need to be busy or laugh or see a movie, and whom to lament with. Different people will fit each of these categories. Then, force yourself to use that list to network and to fight any inclination to cut yourself off from the world and people.

Once you've built your network, learn to take pleasure in your own company. Be able to read a book, watch a rental movie, or cook a meal for yourself. There will, of course, be times when you miss your former job or partner, but recall that they are the same job or partner you resented and found fault with but didn't have the courage to leave on your own. If your loss is a person you valued, think about whether or not he or she would have wanted you to live alone, consumed by depression and cheating yourself out of a future.

Finally, write a letter to yourself that will remind you of the mistakes you made in your former job or relationship. It can help you to alter your behaviors and influence the type of choices you make in the future. Effective use of these insights will help you set firm boundaries for yourself in all your interactions at work and at home. You can then give thanks to your former partner or employer for what you learned from him or her, by virtue of what his or her behavior taught you about yourself.

CHAPTER THIRTY-TWO

GROW UP BEFORE YOU GROW OLD

Leslie is one of the best examples I can provide of someone who finally decided to control her emotions instead of letting them control her. Her decision not only allowed her to grow up before she grew old, but it also provided the impetus for her husband to grow.

John was a real man. He ruled his family with a firm hand and a healthy dose of fear. He saw himself as a wise patriarch, mature beyond his years, who had to assume responsibility for his family. He would have taken pride in being described as a warrior. His wife, Leslie, was a classic "Stepford Wife," passive, obedient, superficially cordial, and a wimp.

As you might expect, John ran the show. He really wasn't a bad human being, but his behavior was. It's true that he never cheated on Leslie, was an exceptional provider, and made a concerted effort to be involved and concerned with every activity and event in the life of his family. At the same time, he was the cause of most of their problems, because he had to control everything, critique everyone, and emphasize every failing. Leslie couldn't exactly put it into words, but she knew she felt suffocated by his presence, a prisoner of his overbearing behavior, and increasingly repulsed by his company.

Their eldest son, John Jr., rebelled, at great personal expense. He had trouble in school, experimented with drugs, and generally estranged himself from the family, particularly his father. Years later, he straightened up and went to college. After graduating, though, he refused all job offers in his hometown and eventually settled down in a city fifteen hundred miles away. His contacts with home are still few and far between and can be described as obligatory, at best.

Their daughter, Stephanie, followed in her mother's footsteps. She became the obedient child, the good kid, the church-attending, religiously grounded youngster who did nothing wrong—on the surface. Underneath, she experienced constant turmoil. She punished herself for even thinking negative thoughts. She was trapped by her own guilt. As a result, her intellectual and social development were severely stifled. Even more, she physically abused herself by tearing at her skin and pulling out chunks of her hair. She became an emotional prisoner in a "body" dominated by her father and was ruled by her conscience, two jailers who cut her little slack and severely chastised her for both her actions and thoughts.

Despite John's deep concern and genuine fears for all their well-being, he reacted to their problems in the only way he knew: he found fault, severely criticized them for their behavior, and rejected them emotionally. In his mind, his sole purpose was to provoke them to improve themselves by virtue of his direction. The result was that their problems became more intense and more destructive, all of which bewildered John. He just couldn't understand why they were unable to see that everything he did was for their own good. He was a concerned warrior but was blind to the fact that he was also a dictator.

When I first met Stephanie in therapy, she was phlegmatic, docile, filled with feelings of futility, and uncommunicative. She was accompanied by her father, who seemed irate over her behavior, and her mother, who was as frightened as a deer in headlights. It was as though she could see what was coming but was unable to move or to escape the inevitable. When I told the parents that their daughter was, in my opinion, severely depressed and in need of medication and possibly hospitalization, at least for a brief period of time, John, as I expected, reacted angrily.

"How much is *this* going to cost me?" he asked.

Leslie, in sharp contrast, blamed herself and seemed totally deflated. Nevertheless, she indicated that she would follow through on my recommendation that Stephanie be seen by a psychiatrist. At the same time, she said, "I also want to see you in therapy for myself."

For Leslie, Stephanie's illness was the straw that broke the camel's back. After several therapy sessions, she said, "I can't live with myself anymore. I'm sick of not knowing what I feel until days later. I hate myself for being too frightened to speak out, even when I know what I think. I feel like a child, and I despise myself for standing by and watching my children go down the drain. John is really a good man on the inside. I think he means well, but he hurts everybody he loves, including me. He's treated me as though I were only another child in the family. But it's not all his fault. I haven't protected my offspring from him. I can't live that way anymore." She was ready to grow up before she grew old.

I was absolutely amazed at her insight, her ability to verbalize, and her level of intelligence. She had never demonstrated a hint of these things in the presence of her husband. But, here she was, right on target.

I cannot begin to tell you how many people I see in therapy who, despite their accomplishments, are still children, at least insofar as their interpersonal relationships are concerned. Like John, they act primarily out of their emotions. They lack insight into the motivations underlying their behaviors and feelings and frequently look to blame others for their actions and shortcomings. Most of all, they live life by attempting to find their identity in others, in their profession, or in their activities. You can't miss them. They are super-active in the PTA, Little League, or their political parties. They control every aspect of their children's lives. They are often seen as pillars of their community, can be charitable, appear to be your friend, and claim to care, but you never really get to know them emotionally, because they don't know themselves.

Oddly enough, they tend to be quite successful. However, what they are successful at is their position, not their person. What they are valued for is their hard work and dedication, not their sensitivity or emotionality. They are people whose image defines them on the outside, even as it hides who they are inside. Their relationships suffer because of their inability to share themselves genuinely.

It doesn't seem to matter to them, because they're primarily "emotional children"; they feel threatened and desperately need to control, lest they appear weak. They cannot afford to let anyone criticize those activities because, once again, what they do is who they are. They are inflexible and have no doubts regarding their own convictions. Thus, they can't permit anyone to behave in a manner different from what they believe to be proper.

Think, for example, about the parents who use their children as their primary identity. They need their children to excel and to perform at school because their performance determines their own self-worth. Or consider the parents who need to keep their children helpless and dependent, so as to reinforce their status as caretakers. Their mantra is "What would they do without me?" It is no wonder that these same parents find it difficult to allow their children to leave home, to go to a college out of town, to speak up, to be independent, or to forget their obligations to their mother and father.

Unfortunately, "emotional children" are more prevalent than you might imagine. Most people grow old long before experiencing the benefit of growing up. They go through life playing the role of perpetual adolescents who use others to excuse their actions or their inaction. They perceive themselves as being controlled by others, sacrificing for others, and not being sufficiently appreciated for their good intentions and efforts. They are quintessential martyrs in their own eyes, but warriors or wimps in the eyes of others. Martyrdom becomes a part of their identity. Without it, they are nothing.

Perhaps the best example I can give you is the pianist who committed suicide after losing several of her fingers in an accident. Her suicide sent the message that, "Without being able to play the piano, I have no identity. Therefore, life isn't worth living."

The examples could go on forever. But in every instance, if you look at individuals of this ilk, you will see they are primarily concerned with themselves. You will also discover that they only become involved in activities or with people when it will enhance their own status. They are, by definition, narcissists who are typically unable to empathize or genuinely invest themselves in their marriages, their children, or their friendships, because they have no real sense of self to invest.

Winners, on the other hand, already have an inherent sense of self. You can always trust what they say, feel, think, and want, because they are able to speak up and express who they are, what they desire, and where they want to go. Having that orientation, they are then able to give or share a part of themselves. As a result, they add to the relationships they become involved in. They don't drain others or have to control, belittle, criticize, or remain rigid, stoic, or strong. Winners lead by example, not by control, intimidation, or emotional abstinence. They are able to be vulnerable. They recognize that gifts and money are possessions to be shared, if they desire, but they're also capable of saying no when they want to. Moreover, they know real involvement comes from sharing oneself with another human being, and they can, because they have a sense of self to share.

The example I always point to is that of Christopher Reeve, star of the Superman movies, who fell off a horse and suffered a severe spinal cord injury. To the surprise of his physicians, friends, and relatives, he made unbelievable progress, because he persisted in his rehabilitation efforts. Later, he went on to act in several made-for-TV movies and became an energetic advocate for other spinal cord injury patients.

Then there's the case of Alex Zinardi, a prominent Formula One driver, who lost both his legs after a terrible crash on the track. Despite his loss, he vowed to race again. He learned to walk on two prosthetic legs. He now lectures on the insight that he gained as a result of his accident. He talks about the increased value that he is able to see in his marriage, his children, his family, and his relationships. He expresses a profound appreciation for life and attributes his accident with opening his eyes to what is really meaningful. He kept his promise: he drove a custom, hand-controlled race car in a trial run that would have placed him in fifth position in the race that followed.

Both of these people and many others are models for "making your losses your gains." Neither would have been capable of taking the steps they took had they not possessed an inner sense of self that was independent of the film industry or the racing circuit. They are shining examples of the need for each and every one of us to develop a sense of centeredness in order to become a *winner.*

Growing up isn't the same for every person. Think back to Leslie and the steps she took to recovery. They can serve as a model you can follow, whether you're a man or a woman, a warrior or a wimp:

1. She stopped focusing on her situation and her spouse. It's an essential, albeit difficult, step to take. It's easier to perceive yourself as a victim. It allows you to blame bad luck; unforeseen circumstances; selfish parents, spouses, or kids; or even God for the pain you're experiencing. However, you can't change any of them. All you can do is gripe and feel trapped. Alternatively, you can give up the victim status and look at yourself.

2. Leslie allowed herself to hurt—not because of what was happening to her, but for how the pain allowed her to see inside herself. In effect, she chose to look inside and to accept responsibility for her actions and her situation.

3. Leslie learned to satisfy her own emotional needs. As a consequence, instead of blaming others for the emptiness she felt inside, she was able to nurture herself. By virtue of accepting who she was, she felt her sense of self-worth grow, which enabled her to begin to take the steps needed to become the person she always wanted to be.

As a result of taking these steps, Leslie's sense of self-acceptance increased to the point where her need to blame others, to fabricate an idealized image, or to obscure her perceived shortcomings, diminished. All of the energy she had previously directed toward these tasks and blaming others could be redirected toward healthy, constructive goals. Instead of retreating into a warrior or wimp mentality, Leslie became a person in her own right. She transformed herself into a winner.

She took a part-time position doing much of the paperwork for one of the city's top realtors until she could reactivate her realtor's license. She polished her tennis game and began painting again. Unbeknownst to me, she was an accomplished watercolorist who had, years earlier, sold her work in one of the top galleries in town. After having children, her husband had discouraged these activities because, "They required too much of her time."

You could say that Leslie began to get a life, an *adult* life. It wasn't that she cared less for John or her children, but she told him without tears, accusations, or anger that she didn't want a relationship with someone who needed to control her or her children. She wanted him, but she no longer needed or feared him.

She said, "The choice, with regard to what direction our marriage will take, is yours."

The jury is still out on their relationship, but whatever happens, Leslie will survive because she breathed life into herself. Her growth didn't occur overnight, and still isn't complete. It probably never is for anyone. But what is important is she learned to give herself C.P.R.—she was able to *Care, Provide,* and *Reason* out what she wanted and where she wanted to go, and all of us can do the same.

All we have to do is follow her steps, one at a time. The pattern of your growth will often be three steps forward, two steps back, but you must not allow yourself to become so discouraged that you quit because of a setback. Just remember that, if you follow the steps, you'll reach your goal. You'll grow up before you grow old.

CHAPTER THIRTY-THREE

THREE MAJOR GIFTS

Rick's means of avoiding emotional vulnerability was silence or humor. His story is one that can provide you with a very positive reason for learning how to give your partner the three major gifts.

It was Rick's second try at marriage. His first marriage died a slow death, due to apathy and ignorance. The relationship with his first wife diminished over the years, because neither of them had the insight, sensitivity, or awareness that might have helped them to be a positive, loving couple. Rick left, leaving his ex-wife to raise their two sons.

After a series of long-term relationships, Rick met Gail, a woman in her late thirties who had almost given up all hope of ever getting married. Although she had dated numerous men, none of her involvements resulted in a meaningful relationship. Somehow, Rick seemed different. There was a sensitive, caring quality about him that was very attractive. The problem was that he displayed that sensitivity infrequently. They went to counseling together, then got married and set themselves up in the home he had owned prior to their marriage. Twelve years and several children later, they still lived there. It wasn't a bad place, but the space was limited and Rick still owned the property by himself.

In fact, over the years, there had been no co-mingling of finances and, even worse, he had very nearly stopped showing his sensitive side to Gail and the children at all. Both factors caused Gail to question his love and commitment, so much so that they returned to therapy.

Rick claimed he didn't want a divorce, that everything was "fine." He also said they had spent considerable money remodeling their present house and he saw no need to move.

After a few months of sessions, their relationship improved. There was a great deal more warmth between them. Rick began to express his emotions openly, and Gail's resentment all but disappeared. They even began to look at houses together—expensive ones—which would not only satisfy their need for space but would enable the children to enroll in an even better school district. Then Rick began to drag his feet, not stopping the process, but keeping his foot on the brake, so to speak. He accompanied Gail to house showings but voiced little enthusiasm, complained about the cost, and accused her of being a social climber.

Then, one day, Rick came to therapy and said, "It's all done but for the signing. I'm not as excited about it as she is, but it's okay. There's loads of room, and it has a lot of positives."

"Do you know what you're doing?" I asked.

"What do you mean?"

"You're making a commitment and making her a partner."

"You know, I haven't given that a second thought."

"Then you're consciously willing to make that commitment?"

"Yes," he replied.

"That's fantastic, but what have you said to her?"

"Well, nothing."

"What do you think she's heard?"

"Well, probably nothing."

"Then you're still playing it safe, aren't you?"

"I must be, because the minute you said that, I knew where you were going. And I thought, if I went home tonight and said something, I'd probably say, 'I hope you're appreciative of what I'm doing and that you recognize how much money I'm putting out and how much effort it's going to take from me, physically, emotionally, and financially.' I realize that's kind of a negative way to put it, isn't it? It's kind of a way of creating guilt, right?"

"Yes," I said, "but it's in keeping with the foot-dragging and negative attitude you've assumed throughout this...should I call it an ordeal or a process? Do you know why you're doing it? I'm asking because I don't believe your words. I think you're happy about the house purchase. I'd go so far as to say you're excited about it but terrified to admit it.

"Well, sure, she could say, 'You should have bought this years ago. Why do you think you deserve credit for buying a house for your family when the place we're living in hardly gives us space to breathe?' I guess I wanted to hear her say she was appreciative and she realized what I was doing for her."

"But the way you wrapped the gift doesn't allow for the reaction you want. Why not go home tonight and tell her what you're really saying?"

"Can I start it with 'I hope you're appreciative'? Maybe I could say, 'That is the way I wanted to start my statement to you, but what I really mean is I hope you know that buying this house is my way of saying I care, I love you, I'm really committed, but inside me is a guy who fears and anticipates being rejected. That's why I can't allow myself to go into things full-speed ahead, with enthusiasm and warmth. I'm afraid I'll wind up running into a brick wall, being hurt and taken advantage of.'"

His words had finally come to match what he felt. For too long, he had difficulty openly expressing what was in his heart, so he said nothing, mitigated his vulnerability, and expected his partner to read his mind. But this prevented Rick and Gail from ever experiencing the love, intimacy, and warmth that's available in a meaningful relationship.

When you say nothing, your partner hears nothing and both of you live with nothing. It's an essential lesson that everyone needs to learn, because it can endow your relationship with the love you genuinely feel but are too frightened to express. You have to give openly of yourself so that you can openly receive love from others.

People might say, "That's great, but how do we do it?"

We must first recognize that we can't change the past, but we can alter our future. How? By giving our partners, families, and friends the three best gifts we can give someone we love. The gifts cost nothing monetarily but are very expensive to give emotionally, because they require us to share ourselves honestly. For many people, this can prove extremely difficult, but the long-term benefit to your relationship, the level of trust that can be developed, and the degree of intimacy you can achieve by giving these gifts makes it well worth your while.

1. *The Gift of Independence.* It's not easy to give. You must be able to give up control. To do so, you must be emotionally secure enough to live with a person whose actions and thoughts may be different from your own.

This type of relationship often proves difficult for both parties involved. I can recall times early in my marriage when I held the peculiar notion that if my wife truly loved me, she would have the same opinions as I did, desire the same kind of food, and enjoy the same kind of people. This wasn't the case, but her sense of individuality had no correlation to the love that she had for me. Sometimes, however, I forgot that. I let myself harbor the same old notion that if she truly loved me, she would also support all my actions and agree with my opinions. On those occasions, I had to realize that I had severely regressed and my inner feelings of insecurity had taken control of my emotions. It is difficult to admit, but nevertheless true, that when you feel emotionally sufficient and worthy of being loved, it is easy to "permit" others to have their own opinions. It is only when you are hurting that you regress back to a point in time when the statement, "If you loved me, you would agree with me," feels like a fact instead of a fantasy.

Control, no matter the motivation, no matter what you call it, is still control. Even if your intention is to help someone learn from your past experiences or to protect him or her from the consequences of the mistakes you experienced in your lifetime, it's still control. Because of that, the bearer of this gift must realize that the freedom to err, to make mistakes, and— we hope—to learn from them is far more valuable than the benefit derived from well-intended attempts to help others to avoid the pitfalls of life. Too often, the price for that help is the other person gives up freedom, remains a child, and accepts being controlled. A far healthier approach is to encourage him or her and be there if and when he or she stumbles.

It's also worth noting that some recipients of the gift of freedom are really not anxious to get it. Emotionally, they may prefer their dependency and be willing to be controlled, rather than take responsibility for themselves. Despite declaring to the world that they resent controlling behavior and desire to be free, they're frightened by independence. They're like the teenager who threatens to leave home but wants his or her parents to continue making the car payments and giving him or her gas money.

You can probably see that in order to be able to allow others their freedom, the giver must first be sufficiently strong so as not to need to control. At the same time, you really can't give freedom to people who can't accept it fully. They have to be sufficiently strong enough to want it. How do they gain that strength? Slowly, by making their own mistakes and learning that you'll still be there to love, support, and accept them.

Warriors learn early in life that if they are strong and self-sufficient, a responsible leader who can solve all sorts of problems, they will be loved. Wimps learn that if they are dependent, helpless, and weak, someone will love them and come to their aid. Later in life, both warriors and wimps unconsciously live according to those assumptions, but not happily, because, at some level, they resent the price they feel they have to pay for love. In order for them to grow, they need to see the emotional trap they've built for themselves and learn that they shouldn't have to pay for love, because everyone is basically worthwhile and deserves it.

In the process of experiencing your own growth, you will discover that you help others to grow as well. The end result is rarely the loss of someone's love. Quite to the contrary, you'll gain the love of an adult who doesn't have to love you but will because you deserve it.

About a year ago, I received a call in the middle of the night. I must have been in a very deep sleep, because I fumbled around to find the phone on the bedside table. I finally answered, though the words that came out of my mouth must have been gibberish. I looked at the clock. It was 1:54 a.m.

The voice I heard sounded like a terrified, almost hysterical, little boy. I was unable to recognize who it was. As my sleep wore off, the voice became faintly familiar. It was Ted, a patient of mine, whose wife, Julie, was hospitalized in intensive care. Her problem was a chronic one, which started years earlier and became increasingly debilitating, to the point that she was only partially ambulatory. To say the least, her prognosis was poor. Ted pleaded with me.

"Call her on her cell, or call the ICU. The nurse will get her on the phone. I'm on my way there now, but there's no telling what she'll do. She'll go against medical advice, despite the IVs. She'll do what she's done before, fire her doctor and leave against medical advice. I'll have to find yet another physician for her."

The curious paradox is that this man is a very fine physician himself. He is respected by his colleagues, and looked upon as a decisive, occasionally too strong-willed, sometimes rigid individual who, once he makes his mind, up finds it difficult to alter his position. That wasn't the case at that moment. Instead, I was talking to a little child, who was overwhelmingly fearful of his wife's reactions and obviously felt incapable of dealing with her in an adult fashion. Perhaps it was a case of "warrior at work, but wimp at home." The wimp was the one on the other end of my phone. I tried to ease his anxiety by assuring him that by the time he reached the hospital, I would have talked to Julie or the nurse on duty in ICU, and, at least in part, alleviated the situation.

When I finally got Julie on the phone, she ranted and raved. She accused her physician of being a pawn, who acquiesced to her husband's desires and agreed to procedures she had not given permission for them to initiate. She complained that it was a conspiracy against her. It wasn't that she was paranoid, she simply felt helpless. Her husband, she said, was going behind her back. In her own words, "After months of therapy, he hasn't learned a thing about honesty and integrity. He's a liar. He obscures the truth by omission, rather than commission."

In many ways, Julie's comments were no different than the ones I had heard from her during the two or three years I had periodically visited with her and Ted. The irony was that she was factually correct. From the time I first met them, Ted's behavior was that of a man who tiptoed around his wife. He frequently censored his words in order to avoid her ire and was terrified of confrontation. Consequently, he often left out essentials in his conversation and justified his actions by not wanting to provoke her ire.

It was only when there was no other recourse, or when he felt his back was to the wall, that he could finally tell Julie the truth. By then, it was too little, too late. She would become angry. He used her anger to rationalize his resentment toward her and to justify his reluctance to tell her the truth in the first place. It was the same way he had dealt with problems his entire life. His explanation was that he didn't want to hurt or upset anyone. He never saw that it was quite the contrary. It was a reflection of his fear of confrontation and, as a result, when Julie, anyone in his family, or his colleagues needed him the most, they were unable to trust him. In the back of Julie's head, there was the constant thought there was something she wasn't being told, that she would learn about at the last moment.

Granted, Julie could often be inappropriately demanding, verbally abusive and emotionally hostile. At the same time, you had to cut her some slack. She'd been sick for over four years. She was in and out of intensive care, but was always intellectually aware of Ted and her doctor caucusing at the other end of the ICU and walking out together through the swinging doors. Ted, who had never been totally truthful, would say, "Everything is fine, there's nothing to worry about." Her thoughts were, "How can I believe him? I'm afraid I'm about to die. I need someone I can trust, who's strong and dependable, who I can lean on, particularly if I'm dying."

It didn't matter that avoiding the truth by tiptoeing around issues was merely a defense mechanism and not a hostile act on Ted's part. It caused everyone around him to distrust him.

2. *The Gift of Self.* Initially, the gift of self sounds relatively simple. It isn't. It requires that you first have insight into who you are, because you can't share what you don't know.

Most of us think we know who we are. I believe, however, that the self we know is merely the one we present to the public. Someone we'd like to be. The real person deep inside is someone the majority of us are too frightened to look at.

Consequently, we're unable to share ourselves with anyone. It follows then, that before we can possibly give ourselves to someone else, we must first give the gift of that inner person to ourselves.

That often creates an additional problem, because most people don't want who they are. They are displeased with who and what they fear they are inside. They expect perfection in themselves and erroneously feel, despite intellectual awareness to the contrary, that anything short of that will be unacceptable to someone else. For that reason, few people ever reveal all of themselves to those you love. Ted was an all too perfect example of this behavior.

In couples therapy, it is not unusual to hear a spouse say, usually after an argument, "He doesn't understand me. All these years and he has no idea who and what I am." On the surface that pretty much sounds like a condemnation of the other party, and often it is intended to be. In my eyes, it is more of a condemnation of the spokesperson. It says, "I have never let you know who I am because I have never felt acceptable enough in my own eyes."

In the heartwarming Christmas story about the gift of the littlest angel, we learn that despite the meagerness of his gift, it was valued most because the littlest angel gave what was dearest to himself. There's a lesson to be learned there: each of us needs to appreciate our own worth, in spite of our fears. We must come to recognize that nobody is perfect, but each of us has value.

It is only when you can recognize and accept yourself as someone of value that you become a valuable gift you can share with yourself as well as someone else.

3. *The Gift of Honesty.* This is perhaps the most precious gift, and also the most difficult to give. Sadly, it is most frequently given during an argument. At those times the gift is usually cloaked in a wrapping of, "I have been meaning to tell you this for a very long time and I am going to get it off my chest now."

Any gift given to me with that wrapping would not be appreciated. Instead, I would receive it with fear and defensiveness. In fact, I doubt that I would view it as a gift at all. Even under the best of circumstances, you need to be very brave, comfortable and emotionally secure to be able to receive the gift of honesty. It is the rare recipient of this gift, even when it comes wrapped in soft loving words, who can say, "Thank you for the constructive criticism."

Let me try to give you an example. One of the things for which I most appreciate my wife is her courage to be honest with me in spite of my initial, often defensive, responses. For example, if she were to attend one of my speeches and find it lacking, she might be prone to say, "It wasn't your best. It was too long-winded and complex."

Intellectually, I wholeheartedly appreciate her honesty but, unfortunately, too often my head doesn't click in until sometime after the emotional child inside me has gone and made a fool of himself. Fortunately, my wife isn't afraid of that insecure little kid. If she were, the gift of honesty would never be in her repertoire.

In order to make the giving of this gift a part of your repertoire you must be able to face your fears of rejection or controversy, and behave in spite of them, not because of them. It requires that you be able to risk the possibility—even the probability—of being criticized and disagreed with by someone whose love and acceptance is important to you. It's dangerous ground to step on but, if you want to give this gift, you have no other choice. Initially, it may appear that it's a lose-lose situation. Speak up and be criticized by someone you love, or "let discretion be the better part of valor," and wind up chastising yourself for being a wimp. The decision rests on which will, in the long run, allow you to sleep better at night and cause you to live better with yourself in the light of day. In every case, timing, humor and genuine care can make the bitter pill easier to swallow.

At the same time, you must be clear about your motivation behind the giving of this gift. All too often, I have seen people deliver so called "constructive criticism" to loved ones that would bring an elephant to its knees. Do not confuse honesty with hostility. They are not the same. You should also try to remember that your observations, particularly when they are right on target, can be very painful. The more you hit the nail on the head, the more it hurts.

Consequently, you can expect the recipient of the gift of honesty to initially retaliate or defend themselves. In these instances, your satisfaction will have to come from the realization that their reaction indicates they heard you. You can only hope that the seeds of your words fell on fertile soil and will bear fruit in the future. In the meantime, be aware that helping someone to see themselves can, on occasion, be a hurtful, thankless task. No wonder it takes great courage to give the gift of honesty.

On the other hand, it takes considerable courage to accept or consider that gift. Warriors who possess old fashioned courage are usually rigid and critical. They avoid emotional truths, fear facing their own reality and abhor suggestions that they may need to change because they view them as attempts to control. The end result is that they behave out of their fears and use confrontation as their major defense. Wimps tend to react as victims. They don't necessarily accept or consider the honest thoughts you give them, they just feel put down and demeaned. They become depressed, feel unjustly criticized, and use flight, or playing dead as their defense.

Neither derives benefit from the gift of honesty. It is only over time that they can appreciate it. So, if you're looking for immediate results, trying to garner someone's gratitude, or trying to demonstrate how insightful you are, don't bother with the gift of honesty. Those are all selfish justifications, and won't take you anywhere on the path to being a winner.

On the other hand, if you truly want to be free of your emotional turmoil, interpersonal conflicts, guilt, and resentment, it is absolutely essential that, in spite of your fears, you give yourself and everyone you love three gifts: *the gift of independence, the gift of yourself, and the gift of honesty.*

CHAPTER THIRTY-FOUR

HAVE FAITH IN YOURSELF

In case you haven't noticed by now, the only solution to relationship conflicts is through yourself. *You* have the power to make your relationships work, to break them, or to merely tolerate them. You have the inner strength, whether you know it or not, to love honestly and forthrightly, and to stand up for yourself. Only *you* can make the decision whether to do so, but make it you must, if you ever want to learn to trust yourself and to love effectively.

In life, the normal inclination is to blame the problems we face, the choices we make and the stands we take, on someone or something else—our upbringing, our lover, or the fact that the world has treated us badly.

For the most part, those are all excuses. It may be true that the world has dumped on you, your childhood was lacking, your partner's behavior needs a major tune-up, or, over time, your emotions have hardened and seem distant and irretrievable. But your feelings aren't dead. They don't just disappear or die from

297

pneumonia or some form of cancer. More often than not, they're buried by old slights and bitter resentment, blurred by fears, or hidden under a host of childhood memories. All of these need to be dealt with up front, discarded, and then forgiven, in order to allow you to get in touch with the desire for and the capacity to love that I assure you is still there inside you.

Dan's behavior exemplifies the problem. He is a forty-eight-year-old confirmed bachelor, as well as a handsome, successful guy most women would see as "a good catch." There is one problem: all of his relationships are short-lived. The longest only lasted three years, and that was only because he didn't know how to leave her without hurting her feelings. He followed his usual pattern of behavior with Anna, but she didn't react in the same manner as the previous women in his life. His pattern was to search out a tall, attractive woman who, despite her outward appearance, lacked confidence—one who had experienced conflict with her father and was either emotionally responsible for, or very dependent on, her mother.

It was no wonder that women were attracted to him. He was gentle, solicitous, generous, and sensitive to their needs. He was also slow to trust, easily hurt, and reluctant to show it. As a result, he built up pools of resentment, which eventually caused him to lose interest. When he did, he retreated emotionally, lost his sexual drive, and spent more time with his male friends and his business. After a while, the woman got the message and left him. In that way, he was never responsible for the breakup, although he was actually the one who initiated it.

In his three-year relationship with Anna, he reached that point on several occasions, but her emotional neediness exceeded her pride. She was willing to accept his neglect and rejection. Finally, he was forced to take a stand, a very difficult step for him, but, in his case, a fortuitous one. It was the first step in the process of his recognition that he lacked trust in himself and, as a result, could neither trust nor love someone else. It took every bit of courage he could muster to ask her to leave. When she expressed a desire to try once again, he reluctantly agreed, only to have to repeat his request several weeks later.

Dan's emotional growth increased by leaps and bounds after their breakup. Several months later, he met and became seriously involved with Nancy. Although she initially fit the bill—she was tall, attractive, and had the prerequisite problem with her father and a dependent relationship with her mother—she was unlike the previous women in his life in that she had a backbone. After a year and a half of serious involvement, she questioned his plans for the future and indicated that she needed some evidence of a commitment. When this was not forthcoming, she called the relationship off, despite his protestations and his vague promises regarding the future. In less than three weeks, Dan actively proclaimed his love. He asked that she reconsider her decision and promised a commitment in the very near future. But before his plan was complete, Dan began to have second thoughts.

"After all," he said during a hastily scheduled therapy session, "she's no pantywaist woman. She's something I really admire, but I'd hate to think how strong she could become. She certainly didn't back down about the breakup. Maybe I'm rushing into this thing too fast."

"You're obviously scared," I said. "I understand that. But before you make any major decisions, please try to determine what the problem really is."

"I don't understand what you're saying. I'm scared to death she'll try to control me. Isn't that enough?"

"Is that the problem? Or is it that you're really frightened that you can't stand up to her?"

"What's the difference? It sounds the same to me."

"There's a huge difference," I said. "On one hand, the problem is between you and Anna. On the other hand, it is between you and your fears."

He was silent for what seemed an interminable period and then looked at me and said, "You're absolutely right! She isn't the problem; it is me. I'll be back for my regular appointment this week, and we'll discuss 'me' issues."

Dan got around to his "me" issues, began addressing them, and eventually married Nancy. I suspect they're doing well. My last contact was a card announcing the birth of their son.

As with all the issues discussed in this book, this one isn't unique to men. Women experience the same blindness with regard to their fears. They are just as likely to search for excuses to justify their actions and any behaviors that they perceive as weak.

Take, for instance, Maureen. She was a paralegal who had a unique way of describing her problems. She said it all in five sentences during her first therapy session. "I have an eighteen-year-old son and twin eight-year-old daughters, yet I feel like I have four children. Let's face it, Dr. Ed, Marc is a good man, but I'm the one who takes care of everything in our house. Sure, he goes to work and brings home a paycheck, but so do I. In fact, I make more money than him. He's like an exchange student we had living with us one summer, except he did more to help at home than Marc does." She then went on to explain, in detail, all of the chores and responsibilities that fell on her shoulders.

She added that her original decision to marry Marc was not an easy one. She was on the rebound from a six-year relationship with an older man who desperately wanted to marry her. "And still does," she added. The only problem was that "the other man" was a widowed entrepreneur used to getting his way. He wanted to care for her, but she knew she wouldn't be able to call all the shots with him. Marc, on the other hand, was an easygoing guy who never questioned her or asked much of her. From the day she met him, she was certain that he would continue to behave the same way after they were married. She was also sure that she could not expect very much from him, emotionally or sexually.

To be frank, she said, "He never stirred me sexually, but I knew he would always be here. Now I'm sorry that he is."

On the surface, it was apparent that Maureen could not afford to take emotional risks. She had settled for "Mr. Steady" and had come to regret it. But Maureen had not gone into the relationship with her eyes closed. She knew exactly what she was doing. Her decision had little to do with the facts. It had everything to do with her emotions. As a child, she had learned to be a caregiver. Much of the responsibility for her younger siblings fell on her shoulders. Her mother was, in Maureen's words, "A child in her own right, who should never have had any children. Most of the time, she was in her own world, which was a lot better than when she tuned into yours and lost her cool."

As a result, Maureen grew up relying only on herself. Her survival technique consisted of never needing anyone so she would never be disappointed. When I suggested that, she replied, "It worked pretty well for the first forty-one years, so why change now?"

"Because somewhere inside is a little girl who desperately wants to be taken care of," I said. "Who wants to lean on someone and to be able to let her emotional guard down, but she is too frightened to risk it."

The solution, however, wasn't necessarily to leave Marc. Before considering that alternative, she had an awful lot of rebuilding to do in herself.

For starters, Maureen is basically a good person, intelligent, professionally successful, and a wonderful mother. But she isn't the confident, loving person she portrays herself to be. Nor is she the victim of Marc's lack of a sense of responsibility. No matter whom she married, she would have eventually trained him to lean on her and to expect her to care for everything. She needed the paradoxical feelings of competence and martyrdom to justify her emotional existence. It provided her with a sense of adequacy, albeit a false one.

Her actions speak for her. They say, "I am capable, and I am needed; therefore, I am. That I sometimes resent the role I have created for myself is true. But I know no other role in life, because I do not trust that anyone will be there to care for me." When I suggested this to her, she vehemently denied it. "I trust and depend on the people I supervise at work, and I certainly know my worth." It was a factual statement, but I wasn't concerned with her intellectual interactions. I was referring to her emotional involvement.

Sad to say, Maureen left therapy because she simply couldn't move on from blaming Marc to looking inside herself.

Dan and Maureen were warriors on the outside, but wimps on the inside. On one hand, Dan couldn't trust himself to stand up for himself. On the other hand, Maureen couldn't trust that anyone else would be there to stand up for her. In both cases, Dan's and Maureen's behavior was the result of the poor self-image they developed early in childhood. Their lack of self-esteem was instrumental in governing their thoughts and actions throughout their adult lives. These patterns of behavior are not likely to change on their own. Their one hope is that, through therapy, they can learn to accept their fears, recognize their worth, and risk becoming involved without having to run from or control their partner.

I hope you have come to realize that if you're a winner, you can trust others because you trust yourself; you don't need to hide behind excuses. But when you do, you understand that excuses are your attempt to justify or defend actions or thoughts whose origins you do not want to confront. You accept that, more often than not, the motivation underlying your overt behavior is the true indicator of who you are on the inside.

To be winners, we must become the guiding force in our own lives. Winners are aware of their inner emotional state, their intellectual wherewithal, and their inherent value. They realize that they must constantly update or modify their beliefs based on their newfound sense of self-confidence.

> If we are ever going to experience a healthy, loving relationship, we have no choice but to become winners. Once again, that requires:
> 1. Being able to recognize and own our feelings and opinions, in spite of how unpopular, politically incorrect, or unacceptable they may be to others;
> 2. Trusting enough in our feelings to openly express them;

3. Exercising our right to take stands, set boundaries, and establish limits for ourselves in all our relationships;

4. Risking the possibility of being disliked or rejected for the positions that we take;

5. Having sufficient flexibility to change our opinions and alter our positions without the feeling that we have given in or are weak and without harboring resentment toward others who disagree with us;

6. Expressing our love to someone in spite of our fear of the real possibility that it may not be returned;

7. Accepting and believing the love we get, without doubt or suspicion;

8. Believing in ourselves sufficiently to show ourselves when we're not at our best: on a bad hair day, with a zit on the end of our chin, when we've erred or failed and everyone knows it, or when we feel weak and needy;

9. Refraining from buying the love of others, emotionally or financially, because we believe we're worth loving for who we are;

10. Admitting we love someone who doesn't love us back, all the while knowing that we won't die because of it and will live to love again, and to share our emotions with another person who will return that love

Essentially, all ten ask that you look inside and see yourself for who you are. They also involve you thinking about how many times you decided not to speak up, express an opinion, or take a stand for fear of it being unacceptable and having others reject you for it. They encourage you to face all the New Year's Eve resolutions you've broken. You know the ones: lose weight; stop drinking, smoking, or taking drugs; get out of an affair; and stop being a couch potato who does nothing, accomplishes nothing, and feels nothing.

In the past, and very likely in the present, you frequently alter the choices you make for yourself in order to be politically correct, to avoid offending others, or to minimize risk and failure. Try to recall the occasions you were cajoled into going out with friends, in spite of all the things you wanted or needed to do at home. Remember the piece of birthday cake you ate, even though you promised yourself you wouldn't. Think of the times you went to the store with your wife when you had been looking forward all week to watching the final round of the golf tournament on television. Remember the jobs you didn't apply for. Each of these incidences are small cracks in the trust you have in yourself. To be responsible, you need to recognize them and take steps to mend them or, more specifically, mend yourself.

The list above should also serve as a reminder that no one is perfect. Everyone can and does err. When that happens, you need to be sufficiently strong to admit your mistakes and, when appropriate, change previous stands, apologize for past acts, or alter your behavior. But, because you are human, you must also accept and forgive yourself for your mistakes. Living by these ten rules will help to rid you of your excuses.

There is one last thing to remember. *It only takes one person to love, if you know how to do it.* Knowing how to love first requires that you trust and love yourself. That is only possible after you have become a loving, responsible parent to yourself. The rewards are far greater than you can imagine. The price you pay is far less than you would expect. The pain that you will rid yourself of by virtue of being sufficiently courageous to behave in accordance with your own thoughts, feelings, and desires will be enormous.

CHAPTER THIRTY-FIVE

A TWENTY-FOUR COW PARTNER

In the final analysis, the questions that require an answer are these: Are the couples and individual patients described in *Warrior, Wimp, or Winner* all examples of people without backbones? Are they weaklings who should be looked down upon, demeaned, or rejected? Are they individuals so lacking in the characteristics traditionally used to define masculinity and femininity that they don't deserve to win the approval and affection of a loving partner?

It's apparent that warriors certainly don't live up to the stereotypic image of a knight in shining armor. After all, in fantasy, that mythical warrior is fearless, without need of companionship or emotion. I've seen a fair number of "knights" in therapy. They were the young men in high school and college who saw themselves as the campus studs. They were labeled "most likely to succeed." They were on the football team. They were president of their fraternity. They had little trouble finding members of the opposite sex but experienced considerable difficulty keeping those women happy, satisfying their emotional needs, or having their emotional needs satisfied in return.

For many of them, what their partner thought or felt was of little consequence. They were insensitive or unaware of their partner's feelings and blind to how hurtful their own ego-centric behaviors could be. They weren't bad people. In fact, many of them would have been appalled by their own behavior had they been aware of it. But for the most part, they weren't, because all their energies and efforts were motivated by their desperate need to polish their armor, so much so that they were oblivious to the effect they had on others or the pain they passed on to those around them. Instead, they were consumed by a quest that men have followed for eternity—the enhancement of their male image by portraying themselves as strong, fearless, successful, all-knowing individuals who were in control of others as much as they were their own emotions. Their purpose was to attract attention and thereby the most attractive, intelligent, sought-after women.

That explains the knight's age-old behavioral pattern, but it doesn't make it acceptable. Domination, lack of emotion, egotistic behavior, and a need to control aren't conducive to establishing a solid foundation for a meaningful relationship. Instead, what is needed is openness, vulnerability, and some degree of introspection, all of which could not occur until a person developed sufficient confidence in his or her own self-worth, despite awareness of his or her insecurities and shortcomings.

Because those behaviors aren't consistent with the attributes typically ascribed to warriors, the decline of the masculine myth and the erosion of his illusion of superiority aren't necessarily curses. It may, in fact, be a blessing. It could be the first step in the alteration of the archaic definition of masculinity that helped to create the war between the sexes in the first place. The new definition will, we hope, reflect the emotional evolution of man from a counterfeit "warrior" to a genuine human being.

Earlier in this book, I noted that behind successful men has very often been a successful woman who supported, guided, and encouraged him to be the person he became. Her role was covert and hidden by a veil that portrayed her as weak and helpless. In this way, she could pose no threat to man's fragile sense of masculinity. She didn't hold the reins, but she directed the guy who did, all the while exclaiming that "Father knows best."

But women wanted the freedom to express themselves, to succeed, and to have the same opportunities and rewards as their male counterparts, and rightfully so. Sadly, women are now just as likely as men to fall victim to the myth of the warrior. In throwing off the yoke of the wimp, they also risk losing many of the most valuable characteristics they formerly possessed—the ability to love, to care, to nurture, to understand, to support, to be sensitive and compassionate, and to uphold the moral and emotional fiber of their families. There needs to be a radical alteration in the definition of femininity as well.

The only viable solution is to establish a new balance between the sexes, one that brings out the best in both men and women and allows them to cooperate without competition. This balance is not only essential to establishing healthier relationships between men and women in marriage; it is equally essential in the public sphere.

The first step requires that men and women feel adequate in their own right. They need a strong sense of sufficiency in self to allow them to be able to see their partners' strengths and to respect one another instead of trying to control or demean each other. Accordingly, men and women need to be able to recognize and forgive each other's shortcomings and to value the virtues they both possess. They're both capable of it.

The solution seems so evident and easy when it's expressed in words. But in practice, human beings have a very long way to go before that end will ever be achieved because change of any kind can be excruciatingly slow. Remember the saying, "Better the devil you know than the devil you don't know"? It's a basic form of survival that humans cling to even when it impedes their growth. It's also one of the major factors that stand in the way of partners establishing the healthy balance necessary for them to interact in an open, loving fashion.

A wonderful example of how this balance might come about is exemplified by Ross and Julie, who just last year celebrated the birth of their first child, a healthy, eight-pound boy. In less than two months, Julie was back to work. On the surface, things couldn't have appeared better. After all, Ross and Julie had every reason to be happy, but that wasn't the case. Julie complained that she was tired all the time and demonstrated signs of postpartum depression. Meanwhile, Ross was conflicted. He felt a mixture of joy and emotional loss. He was delighted to have a son, but he resented the changes in his lifestyle. The amount of work and time the newborn required bothered him. Moreover, he was jealous of the constant attention Julie gave the baby but was embarrassed to admit it.

To say the least, Ross's experience with fatherhood was disappointing. He was incensed by Julie's complaints and dissatisfaction. At times, he even lamented having gotten married to begin with. He wondered if he had made a mistake and if he really wanted all the responsibilities. On those occasions, he meticulously searched for Julie's every flaw or misbehavior. He held on to any statement that could be construed as hurtful or might indicate that she was emotionally rejecting him. It was as though he was searching for issues that he could use to demean her and justify his dissatisfaction.

Intellectually, Ross knew, by virtue of the therapy he had already had, that "we marry who we are." It's a phenomenon that occurs in every marriage and results in spouses holding onto and finding fault with everything they see in their partner that they can't abide in themselves. He also understood that it was his problem and that there wasn't anything wrong with his wife. To the contrary, Julie was an attractive, bright, warm individual, who added a great deal to his life. Nonetheless, he found it increasingly difficult to return home every night. He couldn't stop himself from being critical and pushing her away, physically and emotionally.

Despite his own awareness, Ross felt incapable of changing his home situation. His solution was to concentrate on work, face the problems there, solve them, and feel some sense of productivity and self-sufficiency. I suggested that his behavior only exacerbated his wife's postpartum depression and certainly didn't contribute to her feeling good about their relationship. He was quick to remind me how often he had heard me say, "You can't change anyone else; you can only change yourself. Therefore, you have to look inside to see what you can do differently to resolve the problems in you."

That is still true. You can't change other people, but you can influence their world and their being. You can help them either to feel better and more worthwhile or insufficient and unworthy. To illustrate, I told Ross how, five years earlier, while sitting in the waiting room of a doctor's office, I picked up an old issue of *Reader's Digest*. Inside was the story of Mr. Lingo, which not only related to Ross's problem but seems extremely pertinent to the dilemma presently faced by men and women who compete rather than lift each other up.

A man was in Indonesia on business. After his meetings were over, he decided that prior to returning home, he would fly to an island acclaimed as one of the best bonefishing spots in the world. He had no gear and asked various people who was the best person to contact to help him make arrangements. Everyone's answer was the same: "Mr. Lingo. He's the best bonefisherman on the island. He has the best boat, the finest gear, and the most skill."

Everyone had a small smile on their faces as they sung Mr. Lingo's praises. Eventually, he said to one of them, "Why is it that everyone recommends Mr. Lingo, but can't help smiling? I'm beginning to think you're all putting me on."

"Not at all," the local told him. "Mr. Lingo truly is the most knowledgeable and capable businessman and fisherman in this area. He's tops at everything. But the reason we smile is that Mr. Lingo recently got married to a very nice woman of average beauty. However, for the first time that any of us can recall, Mr. Lingo was outwitted when he bargained for his wife. He could easily have gotten her for four or five cows, but he agreed to pay twenty-four cows. Our humor reflects the small satisfaction we have in knowing that no one's perfect and that even the best of us can be outsmarted."

With that assurance, the traveler set off to hire Lingo. When he arrived, he saw a very tall, muscular gentleman repairing a net.

"Are you Mr. Lingo?"

The man said, "Yes, I am."

"I've been told that you are the best bonefisherman in the area. I'd like you to arrange for my supplies and be my guide."

At that moment, a woman walked past them. She was attractive, strode in an almost stately manner, and gave off an air of royalty.

The traveler turned to Mr. Lingo and said, "Is that your wife?"

Mr. Lingo nodded and said, "We married several months ago."

"I know," the traveler responded. "Everyone told me."

"What did they say?" Mr. Lingo asked.

Hesitantly, the traveler answered, "They said that she was a very fine woman, but that, in negotiating for her, you were overly generous."

"That's correct," Mr. Lingo said.

"But why? You're said to be the best negotiator in the area, and yet you paid twenty-four cows for a woman most people thought you could get for four or five. Why did you do that?"

He simply said, *"Because I wanted a twenty-four cow woman."*

I've never forgotten that story. I am ashamed to admit that, on too many occasions, I fall far short of Mr. Lingo's behavior. My wife and I have been married for over fifty years, but I am embarrassed to think of the times that I have attempted to make her into a three- or four-cow woman because of my own fears, inadequacies, and a need to defend myself. I know that it was because of my shortcomings, not hers. I also know I am not alone in this behavior. Nor are these actions restricted to men. On far too many occasions, I have been in groups where either a husband, a wife, or both have seen fit to find fault, criticize, or undermine their spouse. Sometimes, it was done with humor. On occasion, it was achieved through anger. But I suspect that most of the time, it was done without malice or conscious awareness of the hurtful nature of the behavior or the impact it had on their spouse.

These behaviors can only be corrected by people cognizant of their own actions. Altering behaviors is a secondary goal. Of even greater importance is to recognize the motivation provoking them in the first place. *Warrior, Wimp, or Winner*, at its core, is about providing guidelines to becoming an emotionally healthy person:

1. Look inside yourself and discover where you're coming from and what drives you.

2. Recognize that most of your conflicts, pain, and problems come from within you and that competing with, criticizing, or chastising your partner will never change who you are or the problems inside you. They will only serve as a smoke screen.

3. Be aware that the degree to which you successfully deal with your own problems is the extent to which your problems with others will diminish.

4. Know that it is far easier to deal with your present problems after you've come to peace with your baggage from the past.

5. Learn to trust yourself and to know that you are capable of standing up for yourself in your interpersonal relations with your loved ones.

6. Accept and forgive your shortcomings and fears and love yourself in spite of them.

7. Realize that, despite these shortcomings, you are worthy of being loved by others for who you are.

8. Be selfish. Acquire a rational self-interest that gives you license to set limits and boundaries for yourself.

9. Establish inner harmony by making what you want, feel, think, say, and do congruent with each other. They need to sufficiently overlap to minimize any internal conflict and ensure that all your energies and efforts are pointed in the same direction.

10. Open yourself up to abnormal behavior. Acting in accordance with your "normal" from the past will only impede future change or growth.

In order to establish truly meaningful intimate relationships, we must all start by being accountable to ourselves. That won't ensure that we'll be loved in return, but it will demonstrate that each of us cares and that we love and are willing to risk exposing ourselves to those we choose to love. They may not love us in return, but that needn't stop us from loving them.

It's your choice. You can choose to love anyone you want, and you have a right to declare that love. At the same time, the other person has the right not to return it. That's his or her choice. The same can be said for intimacy. Recall that intimacy can best be defined by the word, itself: "*into-me-see.*" Intimacy can only be achieved by revealing yourself to the object of your affections. The degree to which that's possible is directly related to the degree to which you know yourself. It can't happen if you hide from yourself.

A healthy balance between men and women really can come about in every sphere of life if each of you individually does your part to make yourself emotionally vulnerable. These behavioral characteristics are foreign to warriors and wimps but are inherent to winners, people who are sufficiently emotionally healthy to accept and love themselves and others for who they are, as opposed to the image they present.

Unfortunately, change does not take place overnight—or in a straight line. It's the pendulum effect all over again. I see more and more women in my practice asserting themselves by taking on the stereotypical attitude of masculinity, despite the damage that attitude has historically wrought. Men have become more likely to acquiesce, even though there's nothing inherently weak about stereotypically "feminine" characteristics like tenderness and emotional honesty. Somewhere between these two extremes of warrior and wimp, which are really just two sides of the same coin, revealing the same feelings of insecurity and poor self-worth, is the healthy mean of the winner.

CHAPTER THIRTY-SIX

THOUGHTS ON BECOMING A WINNER

E very four years, a host of dedicated young athletes from all over the globe gather together to compete to determine who is the best of the best. Each of them has already proven he or she is the best in his or her home country. Barring a small slip, a strong wind, a fall, a miscalculation, any one of these individuals could become an Olympic gold medalist and prove he or she is the best in the world (i.e., a *winner*).

In the course of competition, numerous heart-rending stories come to light and are carried over and retold during the next four years. But when the Olympic flame is finally extinguished, I always ask myself what moments most moved me during the competition. Oddly enough, there are two brief vignettes that stick with me far more than any others from all the years I've been watching the Olympics.

The first was a young lady who had just won a medal and was being interviewed when I turned the television on.

I can't tell you which sport she competed in, but it hardly matters. She was as pleased as any human being could be over her success. When the reporter asked what winning the medal meant to her, she said, "Everything. It was the most important single event in my life. It really didn't matter if I won or lost. Being here made me a winner in itself. I have no regrets for the time that I devoted over all these years. It was worth it, even though I had to sell my car to pay for the training I needed to hone my skills." I listened to this young woman, and I thought to myself, "*Here is someone who gave of herself.* Most of all, she bet on herself. Just being able to do that made her a winner even before she came to the Olympics."

The second memorable moment concerned a young woman from Australia who was competing in downhill skiing. She stated that she asked her mother and sister not to come, because it would make her too nervous knowing that they were there watching the event. Despite that, her mother and sister did come, but they hid behind a flag whenever she was even remotely close to prevent her from seeing them. However, in order to buy their tickets, they had to sell the family car. At whatever cost, they wanted to be there to support her, win or lose. I thought to myself, *This young lady is already a winner, as well.* Anyone who receives that love and involvement from his or her family has already won a gold medal in life. That form of support is a springboard for future success. It was a catalytic agent that gave that young lady the resolve to compete. Win or lose, she knew that there were people behind her who would cheer and love her either way.

It's strange, but those two events meant more to me than all the glitz and glitter, all the excitement, the fireworks, and the pageantry, because they told a human story that provides us with at least three lessons that all of us have to learn if we want to be winners. If we are already familiar with the lessons, it can't hurt to have them reinforced.

The lessons are, first and foremost, *success doesn't come easily*. It isn't the result of just chance or luck. Sure, they play a part, but long before you get to the point where you have the opportunity to benefit from the luck, you've got to be able to place yourself in that situation. That requires dedication, commitment, and sacrifice. It requires courage to bet on yourself, a willingness to put out the energy and effort, despite frequent falls and failures, to reach your goals. Oftentimes, it necessitates you giving up things, like your car, social events, free time, and money, in order to finance and facilitate the training you require. Too many of us fail to recognize or appreciate those facts. Even worse, many of us aren't aware of our own talents. But I promise that if we look inside, we'll discover that there are special talents in each of us. Therefore, it behooves us to open ourselves up, particularly to ourselves, so we can see the unique abilities that each of us possesses and learn to capitalize on them.

The second lesson to be learned is that *not all of us can or will excel individually*. Nevertheless, we can be on the team. We can support and encourage others. We can help by cheering them on. We can devote our time and effort and, in our own way, sacrifice just as one mother and sister did, by selling the family car in order to be there to watch their loved one reach for the gold. If I were an Olympic judge, I would have given both her mother and sister a gold medal for their actions. Speaking only for myself, I'm embarrassed to admit that I might not have sold my car. I'd like to think I'd have done other things, but I doubt I'd be deserving of a medal. For a moment, I'd have each of you ask yourself, "How much have I been willing to sacrifice or commit to in my lifetime? Did I waste time feeling the victim, making excuses that I didn't have the talent, the opportunity, or the finances to make big or small things happen for myself?" If your answer is yes, let me suggest it's not too late. Start today.

This brings us to the third lesson: *every one of us has unique talents.* We need to dedicate ourselves to putting those to use and achieving the goals that we desire, either by participating ourselves or lifting those around us to higher heights by participating in their lives. We must genuinely give of ourselves and learn to bask in their accomplishments, not just because of how it reflects on us, but also because it will spur them on to become a winner, just like you.

The moral is that there is a role each of us can play in life and goals each of us can achieve. However, we must first learn to dedicate, to commit, and to sacrifice. After all, that's what success is. It's the culmination of these acts, whether we're on the skis ourselves or helping someone who is by being there to support and acknowledge them. We each have a role, and there are no excuses for not taking part. Going after what we want, running toward the things we desire, is the only way to get there.

If we truly want success, want to feel we achieved in our personal lives, interpersonal relations, jobs, and communities, the rules we need to follow are all the same. If we remember and abide by them, we not only can but *will* contribute to our own good fortune. Let me share some thoughts that I believe can aid us in this endeavor:

1. It's essential to be ourselves, show ourselves, and give of ourselves.

Remember, *Success and achievement are not synonymous with perfection.* On far too many occasions, I have seen perfectionism pull people down. It prevents growth and stops momentum. Needing to be perfect causes human beings to spin their wheels until they're stuck. The perfectionist is a person who is obsessed with avoiding failure, not achieving success. He or she becomes immersed in the small details and frequently spends inordinate amounts of time mulling over the facts. Such people rarely see the big picture.

2. *The ability to achieve is not just something we are born with.*

DNA contributes to our makeup, but self-confidence has to be one of the most important factors contributing to success. Most people tend to associate achievement with success and non-achievement with failure, but that is not accurate. The process of succeeding consists of taking baby steps, while experiencing periodic reversals or failures. None of us ever learned how to walk or ride a bicycle the very first time we tried. We had to fail numerous times until the day we reached a level of success that allowed us to make walking or riding almost second nature. Initially, both represented a challenge that seemed impossible. It's the same for other goals.

3. *In order to succeed at any task, we need to learn to accept the falls and the mistakes that are inherent as necessary to the process of becoming successful.*

The strange paradox is that the lower our confidence, the more perfect we feel we have to be. Conversely, the greater our confidence, the more failure we can tolerate in ourselves. No one ever said it better than Michael Jordan, one of the most successful athletes of our times: "I have missed over four thousand shots. I've lost over three hundred games in my life. I've been trusted to take the game-winning shot twenty-six times, and I've missed. I've failed over and over again in my life, and that is why I succeed."

If we want to be winners, we must heed that message and remember the toughest competition we will ever face is not with others; it's with ourselves. So we must dream, wish, and plan. We must brainstorm and set goals, take action and risk failure, but we mustn't despair over failures, because each mishap we experience is one less mistake we'll make later in the process of becoming a winner.

4. *It doesn't matter what the goal is. What does matter is that we believe we have the wherewithal inside us to reach that goal.*

Whether we want to complete a marathon, win an Olympic downhill ski race, or, more important, improve our relationships and marriages, we have to learn the basics, practice, and find the courage to compete and the initiative to put our own unique spin on our performance.

Warrior, Wimp or Winner has already shared numerous examples of what works and what doesn't. It has presented the basic guidelines for you to follow, as well as rules of thumb on how to work at a relationship. You have to supply the courage and initiative. Lastly, it has repeatedly attempted to leave you with one essential message:

> Neither a warrior nor a wimp be. Strive instead to be a winner, a person who:
>
> Has found himself, believes in himself, loves himself, and gives of himself to others.

CHAPTER THIRTY-SEVEN

SO WHO ARE YOU, A WARRIOR, A WIMP, OR A WINNER?

When I first shared the title of this book with several friends, they suggested that the word "wimp" was a poor choice. They felt that men in particular, would find it offensive and reject the entire notion. Despite their suggestions, and my feeling that there was validity to their thoughts, I decided to include it. First, because it fit, and second, because I thought it might not prove quite as offensive if I provided several examples.

The first concerns an individual I'll refer to as Austin. He was a tremendously successful man. He was the executive president of one of the largest banks in Houston, Texas some forty years ago. No one would ever have considered him a wimp. In fact, to have used that word in reference to him would have been viewed as a total misrepresentation of the man and the reputation he had earned throughout the years. He was a community leader, actively involved in charitable organizations, and a very politically savvy individual.

One particular day, he called his wife, as was his custom before leaving work, and said, "I'll be home in about 40 minutes. I'm packing my things and I'm leaving now." As he was about to leave the executive floor of the bank, a vice president rushed over to him and said, "Austin, I've got to talk with you. An issue has come up in one of our branches that requires your attention." They sat down and, 40 minutes later, their conversation was still going strong. Those were the days before cell phones and, in his haste to leave, he neglected, or felt it more prudent, not to call her. On the way home, he suddenly found himself feeling tremendous pressure. He was driving in a manner that was atypical for him, speeding, cutting in front of cars and, believe it or not, breathing hard. It was obvious to him how pressured, anxious and intimidated he felt. Needless to say, he made it home in record time. He got out of his car, retrieved his briefcase from the back seat, and started to walk to the front door. Then he stopped, without any conscious thought or preplanning, rubbed his hands on the tires, and walked into the house, announcing that he'd had a flat tire and had to fix it.

This was the story he related to me several days later, during a therapy session. In the process of telling the story, he himself used the word "wimp" to describe his behavior. He ended by stating, "I never realized how intimidated I am by her, how much I need her approval, fear her rejection, and act out of those emotions, rather than standing up for myself. I'm embarrassed, but even more importantly, I'm surprised at the person I discovered inside me. Not one of the almost 400 people working for the bank would have ever believed me capable of this, and I'm one of those employees."

The second story is about Claude, a design engineer working for an architectural firm. Physically, he was a brute of a man. To see him, you would have suspected that he was a linebacker for a football team, or a martial arts instructor. But his size belied his behavior. Here is Claude's story:

"I came in to work Monday morning and John, one of my co-workers, pulled me aside and said he and Harry, another co-worker, were going off on a fishing trip, to a fishing cabin Harry owned about 200 miles south of Houston. He said that they were both taking off Friday, leaving Thursday night, and planned to wet a line early the following morning." Without giving it a thought, Claude's initial response was "Count me in." Almost immediately, John replied, "Harry and I already have. It's going to be a blast."

That night when Claude arrived home, he found his wife in a tizzy. The dog got sick, she took it to the vet; one of the kids cut his hand and she went to the "doc in a box"; dinner was late, and she was totally beside herself. By the time things calmed down, he forgot to mention the fishing trip planned for the next weekend.

The following day, he promised himself that when he got home, he'd tell her all about it, but Tuesday night was swim team for the kids and there was a PTA meeting that either he or his wife had to attend. So, once again, their schedule undermined his good intentions.

Wednesday, he realized that he had no alternative but to tell her his plans for the weekend. But, would you believe it - they were scheduled to go out with friends for a quick dinner and he never got around to discussing it because he had a little too much to drink and immediately fell asleep when they got home.

Thursday morning, he found himself in a quandary. 'I've got to tell her, or I've got to back out with the guys. I don't want to back out, and it's evident, even to myself, that I really have walked on tiptoes around her with regard to this trip." Having discovered that, he felt himself trapped, angry at her, because he felt the need for her approval, and frightened to verbal-ize his plans because of his fear (note that word again) that she would object, and most certainly would be critical of his not sharing his plans earlier. Sometime later that morning, he called her, they got involved in a discussion about her mother's forthcoming visit, and somehow, tempers flared. Each of them became agitated, and when the emotions reached a crescendo, he ended with the following statement. "To hell with you, I'm not coming home. I've had enough of your control. I'm going fishing with the guys this weekend. I'm leaving tonight."

The following Tuesday during a therapy session, Claude related the whole story. I might add that when he returned home mid-day Sunday, there was a great deal of tension and anger. He apologized and, for the most part, the immediate issue was resolved, but, the long-term problem wasn't even discussed.

Neither Austin nor Claude could be looked upon as a wimp, and to be sure, at work, with friends and co-workers, they were looked up to, seen as strong male role models, and admired for the success each of them had achieved up to that point in their lives. The problem was, none of those views said anything about the way they interacted with people they were emotionally close to, whose approval they desperately needed, and whose rejection they feared. Think about it. Maybe wimps aren't 100 percent wimpy. Perhaps the term and the status only applies to their behavior and their emotions in selective arenas of their lives. For some, that arena might be a very small one. For others, it might be generalized to every area of their existence. Are they wimps? You would have to say yes. Are they warriors? Claude's wife would certainly testify to that notion. To what degree could you apply either of the terms to these individuals? It's difficult to say. But, if I were to ask you, "are they winners?", the answer would have to be most certainly not.

Having said this, I'd ask each of you, whether male or female, to look at yourself, judge your behavior, thoughts and feelings in order to determine whether you are a warrior, a wimp or a winner. Then I'd like you to take a breath and try to think of and accept that label as reflective of behavior, not as a condemnation of you as a person. You see, in the end, the rule of thumb has to be:

> Good people often behave as warriors, and equally good people display wimpy behavior. But emotionally healthy people become winners.

People who behave honestly, openly, transparently, and aren't ashamed of their feelings, their fears, the emotions they harbor, and the shortcomings they may have. Why? Because they recognize that to be human is to be imperfect, and they know that imperfect people have the right to be loved and are worthy of being taken seriously and respected for who they are as a total human being who can in part be either a warrior, a wimp or both, and still be a winner.

INDEX

p.   Hanna Rosin
            The End of Men: And the Rise of Women
            Riverhead Books/The Penguin Group
            September, 2012

p.   David Brooks
            The New York Times
            Why Men Fail
            September 10, 2012

p.   Charlie le Duff
            The True and Twisted Mind of the
            American Man
            Penguin Books
            March 2008

p.   National Marriage Project
            Rutgers University 1997-2005
            University of Virginia 2009-Present

p.

AARP Magazine
The Divorce Experience
A Study of Divorce at Midlife and Beyond
May 2004